THE CARBON BUBBLE

ALSO BY JEFF RUBIN

Why Your World Is About to Get a Whole Lot Smaller
The End of Growth

JEFF RUBIN

—

THE
CARBON
BUBBLE

RANDOM HOUSE CANADA

PUBLISHED BY RANDOM HOUSE CANADA

www.penguinrandomhouse.ca

Random House Canada and colophon are registered trademarks.

Library and Archives Canada Cataloguing in Publication

Rubin, Jeff, 1954–, author
The carbon bubble : what happens to us when it bursts
/ Jeff Rubin.

Includes bibliographical references and index.
Issued in print and electronic formats.

ISBN 978-0-345-81469-2
eBook ISBN 978-0-345-81471-5

1. Canada—Economic policy—21st century. 2. Energy policy—Canada. 3. Climatic
changes—Economic aspects—Canada. 4. Industrial priorities—Canada. 5. Petroleum
industry and trade—Canada. 6. Canada—Economic conditions—21st century.

I. Title.

HC115.R76 2015   338.971   C2014-906397-0

Book design by Andrew Roberts

Cover image: © Level1studio / The Image Bank / Getty Images

Printed and bound in the United States of America

10 9 8 7 6 5 4 3 2 1

 Penguin
Random House
RANDOM HOUSE CANADA

To Jack and Margot—my guiding lights

[CONTENTS]

POP GOES THE BUBBLE

IF YOU WANT TO KNOW a thing or two about bubbles, just ask a kid. At some point or other, many of them have mixed dishwashing liquid with water and hit the backyard running, with a small plastic wand. The result can seem a little like magic: weightless, ephemeral balls floating on the breeze.

What any kid will tell you, though, is that bubbles aren't built to last. As they float ever higher in the sunlight, they inevitably pop. In a flash—*poof!*—they are gone.

Canada's carbon bubble, like its backyard cousin, is popping. For nearly a decade, the country has been chasing Prime Minister Stephen Harper's dream of becoming an energy superpower. It's a dream the Conservative leader laid out shortly after assuming office in 2006. At the time, it seemed a solid-enough plan: the world needed oil to power economic growth, and Canada had oil, in spades. And for a while at least, it seemed to work. The oil sands— the Harper government's anointed engine for the country's economic growth—ramped up production. Oil prices rose to unprecedented triple-digit highs and took the Canadian dollar along for the ride. Investment dollars poured into the oil sands, oil royalties poured into the Alberta Treasury, and Fort McMurray became a 21st-century boomtown. On the surface, everything seemed to be coming up roses.

But from today's vantage point—with world oil prices dropping to levels not seen since the Great Recession and demand for the fuel softening even in traditionally solid markets—it's clear that the journey to realizing Harper's vision wasn't destined to be all smooth sailing and fair weather. The country's master economic plan was predicated on some key assumptions: that oil prices would inexorably move higher; that our neighbour and the world's largest oil-consuming nation, the United States, would continue to have an insatiable appetite for our high-cost fuel; that the economy of the world's second-highest oil-consuming country, China, would grow indefinitely at double-digit rates, single-handedly driving world demand for oil as it had once done for coal; and that emissions from the extraction and processing of bitumen, one of the dirtiest carbon fuels on the planet, would not count in the face of the world's laissez-faire pursuit of growth.

Since 2006, one after the other, each of these assumptions has fallen by the wayside, and Canada's oversized oil industry—and its whole oil-driven economy—is paying the price. As the carbon bubble bursts, billions of dollars of investment and government royalties, not to mention thousands of jobs, are vanishing just as quickly as that iridescent sphere that once floated even higher in the sunlight. *Poof!*

Financial bubbles are, of course, nothing new. They have been a recurrent theme throughout modern history. While they've taken different forms over the centuries, at their core they are essentially the same.

- In the 1600s, Holland's upper classes went berserk for an unusual status symbol: tulip bulbs. By 1636, the bulbs were trading on the stock exchanges of many Dutch towns and cities, encouraging everyone to speculate. At the height of the craze, the rarest bulbs commanded as much as six times an average person's salary. Ten years later, prices dropped and a massive sell-off began, leaving many people in financial ruin.

- In 1711, the South Sea Company presented the British government with an IOU for £10,000,000 in exchange for the rights to handle all trade with South America. Investors swarmed, paying as much as £1,000 per share. Nine years later, those shares were worth nothing. South America remained firmly under Spanish control and the British trade rights for the region were worthless.

- More recently, the world witnessed the greatest financial meltdown of the postwar era when securities financed by subprime mortgages given to unsuitable borrowers crashed as delinquent payments triggered a collapse in US housing prices. The mortgage-backed securities, which had been assigned the highest rating by credit rating agencies, were widely held by financial institutions around the world, many of which failed or required massive, publicly funded bailouts.

All of these bubbles had something in common: like Canada's current "energy superpower" dream, they were built on false premises. People just weren't going to continue sinking years' worth of earnings into a status symbol that bloomed for two weeks and then went into hibernation. They weren't going to keep pouring money into a company whose British charter to control trade was meaningless in a Spanish-ruled region of the world. And US real estate values simply weren't going to climb forever, particularly when insolvent homeowners financed by subprime mortgages mailed in their keys and just walked away from their payments. In all of these cases, a correction was bound to occur, and occur it did, with horrific repercussions for those who failed to see the writing on the wall.

And now it's our turn. No sooner have we turned the page on the subprime mortgage bubble than we find ourselves facing what could be an even more daunting one. While Canada escaped relatively unscathed from last decade's Wall Street–centred crisis, it won't be so lucky this time around. The country's oil sands–leveraged economy is at the epicentre of the bursting global carbon bubble. No oil industry in the world is more vulnerable to plunging prices than the oil sands, home to one of the planet's most costly and emissions-intensive oils. In today's convulsive oil market, where record-sized boom-bust price swings have become the norm, those high costs leave the oil sands' future very much in doubt—and the Canadian economy suddenly in need of a new engine for its growth.

This, then, is the fallout of chasing Harper's dream. How did we get here? And what does it mean for the future of the economy, not to mention your investments? That's what we're going to explore in the pages that follow. We'll start, in part 1, by taking a hard look at the pressing challenge of sustaining economic growth in the face of an ever more urgent need to halt carbon emissions and avert the worst consequences of warming global temperatures and rising sea levels. That dilemma has put the needs of the economy and those of the environment on a collision course like never before. We'll see how countries around the world are coming to recognize this challenge, and how the goalposts are shifting when it comes to the use of fossil fuels. We'll examine how Canada's record on this front sticks out like a sore (and definitely not green) thumb. This country's leadership—unlike, say, the US president or even, surprisingly, the Chinese government—has followed the time-honoured dictum that growth and "green" are mutually exclusive concepts, despite mounting evidence that, quite to the contrary, perhaps the only way to grow in the future will be to grow green.

As Canada was busy putting all of its economic eggs in one oily basket—ramping up oil sands production to unprecedented levels—the warning signs were already plain to see (and had been for some time) for anyone who cared to look. In part 2, we'll explore how a technological breakthrough spurred a boom in oil production south of the border, a boom that suddenly stole the primary market for the oil sands' huge expansion. And we will see how the ensuing desperate search for a way to get oil to tidewater and find new overseas markets thrust discussion of the pros and cons of new pipelines, and turning railways into veritable ones, into the spotlight of the nation's political debates. But none of these difficulties put a brake on production, and backed by all of that Alberta oil, the Canadian dollar rose to parity (and, briefly, beyond) with the US greenback, taking a heavy toll on other industries and regions of the country left in the shadow of the oil sands boom.

In part 3, we'll talk about how, when and why things went wrong for this problematic resource. We'll discuss how the very high prices that the oil sands and other unconventional oil sources require to recover their extraction and processing costs affect economic growth and, hence, demand for the fuel. We'll explore what that implies for oil companies that have spent the last decade sinking billions of your investment dollars into the search for increasingly costly reserves. We'll look more closely at those shifting goalposts we mentioned, and note the growing similarities between what has already occurred in the world coal industry and what is now occurring in oil—the two heavyweight fuels that have provided the global economy with the bulk of its power. We'll see that instead of a world that will always burn more of these fuels, we are likelier to live in a world that burns a good deal less of them. That prospect leaves fossil fuel industries, and in particular high-cost and emissions-intensive segments like the oil sands, facing their sunset phase. Given the oil sands' oversized imprint on the country, there will be important repercussions for the Canadian economy, the Toronto Stock Exchange (one of the most oil-intensive bourses in the world) and your portfolio.

Finally, we look to the future. How can you, as an investor, manage the turbulent times that a bursting carbon bubble brings, and how can the Canadian economy weather the storm? While slower growth and a warming climate may indeed sound the death knell for what until now has been seen as the country's most valuable economic asset, the latter, at least, could offer more than a silver lining or two.

As a high-latitude country, Canada's climate will change more than most, and as it does, new economic opportunities will emerge. In fact, the climate change that the Harper government has been so fervently trying to deny may present far greater economic opportunities for Canada in a carbon-constrained future than we ever had in our oil-soaked past. In seizing these opportunities, we will soon come to realize that oil is not our most valuable resource after all. That title will soon belong to something Canadians often take for granted, but that others—like residents of, say, California—no doubt wish was a little more abundant in their neck of the woods. Water, it turns out, is about to become a whole lot more valuable and important to our economy than it's ever been before.

Recently, one of this country's national newspapers dubbed the oil sands the "business story of the decade." But the headline told only half of the story. The rise of the oil sands is certainly one of the biggest business developments ever to grip the Canadian imagination. And why not? Enormous expansion, huge numbers of jobs, a steady stream of revenue: it's compelling, to be sure. Today's newspaper headlines, however, are telling the other half of that story—the fall. And this part reads very differently. Instead of stories of massive expansion con-nected to gleaming new pipelines, we're reading of extensive layoffs, abandoned projects and scaled-back operations. As the world turns away from high-cost fuel and carbon emissions, the oil sands' imprint on both the landscape and the economy is going to get a lot smaller.

It may seem hard to imagine a future beyond the carbon bubble— when the economy and the country's ambitions are no longer all about oil. But you're about to discover that this future is closer than you think.

PART
ONE

MAKING YOUR WAY through a conversation about climate change, fossil fuels and the economy can be a bit like navigating the tricky terrain of J.R.R. Tolkien's Middle Earth. The landscape is rocky, there are fire-breathing dragons at every turn, and you'd better be on the alert for enchantments that can make the truth seem like fiction, and vice versa. Partway through, you find yourself wanting nothing more than a map marked with a big red dot and three familiar, comforting words: *You are here.*

As any traveller can tell you, knowing where you are is important— in Middle Earth or anywhere else. If you don't know where you're starting from, how can you figure out where you're going? How can you avoid getting stuck in the no man's land between Bag End and Mordor? Or, more to my point, between a carbon-shrouded past and a renewables-fuelled future?

So, where are we? The answer to that question, unfortunately, is "in a bit of a mess." For decades now, we've looked the other way as global temperatures and sea levels have risen, as the ice caps have shrunk, and as greenhouse gas emissions have grown unchecked. Despite mounting evidence to the contrary, we've chosen to believe that we can go on living the way we've always done. We can't. Our past choices are catching up with us, quickly.

If you happen to call Canada home, things are bleaker still. You reside in a country whose government has not only been wilfully turning a blind eye to the problem but has also been building the country's economic future on a foundation of high-cost, emissions-intensive heavy oil—a foundation that can't possibly hold as climate change forces us to move away from our unhealthy reliance on fossil fuels.

This failure to truly see where we are, and to act accordingly, is going to have repercussions—for the economy as a whole, and for you. In order to avoid those repercussions, you first need to understand them. You need to know, in other words, where you are. Here's my best attempt to describe exactly where that is.

[CHAPTER 1]

RUNNING OUT OF TIME

MONDAY MORNING. The alarm goes off at 6 a.m. You hit the snooze button twice before you drag yourself out of bed into a long, hot shower and then down to the kitchen to make coffee. You turn on the tele—vision or radio to hear the news and the weather, or find out if the Canadiens or Jays or Roughriders won last night. You check your email. You dry your hair and iron a shirt. Maybe you throw in some laundry before you leave the house, or run the dishwasher. Then you get into your car and make your way to work, hitting up the drive-thru for a double-double on the way. It's going to be a long ride. Not that it will make you feel any better, but you've got company on that com-mute: more than 15 million of your fellow Canadians are on the road too, and it takes them, on average, about twenty-five minutes to get to the office.[1] Once they get there, they turn on lights, fire up computers and photocopiers, and start doing whatever it is they get paid to do.

A pretty familiar morning, right? It's a pretty carbon-intensive one too. From turning on the lights to turning over your car engine, a huge number of your daily activities are powered by carbon-based fossil fuels—in the form of oil, coal or natural gas. These same fuels supply more than 80 percent of the energy that powers the world economy.[2] For all of the talk about weaning ourselves off carbon and replacing it with cleaner and renewable energy sources, the world economy is as dependent on these fuels today as it was a quarter century ago. Our whole world is based on burning carbon.

That may sound like good news for oil, gas and coal companies, or those who invest in them, but scratch that shiny surface and a different story begins to emerge. Turns out we've burned a lot of carbon since the days of the Industrial Revolution, and although we didn't realize it at the time, we were on a budget. Unfortunately, a carbon budget works like any other kind of budget—think dollars, or calories, or cigarettes, if you're trying to quit and hold yourself to a certain number per day. The more you smoke in the morning, the fewer you can light up at night. It's the same deal with carbon: all of the carbon we've already emitted into the atmosphere is soon going to force us to find another way to power our economies. For the first time since the Industrial Revolution, we are going to have to adapt to burning less fossil fuels as opposed to always burning more. That means less electricity from coal-fired power plants, fewer automobiles running on gas and diesel, and fewer homes heated with natural gas.

If this comes as a surprise, it shouldn't. Carbon readings in our atmosphere have been sending us this message for decades. We've been doing a decent job of ignoring it, but we can't do that anymore, given that Mother Nature's missive is now being driven home by some pretty convincing evidence of climate change. Consider:

- the earth's surface temperature has warmed since 1880, but most of that has occurred since 1981, with ten of the warmest years on record occurring in the past twelve, and 2014 clocking in as the warmest year on record;
- global sea levels have risen about eighteen centimetres in the last century, but the rate of change over the last ten years is nearly double that of the previous one hundred years;

- the world's oceans are warmer now than they have been at any point in the last fifty years;
- glaciers are retreating around the world; and
- the extent and thickness of Arctic sea ice has declined rapidly over the last several decades.[3]

While at first we blamed factors beyond our control—such as solar flares from violent sun storms or random volcanic eruptions—scientific evidence now incontrovertibly identifies human activity as the primary culprit.

Atmospheric carbon was stable at around 280 parts per million (ppm) from the time of the last ice age, roughly ten thousand years ago, to the dawn of the Industrial Revolution.[4] But carbon readings began climbing steadily when we started burning coal—first with the advent of the steam engine and then later with the development of the oil-burning internal combustion engine. More recently, we added natural gas to our fossil fuel repertoire. In the summer of 2013, atmospheric carbon was measured at the Mauna Loa testing station in Hawaii at 400 ppm.[5] Clearly, we're burning on all cylinders.

CLIMATE CHAOS

We've all heard about the main culprits in this bad-news situation: greenhouse gases (GHGs). These heat-trapping gases—including CO_2, methane, nitrous oxide and fluorinated gases—retain much of the solar energy that penetrates the atmosphere. GHGs do us some favours: without them, the average global temperature would be more than 15 degrees Celsius colder, making most of the planet too cold for human habitation.[6] But with them, the planet becomes warmer. The greater their presence in the atmosphere, the warmer it gets.

Of all the greenhouse gases, CO_2 is by far the most significant; it's the most prevalent, and it sticks around the longest. It's an unavoidable by-product of combusting fossil fuels such as oil, natural gas and coal. The more of these fuels we combust, the greater the concentration of CO_2 in the atmosphere and the warmer the climate.

While certainly not all increases in global temperatures in the past can be attributed to rising CO_2 levels in the atmosphere, unfortunately the converse is true: all past increases in the concentration of atmospheric carbon have brought with them increases in global temperatures.

The impact on temperature of rising levels of atmospheric carbon doesn't show up overnight; it occurs gradually and cumulatively over time. Since 1880, world temperatures have increased by about 0.8 degrees Celsius.[7] Scientists estimate that we will see another half to a full degree of warming as a result of the carbon that has already gone up smokestacks since the Industrial Revolution. So even if we stopped burning carbon fuels today, we'd still have to contend with a changing climate.

Contemplating a slightly warmer winter and coming to the conclusion that it doesn't sound so bad? Before you toss your Canada Goose parka and stock up on sunscreen, think twice. It's not just the average temperature that is changing. Rising carbon levels in the atmosphere create a whole array of major climate effects that will raise sea levels, lead to increasingly violent tropical storms and fundamentally change precipitation patterns around the world, leaving many of today's breadbaskets drought-stricken while deluging heavily populated floodplains with record rains. While there are many complex processes at play, temperature changes are often the trigger.

Still wondering what the big deal is? It's worth remembering that climate change isn't just about the weather. We've already had a small taste of the economic, social and political chaos climate change can bring. A supposedly once-in-a-century drought in northern China in 2010 sent world grain prices through the roof. With today's globally integrated markets, a shock in one part of the world quickly resonates in another. The top nine wheat-importing countries (on a per capita basis) are all in the Middle East.[8] Food riots sparked revolts in seven of them and, in the cases of Libya and Egypt, contributed to the toppling of long-standing dictatorships.

The food crisis got so bad in 2010 that many grain producers, such as Russia, banned exports, which only sent prices higher. By February 2011, Bloomberg was reporting that wheat prices had jumped by 83 percent over the previous year's prices on the Chicago Board of Trade exchange.[9] It didn't take long before those prices were reflected in the cost of dietary staples such as tortillas and pasta, provoking mass demonstrations against rising food prices from Mexico to Italy.

And this may be only a hint of what lies ahead. Many of the hallmarks of expected global climate change—the loss of arable land, crop-killing heat waves and drought—will challenge our ability to maintain current rates of growth in world food production, even as the global population moves inexorably closer to the 9-billion mark sometime this century.

The counterpoint to record droughts in some parts of the world is record flooding and tropical storms in others. In 2013, flooding in western Europe left many insurance companies with huge bills, and reconsidering whether they want to continue to cover damage to property in Europe's heavily populated floodplains. The severity of recent tropical storms and typhoons—like Superstorm Sandy, whose surge crashed into New York City, or Typhoon Haiyan, which left a trail of devastation across the Philippines—dwarfs anything seen during past decades.

Not only are the seas getting stormier, they are rising as well. Sea levels had stayed pretty well constant for two thousand years, but they rose more than fifteen centimetres during the last century as warming temperatures caused ice sheets the size of Manhattan to sheer off glaciers from Greenland and Antarctica. In May 2014, scientists reported that a mammoth and rapidly melting section of the West Antarctic Ice Sheet appears to be in irreversible decline and will eventually collapse into the Amundsen Sea.[10] The area of that section contains enough water *on its own* to raise sea levels by over a metre. Even without this impact, the Intergovernmental Panel on Climate Change (IPCC)—the leading international scientific body for the assessment of climate change, working under the auspices of the United Nations (UN)—expects ocean levels to rise between thirty and ninety centimetres by the end of the century, due to the loss of Arctic ice and the thermal expansion of water that comes with warming sea temperatures.

Melting ice may have oil companies salivating at the prospect of newly accessible Arctic reserves, but if you are one of the nearly 400,000 or so people living on the Maldives in the Indian Ocean, or in the Pacific's Kiribati islands, rising seas are already lapping at your shores. Leaders from those island nations are accusing the carbon-burning world of genocide. The rise in sea level the IPCC is expecting will not only submerge those islanders but also put the world's coastal populations at risk. The numbers are mind-boggling. Nearly 25 percent of the world's population currently lives within a hundred kilometres of a shoreline, while roughly 600 million people make their homes in coastal regions that are less than ten metres above sea level. Thirteen of the world's fifteen largest cities are on coastal plains. In the United States alone, Boston, New York, San Francisco, Miami, Seattle and New Orleans are all at risk. Globally, Mumbai, Alexandria, Osaka–Kobe, Shanghai and Ho Chi Minh City are in the danger zone.[11]

At the very minimum, protecting these areas and others would require the construction of giant seawalls to prevent flooding. New York City may be able to afford a $10-billion barrier to save itself from the next superstorm, but what will places like Dhaka in Bangladesh—home to 12 million—do when tsunami-like waves start heading for shore?

Whether seawalls will be able to withstand the height of superstorm surges is another question altogether—and one that will be asked with increasing frequency. What were once considered storms of the century are becoming annual events. When a storm the size of Sandy hits a coastline (its winds covered an area of 1,600 kilometres), little can stand in its way. Sandy's storm surge rose to heights of between one and three metres—flooding New York's subway system and temporarily putting the lower end of Manhattan underwater.[12]

All of this *without* that extra degree of warming scientists say is already coming at us. What else may be in store is difficult to predict and certainly open to debate. But there is near unanimity in the scientific community that anything greater than a 2-degrees-Celsius rise in average global temperature would overwhelm our capacity to adjust, putting the human population—not to mention countless other species of animal and plant life—at risk.

THE CARBON BUDGET: CRUNCHING THE NUMBERS

So we've established this much: First, temperature change is directly related to how much carbon is in our atmosphere. Second, too much carbon—and too much global warming—is bad. But how much is too much? When do we pass the point of no return? According to the IPCC, that point is 450 parts per million. Anything beyond that and the 2-degrees-Celsius threshold will be breeched.

In its fifth and latest assessment report, released in 2013, the IPCC calculated how much carbon we could burn without exceeding that threshold. The organization called this total our carbon budget: the point at which we either have to stop burning carbon altogether or find a way of no longer emitting its waste products into the atmosphere when we do.

And what is our carbon budget? According to the IPCC, we cannot emit more than 2,900 gigatonnes (GT) of CO_2 if we want to stay out of the danger zone. But here's the unfortunate part: the countdown on that 2,900 GT carbon budget started at the dawn of the Industrial Revolution—some 250 years ago, when we first started burning coal and emitting its by-product, carbon dioxide, into the atmosphere. We have already emitted well over half of that amount—some 1,900 GT of CO_2. That means we've got about 1,000 GT left.

One thousand gigatonnes may sound like an incredibly large number—and it is. A gigatonne is a billion tons, and talking about billions of anything can offer a false sense of security. But those numbers don't seem so huge when they are scaled to the pace at which we're currently emitting. Human-made emissions are now running at around 37 GT of CO_2 a year.[13] If we continue at today's pace, we've got twenty-seven years left to burn carbon. After that, we either have to shut down the global economy as we know it or prepare for a much larger than 2-degree global temperature rise, and everything that entails.

We can extend that carbon-burning horizon considerably by easing off on our emissions over the next two decades. If we could cut our annual emissions in half, for example, we would double the number of years left before our carbon budget runs out. Even so, we would only be able to combust carbon fuels for a little longer than fifty years. The longer we wait to reduce our emissions, the shorter the time we have left to power our world by burning carbon. And, unfortunately, the trend in annual emissions is moving in the wrong direction.

Between 1990 and 2000, global CO_2 emissions grew at a rate of about 1 percent a year. Since then, emissions growth has been on a tear. As the rapid development of China and the other so-called BRIC countries (Brazil, Russia and India) shifted global economic growth into overdrive, it shifted CO_2 emissions growth into the same gear. Between 2000 and 2009, annual emissions growth more than tripled, to over 3 percent. The 2009 recession put a temporary kink in that growth, but it didn't last long. Once the recession was over, emissions growth quickly recovered. In 2014, emissions grew at a very robust rate of 2.5 percent. And with every passing year in which emissions grow, the chances of holding atmospheric carbon to the 450-ppm threshold fade.

That's bad-enough news on its own, but it gets worse when we consider that even holding carbon to 450 ppm is no surefire guarantee that we'll able to hold the increase in average global temperature to 2 degrees Celsius. Given the complex interactions between climate variables, known as *feedback mechanisms* in the scientific community, the IPCC's carbon budget is a probabilistic estimate. That means the budget shrinks or increases depending on how sure we want to be of the results. The IPCC scientists figure that the 1,000 GT estimate of the remaining carbon budget gives us a two-thirds probability of staying within that 2-degree range. If we want better odds, we have even less carbon to emit.

Of course, we could just do nothing and merrily go on pumping ever-increasing amounts of carbon into the atmosphere. But the more we emit, the hotter it will get. With atmospheric carbon levels between 480 and 580 ppm, we will experience more than 3 degrees Celsius of warming. Ramp up to between 580 and 720 ppm and we're talking something closer to 4 degrees—almost double the increase in average global temperature that the scientific community warns against.

The scariest part is that we've backed ourselves into a corner with our own complacency. Most of the carbon-burning infrastructure (think coal-fired plants) needed to take us past the 450-ppm threshold either is already built or will be built by 2017.[14]

And if emissions keep growing at their current pace, we are on target for 700 ppm of carbon in our atmosphere by the end of the century, and a nearly 4-degree rise in average global temperature.

LOOKING FOR SOLUTIONS
IN ALL THE WRONG PLACES

It's a worrisome situation indeed for a world on the brink of environmental and economic disaster. We should be moving as fast as we can
toward a carbon-free future. Instead, we're sticking to our same old
bad habits—and are primed to continue doing so into the foreseeable
future. Something's got to give.

When faced with news like this, one's natural inclination is often
to look for a quick fix, a no-fuss, no-muss solution. It's the same
mentality that drives those desperate to lose weight or get in shape to
try the latest diet pill or exercise gizmo (remember the Thigh Master?).
The fact that these shortcuts rarely work is no deterrent. We deny all
logic and convince ourselves that they stand a chance. We try, we fail,
and then, maybe, we get serious about putting in the time and effort
required to effect real change.

When it comes to carbon, it seems we're still in the denial stage,
looking for solutions in all the wrong places.

Not-So-Clean Coal

Clean coal is a perfect example. You hear the term bandied about
a lot these days, usually from the lips of coal company executives.
But the only way that coal can be made clean, at least from a GHG
perspective, is if you capture the CO_2 emissions that are released
from combusting the fuel and store them in underground caverns.
Given the over 8 billion tons of coal the world burns ever year, the
vastness of that task is absolutely staggering. To capture even a
tenth of the world's coal-fired emissions would require pumping
the same volume of CO_2 into the ground as the volume of oil we
currently pump out.[15]

If the physical requirements of carbon sequestration and storage
seem absurdly gargantuan, imagine the cost. It would require at least

a \$100-a-ton tax on carbon emissions for the technology to make any commercial sense to a CO_2-emitting power utility. Currently, CO_2 emission prices in the European Union Emission Trading System are under \$10 a ton.

And even if we were willing to levy that tax, we're nowhere near ready to push the "go" button. At the time of this writing, there is only one commercial-scale coal-fired power plant in the world with capture and storage capacity, and it happens to be in Saskatchewan.[16] But the economics behind this project are unique and not readily applicable to capturing and storing carbon emissions from most coal plants. As it turns out, the CO_2 captured from SaskPower's Boundary Dam coal-fired power plant will be used, through a process known as enhanced oil recovery (EOR), to pump out otherwise unrecoverable oil from a nearby Cenovus Energy property. In addition to the value created by the otherwise unrecoverable oil, the project requires a \$240 million dollar subsidy from the federal government.

Without enhanced oil recovery or massive public subsidies, carbon capture and sequestration does not make financial sense. That reality was acknowledged by Alberta's newly appointed premier, Jim Prentice, who abandoned the province's plans to consider as many as four carbon-capture projects, calling the exercise a "science experiment" and rightfully questioning its economic viability.[17] Another North American site—the Kemper County integrated gasification combined cycle facility in Mississippi—will eventually capture over half of its coal-fired emissions and sequester them in neighbouring oil fields. Unfortunately, the plant, financed in large measure by a grant from the US Department of Energy, is massively over budget.[18]

A Bridge to a Carbon-Free Future?

So clean coal, it would seem, is a non-starter when it comes to dramatically cutting emissions—at least in the short term. But what about cleaner fossil fuels? Of all the hydrocarbons, natural gas leaves the faintest carbon trail when burnt, emitting about half the carbon that coal does for a comparable unit of energy. This means that switching from burning coal to burning natural gas can give you twice the amount of energy for a given level of emissions, and presumably that much more economic activity as well. For that reason, natural gas has often been described as a bridge to a carbon-free economy, a way to buy the time needed to transition to non-emitting energy sources such as wind and solar.

Whether natural gas is really that much cleaner than coal is now a subject of growing debate. The fracking of shale gas, which now accounts for about 40 percent of US gas production, and is soon expected to represent a growing proportion of world production as well, has been associated with the unintended release of substantial amounts of methane. Methane, the principal component of natural gas, is a greenhouse gas that is about twenty times more potent than CO_2 when it comes to its heat-trapping properties, although it doesn't remain nearly as long in the atmosphere.

Studies done at Harvard and Stanford have found that fugitive methane emissions from gas wells in the United States are likely to be 50 percent greater than acknowledged by the Environmental Protection Agency (EPA). So the supposed emissions savings from switching to natural gas may turn out to be largely bogus.

It probably won't matter. There simply isn't enough natural gas around to replace all the coal the world burns. Consider the numbers: On an energy-equivalent basis, 1 billion metric tons of coal is equal to .761 trillion cubic metres of natural gas. At that energy exchange ratio conversion, the 4 billion tons of coal China presently burns each year is roughly equal to the energy from combusting almost 3 trillion cubic metres of natural gas. But that's almost as much as China's total estimated gas reserves of 3.1 trillion cubic metres. In other words, the country could switch from coal to natural gas for just a single year before it would exhaust its reserves and have to switch back to burning coal.

If natural gas is a bridge to a carbon-free future, it's a pretty short bridge.

THE HEIR(S) APPARENT

In the war against emissions, there are no quick fixes, and no short-cuts. The IEA estimates that if we are to hold atmospheric carbon to the 450-ppm threshold, there will have to be a quantum increase in the use of non-carbon fuels. In fact, such fuel usage would have to more than double from current levels, to the point where it meets more than 80 percent of the expected increase in energy demand over the next two decades.[19] While there is much that is promising in the works, this road to a carbon-free future is full of twists and turns, and more than a few potholes.

Until 2:46 p.m. on Friday, March 11, 2011, the most likely candidate to lessen our overwhelming but unsustainable dependence on burning fossil fuels was nuclear power. At that moment, a rare double earthquake registering 9.1 on the Richter scale unleashed a fifteen-metre-high tsunami 130 kilometres off the Japanese coast. The wave crashed over an almost six-metre breakwater barrier protecting the Tokyo Electric Power Company's nuclear generating station in Fukushima (the largest power utility in Asia) and flooded the reactor buildings, shutting off all electric power. Without power, the cooling system failed and three nuclear reactors melted down. The ongoing contamination of local groundwater and surrounding seawater with radioactive material may ultimately prove to be the greatest nuclear disaster in history.[20]

Before Fukushima, most people considered nuclear energy the most economically viable alternative to burning carbon fuels. Some still do. But aside from China, India and South Korea, no one seems to want to build new reactors anymore. Since the Fukushima reactor meltdowns, many countries are actively shying away from the nuclear option. Japan has shut down its entire network of reactors, which accounted for roughly 30 percent of the nation's power. France recently voted to reduce the amount of electricity it generates from nuclear by a third—from 75 percent to 50 percent—over the next eleven years. To do so, the country will need to shut down nearly a third of its reactors.[21] Germany has permanently shuttered several of its older nuclear power plants and has announced its intention of becoming nuclear free in the future. But so far at least, this move away from nuclear has led to a greater use of fossil fuels, as countries such as Japan and Germany have ramped up imports of liquefied natural gas (LNG) or coal to fill the power void.

So if nuclear isn't going to be the answer (at least for now), what else is on the table? An expanded role for hydroelectric power is another option to decarbonize our economies. Hydropower is created by the movement of water downstream—movement that is harnessed and used to drive turbines. The more water is moving, and the greater the height from which it drops, the more power is produced. Typically, hydropower stations dam rivers and create reservoirs in which to store water, so that levels can be adjusted in accordance with power demand.

Currently, hydro accounts for just over 15 percent of world power generation, but in some places, like Brazil, it provides almost 80 percent of a country's power needs. In Canada, 60 percent of the country's power needs are currently being met by hydro, and the Canadian Hydropower Association estimates that tapping more potential sources of hydroelectricity could double the current capacity.[22] Of course, not every country has undeveloped hydroelectric potential. With a few notable exceptions—including Canada, China, Russia and Brazil— most countries have already developed their prime hydroelectric sites. Moreover, hydroelectric power comes with its own environmental and social challenges. The controversial Belo Monte dam on the Xingu River in Brazil, which when completed will be the third largest in the world, will flood hundreds of square kilometres of jungle. Thousands of indigenous people will lose their traditional livelihoods so that urban consumers in Brazil's sprawling metropolises can consume more power.

Right now, wind and solar are our most promising options for clean and renewable power, and both have established permanent beachheads in today's energy grid. Wind power is the world's fastest-growing source of energy. In 2011, Europe led the world in the production of offshore wind energy, and estimates suggest that the capacity installed by the end of 2013 could produce enough to cover 8 percent of the European Union's (EU) electricity consumption.[23] Europe is also on the cutting edge with solar. The continent features nine of the fifteen largest solar markets in the world, with Germany leading the way in solar power capacity.[24] By 2020, the EU aims to get 20 percent of its energy from renewable sources.[25] Countries such as Germany, France and Spain are already past that threshold.[26]

What is happening in Europe, however, may pale in comparison with what's about to happen in Asia. Some estimates suggest that installed solar capacity worldwide will almost triple by 2018, with much of the growth coming from Asia, which knocked Europe off its perch as the world's biggest solar market in 2013.[27] China alone installed 12.9 gigawatts of solar electricity generation—the largest amount ever by one country in a single year.[28]

Both wind and solar power could potentially post huge gains in the future, particularly if advances in battery technology allow for greater storage capacity of energy when the wind isn't blowing or the sun's not shining. They could also pose a serious challenge to the business models of large electric utility companies that transmit power. Solar-powered households in particular could simply disconnect from the grid, or drastically reduce the amount of power they draw from it. The more households that do disconnect, the more remaining ratepayers will have to pay to cover the huge fixed costs of building massive transmission lines. The resulting hike in hydro bills would, in turn, encourage even more ratepayers to switch.

Or perhaps the answer to our carbon problem will come via breakthroughs in new technologies, like nuclear fusion, or through the redevelopment of older technologies, like thorium-based reactors that don't emit deadly radiation.

Dramatically reducing our reliance on fossil fuels over the coming decades is obviously a very bullish scenario for companies developing renewable energy sources that don't emit carbon, if they can fill the energy gap; if they can't, it's a very bearish outlook for world economic growth.

CHAPTER 2

GROW GREEN OR DON'T GROW

TESLA MOTORS' CEO, ELON MUSK, probably wakes up happy most mornings. Since the company's initial public offering in 2010, its stock has shot up an astonishing 1,400 percent,[1] and its electric cars—despite price tags upwards of $100,000—are among the most loved on the market.[2] When it comes to brand popularity, Tesla may soon be giving Apple a run for its money.

There's no doubt that part of the company's appeal is its whole-hearted embracing of the "green" ethos—the idea that we're going to have to do things differently if we want to . . . well . . . keep doing things at all. For those who have been preaching this gospel for decades now, the Tesla story offers hope, an indication that perhaps the public is ready to begin embracing the switch to renewables that's necessary if we're going to avoid the doom-and-gloom scenarios that come with too much global warming. It also offers hope on an economic level. If a company like Tesla can succeed so spectacularly, perhaps it means that the hitherto-elusive concept of green growth is, in fact, an option.

A GREEN LIGHT FOR GROWTH?

Not so long ago, a green economy and a growing economy were considered to be mutually exclusive. It's easy to see why. Economic growth is a powerful driver of carbon emissions. We can see this just by looking at what happens when our economies stop growing. Emissions invariably fall during recessions, even though environmental standards are usually relaxed or ignored in times of economic hardship. The rate of economic growth, it seems, is a lot more important in determining our emissions levels than any policy choices we've made about energy use. But most of us who are concerned with carbon emissions and climate change don't want to see recessions any more than anyone else does. Even the prospect of slower growth isn't that appealing. Economic growth means jobs and income and, most of all, consumption — things most of us consider essential to our well-being.

If growth requires energy and that energy can't come from burning hydrocarbons, the preferred solution, as we saw in chapter 1, is a massive shift to renewable and clean sources of energy. That way, our economies can continue to grow, and we can continue our energy-intensive lifestyles — all without further burdening our already carbon-laden skies.

At least for the moment, however, this "having our cake and eating it too" option isn't feasible. Americans alone currently use over 18 million barrels of oil a day, along with 2.7 million tons of coal and 63 billion cubic feet of natural gas. More than 84 percent of the country's total energy use is provided by fossil fuels. In comparison, nuclear energy supplies 8.5 percent, while renewables bring up the rear with 7.3 percent.[3] The numbers vary in other countries,[4] but the overall message is consistent: renewable energy sources are becoming more cost effective, and they are undoubtedly clean, but they just don't have the capacity to replace carbon — at least not yet. And so we're back where we started, facing the undesirable but inevitable scenario of limited growth.[5]

In a world of much slower economic growth, we don't have to be so green to achieve our desired carbon emissions targets. Slower growth means fewer energy inputs are needed, and since most of the world's energy inputs currently come from carbon-emitting fossil fuels, it's only natural that demand for these fuels will bear the burden of any adjustment in energy use. That's why emissions always fall during recessions.

Economic growth is measured by the annual rate of change in gross domestic product (GDP), while the carbon intensity of our economy is measured by emissions per unit of GDP. Since an already-changing climate is forcing us to halt the rise in emissions, the only way we can grow is by reducing emissions per unit of GDP. The less carbon emitted per unit of GDP, the more GDP can be squeezed into a country's carbon budget.

If, for example, a country wants to hold its carbon emissions constant over time, it must decarbonize at the same pace that it is growing. In other words, emissions per unit of GDP must decline at the same rate at which GDP is growing. Keeping that relationship in mind, the more you can reduce emissions per unit of GDP, the more room you have to grow.

That is a very different relationship between environmental stewardship and economic growth from the one to which we've grown accustomed. For years, we have been warned that switching to greener energy sources reduces economic growth. But now that the clock is ticking on our carbon budget, that is precisely what governments around the world will have to do. In a world in which global carbon emissions are constrained, the old trade-off between doing what is right for the environment and doing what is right for the economy gets turned on its head. In the past, going green came at the expense of economic growth. In a carbon emissions–constrained future, the greener the economy, the more room it has to grow.[6]

To be sure, world leaders will try to reduce emissions in the least disruptive way possible. But, like it or not, they will need to act, and those actions are going to hurt the carbon-burning components of their economies, most of all the fossil fuel industries themselves.

NO MORE BUSINESS AS USUAL

All of this is certainly bad news for industries that rely on burning carbon for power, but it's even worse news for the companies that supply them with their fossil fuel. The International Energy Agency (IEA),[7] the world's leading authority on, and tracker of, energy usage and supply, calculates that if world emissions are to be held to 450 ppm, world coal consumption would have to fall by a third by 2035, while global oil consumption would have to peak as early as 2020 and decline steadily thereafter, falling to around 80 million barrels a day (mbd) by 2035—an almost 15 percent reduction from 2014 levels. Those forecasts suggest a very different trajectory for future fossil fuel demand than the ones guiding investment decisions in the coal and oil industries today.

Rather than planning how to adjust to a shrinking market, these companies are instead preparing to meet the demand from business-as-usual growth in global fossil fuel combustion. Indeed, the notion that there is no limit to the amount of carbon we can emit into the atmosphere is the bedrock of the business plans those firms have put together. And it's those very business plans in which shareholders are investing.

The notion of unlimited growth powered by unlimited emissions has pretty well guided the business practices of the carbon industry since its inception. It stems from the undeniable fact that economic growth has required the combustion of ever-greater amounts of fossil fuel. And since the lead times between the discovery of new reserves and actual production could often exceed a decade, business planning dictated that oil, coal and natural gas producers needed to be continually finding new reserves today if they were going to be filling your gas tank or heating your home tomorrow.

It's a valid business model for a world that will always want to combust more fossil fuel. But in a world that will soon have to adapt to a carbon budget, it's a business model that no longer makes any economic sense.

Compare what is left of our carbon budget with how much fuel we have already found—proven reserves that have been earmarked for extraction—and you may be astonished to learn that we don't have to find any more coal, oil or natural gas. Depending upon what odds we want to place on our ability to hold carbon at the 450 ppm mark, anywhere from two-thirds to over three-quarters of all the proven reserves of fossil fuels *cannot be burned*. We simply can't afford the carbon trail.

If we want to have a 50 percent chance of holding the rise in average global temperature to no more than 2 degrees Celsius, the IEA calculates that two-thirds of our reserves should be left untouched. It's a safe bet that most of us will want to have more than coin-toss odds when the full impacts of climate change start knocking at the door. If so, we should burn even less of those reserves than the IEA suggests. Erring on the side of caution, the IPCC estimates that if we want an 80 percent chance of holding carbon to 450 ppm, over three-quarters of our proven fossil fuel reserves must stay in the ground.

So why are oil, coal and natural gas companies spending over $674 billion each year to scour the globe for new and increasingly hard-to-access hydrocarbons?[8] Instead of wasting all that money on unnecessary exploration and development budgets for fuel no one will be able to burn, why don't they just kick back and pay out those billions to their investors? After all, once stock markets figure out how much these carbon companies own in unburnable reserves, management won't have to worry about maintaining adequate reserve ratios for their investors. Or, better yet, they could take some of those billions and put them toward the development of fuel alternatives.

As we've seen, leaving the majority of the world's proven reserves of fossil fuels in the ground implies either a massive shift to alternative fuels or just as massive a reduction in the rate of economic growth, and hence world fuel consumption. Neither route is particularly appealing to fossil fuel energy firms. If we don't decarbonize our economies sufficiently and are forced to reduce growth, oil, coal and natural gas companies may be able to hold on to their huge share of the energy pie, but the size of the pie, along with the size of the economy, won't be growing anymore. Alternatively, if we are successful in engineering a massive shift to cleaner fuels, fossil fuel firms may in fact be looking at a bigger energy pie, but their slice will be a whole lot smaller.

BACK TO $40 A BARREL?

If we can't keep burning oil, coal and natural gas, the demand for these fuels will fall. Fewer factories running on coal-fired power, fewer vehicles powered by gasoline and diesel, and fewer homes heated by natural gas will translate into falling oil, coal and natural gas prices—not exactly the scenario that fossil fuel producers are counting on in their business plans.

For carbon companies, especially oily ones, a world of falling fuel prices is a whole different business paradigm from a world of rising prices. Declining prices are challenging enough for any business, but they become downright lethal in an industry whose costs are at the same time sharply rising. Yet that is precisely the position most oil firms find themselves in today.

Why all of this massive spending to find new reserves? Well, it turns out you have to spend a lot more these day to find and develop new reserves than you did in the past. Conventional, easy-to-access, low-cost oil peaked about a decade ago. While world oil production has grown since 2005, all of the increases in global supply have come from high-cost unconventional sources such as oil sands, shale formations and deepwater wells. That's no problem if oil prices just keep on rising. According to the British think tank Carbon Tracker, oil industry capital outlay rose by 90 percent between 2005 and 2012, while oil prices over the same period rose 75 percent. Between 2011 and 2013, capital expenditures (cap ex) rose another 20 percent.[9]

But if prices start falling, as they have since 2014, a whole different scenario emerges. If high-cost unconventional production accounts for a greater share of world oil supply with each passing year, then more and more of the world's oil production is in fact vulnerable to the falling oil prices that go hand in hand with the steadily reduced rations of fossil fuel that our dwindling carbon budget will allow us to burn.

World oil demand has been growing at an annual rate of roughly 1 percent for the last several years. Even with much slower growth in the future, the IEA estimates that world demand will easily exceed 100 mbd within the next two decades. Yet the same agency calculates that if we are to cap atmospheric carbon at 450 ppm, world oil consumption will instead have to *drop* by almost 15 percent over the same time period, to 80 mbd. Those two scenarios pose very different outlooks for oil prices.

What does a reduction in consumption imply for prices over the period? If you want a benchmark, look at what happened during the last recession. World oil demand fell by 3.5 mbd between the first quarter of 2008 and the second quarter of 2009. During that same period, crude prices fell from nearly $150 per barrel to, briefly, below $40 per barrel.

A nearly 15 percent reduction in world demand is over *three times* the decline suffered during the Great Recession. Moreover, world oil prices sprang right back to the triple-digit range once the global economy began to recover. In the emissions-restrained future we are talking about, however, there can be no cyclical bounce back.

But how do we achieve this? How do the laws of supply and demand get us to a more sustainable level of oil consumption? In today's world of plunging oil prices and a weakening global economy, it's not too hard to see how we might get back to $40-a-barrel prices. The current global economic slowdown has already seen oil prices drop below $50 a barrel, in sight of the lows reached during the last recession. It's harder, though, to see how demand won't spring back like a jack-in-the-box when those low oil prices start showing up at the pumps. How many cars will Tesla sell once filling up a gas-guzzler no longer burns a big hole in your wallet?

ALCOHOL, TOBACCO . . . AND CARBON?

Unless, of course, those low pump prices don't hang around for very long. Just as the cost of cigarettes today isn't dependent on the cost of growing tobacco, or the price of a bottle of rum on the price of sugar-cane, the cost of filling your car should not depend so heavily on the price of oil.

Governments tax alcohol and tobacco prohibitively. It's known as a "sin tax," a state-sponsored levy on items generally believed to be detrimental to our overall health and well-being. In a carbon-constrained future, emissions are going to have to be treated in the same way. Right now, we're paying only for the cost of extracting and processing the fuel. We don't pay for our emissions when we combust that fuel, or for the costs that will accrue from the resulting climate change. That's got to change, and soon.

Even the International Monetary Fund (IMF), not known as a carbon-management advocacy group, has urged a 50 percent increase in fuel taxes across 156 countries to encourage more rapid growth in renewable energy.[10] While motorists will feel those increases every time they fill up at the pump, it's worth noting that the IMF and others who advocate higher carbon taxes are also calling for equivalent income tax cuts. In effect, the call to raise carbon taxes is a call to shift the tax base from income to carbon emissions. If you actually cut back on your fuel consumption—which is what carbon taxes are intended to encourage—the accompanying income tax cuts would in fact leave you with more disposable income to spend on everything else. That's not just a win for the environment; it's a win for your pocketbook as well.

However things develop, the upshot is that we're heading into a future where the time-honoured machinations of the free market cannot be left to play out on their own. One way or another, the global economy will have to combust less oil in the future. And that points to a world of much lower oil prices than today. But it certainly won't be because oil has suddenly become cheap and plentiful. On the contrary, at those prices, oil will never have been scarcer. The vast majority of the world's oil supply—including much of the largest-known oil reserve (Venezuela's Orinoco belt) and the third-largest reserve (the Canadian oil sands)—will no longer be economically viable. Tight oil from fracked shale formations or deepwater wells will also be at risk.

Ultimately, prices determine where oil can be profitably extracted and where it will have to stay in the ground. Even with low oil prices, it is still economically profitable to extract oil from fields in the Middle East, given that those fields have the lowest production costs in the world. For all the talk in the media these days about how newfound North American oil supplies from shale formations and oil sands will lessen the strategic importance of Middle Eastern oil, it's Middle Eastern oil that is the least likely to be affected by plunging oil prices.

The rest of the oil industry will fare much worse. A study by HSBC's Global Research Department estimated that even with prices at $50 per barrel, some of the largest publicly traded oil companies would stand to lose anywhere from 40 to 60 percent of their stock market value.[11] Of course, not all oil companies would be equally exposed to that decline. Those hit hardest would be bitumen and other heavy-oil producers. Not only is their fuel more emissions intensive than other oils but, more important, their high-cost production structure would make them economically untenable at low oil prices.

Someone should have mentioned this to Stephen Harper.

CHAPTER 3

PARIAH

MANAGING GLOBAL EMISSIONS is an international task. Since there are no borders in the atmosphere, every country's emissions are every other country's concern. Global climate change won't affect only those countries that fail to give up their carbon-burning habits; it will happen everywhere. In fact, the countries that are likely to experience the most dramatic climate change effects, such as those with low-lying islands and coastal regions, aren't necessarily the ones responsible for emitting the most carbon.

That said, there is an emerging global consensus that it must fall to the world's rich, developed countries to decarbonize their economies first, allowing developing countries to use what's left of the dwindling global carbon budget to raise living standards.[1] Not only are affluent, developed countries better able to afford the transition away from fossil fuels, but, by and large, these are the countries that industrialized the earliest and have been emitting carbon the longest. And so, the argument goes, it's only fair that developing countries get to use what little is left of our carbon budget.

Most advanced industrial nations seem to be on board with this line of thinking, and many have already committed to significantly reducing their emissions. The EU, for example, has pledged to reduce its emissions by 40 percent from 1990 levels by 2030. In the United States, President Barack Obama has announced plans to cut economy-wide US greenhouse gas emissions by 25 percent by 2025; Environmental Protection Agency data shows that US power plants have already reduced CO_2 emissions by 13 percent since 2005.[2] But among the world's wealthiest developed nations, one country's carbon trail stands out like a sky-written message on a crystal-clear day. Instead of reducing its share of global emissions, this pariah plans on hogging even more. In fact, by 2030, it intends to emit about 40 *percent more* than it did back in 1990, the benchmark year for the targets set by the original Kyoto accord.

That country is Canada.

NOT YOUR TYPICAL BAD GUY

You can be excused if you need a moment to take that in. Canada, after all, is not normally viewed as a pariah state in the international community. For years it was known for its peacekeepers and its commitment to the UN and multilateralism, for fairness and abject apologies, for maple syrup and polar bears and hockey. And like the country's obsession with its unofficial national sport, Canada's environmental record used to be a point of national pride. Under Liberal prime minister Jean Chrétien, Canada was one of the world's most enthusiastic supporters of—and an original signatory of—the Kyoto accord.

Yet in recent years, Canada's emissions record has taken a major hit. In 2006, the new Conservative government of Prime Minister Stephen Harper abandoned the targets set under the Kyoto accord and didn't waste any time putting the whole idea in the rear-view mirror. (Canada initially pledged to reduce its GHG emissions by 6 percent between 1996 and 2012; instead, they have risen by 26 percent.) It then set about blocking a Commonwealth resolution to support binding targets for industrialized nations. In 2008, after the climate talks in Poznań, Poland, Canada was awarded the Fossil of the Year Award, presented by environmental groups to the country that had done the most to disrupt progress at the talks. By 2009, a number of prominent scientists and politicians were calling for the country's expulsion from the Commonwealth.[3] At the 2013 UN Climate Summit in Warsaw, the Climate Action Network awarded the country its "Lifetime Unachievement" Fossil Award, in recognition of Canada winning the annual award six years running.[4]

How did Canada go from full-out support of Kyoto to environmental pariah in less than a decade? It all started with Harper's vision.

AN ENERGY SUPERPOWER

On July 14, 2006, Stephen Harper stood to address the Canada–UK Chamber of Commerce in London, England—his first international speech since being elected prime minister five months earlier. After thanking his hosts and outlining the deep historical connection between the two countries, Harper turned to meatier fare. In what was no doubt a reflection of the times, he first addressed issues of foreign policy, defence and national security. Then he moved on to the topic at hand: Canada's appeal as a place to do business.

> One of the primary targets for British investors has been our booming energy sector. They have recognized Canada's emergence as a global energy powerhouse—the emerging "energy superpower" our government intends to build.
>
> It's no exaggeration.
>
> We are currently the fifth-largest energy producer in the world. We rank third and seventh in global gas and oil production respectively. We generate more hydroelectric power than any other country on earth. And we are the world's largest supplier of uranium. But that's just the beginning.

Our government is making new investments in renewable energy sources such as biofuels. And an ocean of oil-soaked sand lies under the muskeg of northern Alberta—my home province. The oil sands are the second-largest oil deposit in the world, bigger than Iraq, Iran or Russia; exceeded only by Saudi Arabia.

Digging the bitumen out of the ground, squeezing out the oil and converting it into synthetic crude is a monumental challenge. It requires vast amounts of capital, Brobdingnagian technology, and an army of skilled workers. In short, it is an enterprise of epic proportions, akin to the building of the pyramids or China's Great Wall.

Only bigger.[5]

And there it was, first spoken and then reported in newspapers both in Canada and around the world. Harper had plans, big plans (Wall of China big, Brobdingnagian big): Canada was going to become an energy superpower, not by focusing on the development of renewable energy such as wind or solar power, or even nuclear or hydro (even though the country has a considerable amount of both). No, Harper was talking about Canada becoming a petro power. Only the petro he was referring to wasn't the kind that gushed out of oil wells; it was the kind that had to be extracted from a vast reservoir of oil-drenched sand, known for decades as tar sands, which until the last decade the oil industry had largely ignored.

Whether the prime minister realized it or not, he was tapping into a rich vein in Canada's history.

THE BIRTHPLACE OF NORTH AMERICAN OIL

I'm sitting on Charlie Fairbank's porch looking out at the site of the first oil well in North America. Only it's not in the hills of Pennsylvania, where Americans claim oil was first drilled on the continent. Instead, I'm gazing at the pastoral countryside of south-western Ontario. In 1858—a full year before Colonel Drake drilled his first well in Titusville, Pennsylvania—oil was flowing from wells drilled in Oil Springs, Ontario. Some of those wells, like Charlie's, are still producing over 150 years later.

No one would confuse Charlie's operation with the brutal terrain of northern Alberta, where giant tailing ponds litter a destroyed landscape. His wells are on 650 acres of typical southwestern Ontario farmland. There is even a llama parading around, on guard to scare away any coyotes that might be stalking the farm's animals. Aside from the pungent smell of sour oil, the bucolic scene could be lifted from the set of *Green Acres*.

Charlie, a fourth-generation oilman, comes from a family that has been pumping oil for over a century. He can't smell the stuff anymore, even though its odour is everywhere. He tells me his nose stopped working a long time ago, and it's not hard to see why: he has been whiffing such fumes for his entire sixty-eight-year life. Today, he is still producing about twenty-four thousand barrels a year using the same jerker-line system[6] his great-grandfather, John Fairbank, invented over a century ago.

Even back in John Fairbank's day, the existence in southwestern Ontario of oil springs and bitumen outcrops (then called gum beds) had already been known for some time. As early as 1793, the first lieutenant-governor of Ontario, John Simcoe, noted the presence of oil springs along the banks of the lower Thames River on his travels through the region. But it was Thomas Hunt, working for the Geological Survey of Canada in 1850, who first brought widespread attention to the area's bitumen outcrops. It wasn't long before the news travelled stateside and attracted a steady stream of adventurers and entrepreneurs. One of these was Charlie's great-grandfather, who purchased land in Oil Springs in 1861.

At first, only the surface bitumen was exploited, the same substance that is now the backbone of Canada's production in Alberta.

Back then, however, the only commercial use for bitumen was asphalt. After displaying its product at the Universal Exhibition in Paris in 1855, the region's biggest bitumen producer actually received an order to provide enough of the tar pitch to pave all the streets of Paris. Unfortunately, logistics prevented the order from being filled. There was no way to get the bitumen out of the muddy backwoods of southwestern Ontario and across the Atlantic Ocean to Paris. Even in those days, getting bitumen to foreign markets was a problem.

Not only was the first oil well in North America drilled in Canada, but it was also a Canadian, Nova Scotia's Dr. Abraham Gesner, who first developed a process for producing kerosene from crude. Dr. Gesner's breakthrough discovery immediately created a more valuable use for oil than paving roads with bitumen.

It didn't take long for that technology to hit the bitumen fields of southwestern Ontario. In the summer of 1858, James Williams—digging a well over four metres deep atop a surface outcrop of bitumen—hit the real stuff: gushing oil. News spread fast, creating a mini rush. Within two years, there were no fewer than four hundred wells in the Oil Springs area.

Depletion was something the oil industry had to deal with even in its infancy. Production in Oil Springs quickly fell off, prompting exploration and discovery in nearby Petrolia, where the deposits, while deeper under the ground, were larger. Petrolia became the new focal point for Canada's burgeoning oil industry as technological improvements allowed for the digging of much deeper wells, some over thirty metres down.

Petrolia's day in the sun was brief. An economic depression hit in the 1870s, reining in demand for oil while depletion steadily sapped production. Over the ensuing decades, there was a diaspora of Ontario oilmen from Enniskillen township who took their experience and technology around the world. From the Dutch East Indies (now Indonesia) to Borneo, the Hard Oilers, as they were known, toiled through jungles infested with malaria and yellow fever, bringing Canadian drilling technology to the tropics. In central Europe, their search for oil put them in the crossfire of warring armies during the First World War. Others scoured the sand dunes of the Middle East and the mountains of Persia searching for oil, often getting a hostile greeting from the locals. Petrolia was probably Canada's most cosmopolitan small town by virtue of its swashbuckling oil explorers scattered around the world. Among them was William McGarvey, who went to the Carpathian mountains in Galicia (today part of Poland) and made a large-enough fortune, through his Galicia-Carpathian Petroleum Company, that he was able to marry off his daughter to a European royal with a dowry of a seven-hundred-acre estate complete with castle.[7]

On the home front, however, trouble was brewing. Rockefeller's Standard Oil had monopolized the petroleum business in the United States, and the company intended to achieve the same market dominance north of the border. It moved aggressively into Canada, building the country's largest refinery in Sarnia, Ontario.

To ward off the threat from Rockefeller, nineteen of the largest Oil Springs and Petrolia producers banded together to form the Imperial Oil Company. The new company was incorporated in London, Ontario, which, with fifty-two plants, was the refining centre for the region. The company's mandate was ambitious from the start: from its perch in oil-rich southwestern Ontario, Imperial sought to be Canada's primary producer, refiner and distributor of petroleum.

Even back in the industry's early days, oil was a scale business requiring lots and lots of capital. Soon enough, the fledging Canadian company was dwarfed by Rockefeller's behemoth, and in 1898, Standard Oil bought out Imperial. (Its successor company, Exxon, still owns two-thirds of Imperial Oil and controls its management.) Shortly after the takeover, Imperial moved its refining operations from Petrolia to Sarnia, which grew to become not only the nation's primary refining site but also the petrochemical centre of the country.

The oil fields in southwestern Ontario, like those south of the border in Pennsylvania, were quickly sucked dry, forcing the industry to move west. In the United States, the oil industry relocated to Texas. In Canada, it found a new home in Alberta. In 1947, Imperial hit a big gusher at the Leduc Well, just south of Edmonton, and the focus of Canada's oil industry subsequently shifted to Alberta's Western Canadian Sedimentary Basin (WCSB), which quickly became the mainstay of the country's oil production.

Not surprisingly, the WCSB posed the same problem as today's oil sands: it was located thousands of kilometres from its principal markets. Most of the Canadian population and the country's industry, and hence the country's oil demand, were in central Canada. At the time, shipping oil by rail was about four times more expensive than shipping through a pipeline, so the Interprovincial Pipeline Company (the precursor of today's Enbridge) built a pipeline from Edmonton to Sarnia. In 1956, this line was extended to energy-hungry consumers in Toronto. Measuring over three thousand kilometres, it was at the time the world's longest pipeline.[8] In 1953, a second pipeline was built, to connect Alberta's oil with the Pacific coast. The 1,150-kilometre TransMountain Pipeline, which ends in Burnaby, BC, just outside Vancouver, is now owned by the American pipeline company Kinder Morgan.

Just as the oil fields of Petrolia and Oil Springs became depleted in the pioneering days of the Canadian oil industry, so too did the much larger Western Canadian Sedimentary Basin. As with most conventional oil fields in North America, production peaked around the 1970s and then began a gradual but persistent decline. With the aid of generous federal government financing, an offshore oil industry developed on the east coast, but production was relatively small and expensive, and the work could be hazardous. In 1981, the *Ocean*

Ranger platform capsized in a storm off the coast of Newfoundland, killing all eighty-four on board.

Given Canada's history as an oil-producing nation, it is perhaps understandable that an ambitious prime minister from Alberta would look to this particular resource as a path to economic security and prosperity. And, truth be told, things might have progressed without a hitch but for one key fact: when Prime Minister Harper started musing about the country becoming an energy superpower, he wasn't referring to the offshore oil in the Atlantic or the already depleting WCSB. He was talking about what the International Energy Agency had just identified as the third-largest oil reserve in the world—the vast Alberta oil sands.

THE TROUBLE WITH BITUMEN

Canada's oil sands are one of the most emissions-intensive and costly sources of oil in the world.[9] Found primarily in three deposits—Athabasca, Peace River and Cold Lake—they are a mixture of sand, water, clay and bitumen. It's bitumen that causes all the problems. At about 10 degrees Celsius, bitumen has the consistency of a hockey puck, which makes it pretty inconvenient to extract and ship. Further complicating things is the fact that bitumen isn't just lying around waiting for us to come and pick it up. Some lies fairly close to the earth's surface (within sixty metres), but the majority is much deeper underground.

At first glance, however, the sheer immensity of the proven reserves in the oil sands and the fact that the area is located next door to the world's largest oil-consuming market made the whole idea—extraction challenges and all—seem like a no-brainer. The oil sands contain an estimated 170 billion barrels, behind Venezuela's 298 billion and Saudi Arabia's 266 billion but well ahead of Iran's 157 billion.[10] In Harper's vision, these vast bitumen deposits would become an engine of huge resource wealth and economic growth for the whole country.

While commercial development of the area is fairly recent, the oil sands were hardly a new discovery. As early as 1920 there was a pilot project to extract bitumen there, but it wasn't until much later that anyone tried to make a go of it on a commercial basis. In the 1960s, the Great Canadian Oil Sands Company tried to commercially upgrade bitumen into crude oil, but before it got very far, it was gobbled up by the Sun Oil Company, the ancestor of Suncor, the sector's biggest player and Canada's largest energy firm.

Still, until oil prices started soaring a little over a decade ago, the resource, vast as it was, went largely ignored by the petroleum industry. (The same, incidentally, can be said of Venezuela's Oronoco Heavy Oil Belt, recently renamed the Hugo Chávez Reserve.) No one doubted that there was an ocean of oil buried in the sands; what people questioned was whether it could be extracted and separated at a cost that made any commercial sense. Of course, what does and doesn't make commercial sense in the oil industry depends very much on the price of oil. At $100 a barrel, the oil sands are a huge untapped reserve. At $20 a barrel, they're not worth the bother.

There was good reason why no one was interested in the oil sands when oil was trading in the low double digits. The region's deposits lie between 100 and 400 metres belowground. In order to access them, bulldozers have to scrape off the boreal forest overburden that lies on top of the oil sands. "Overburden," by the way, is one of the oil industry's most ingenious euphemisms. What we're talking about here is *nature*: trees and rocks and soil and peat and clay, all of which are supposed to be there and all of which serve an ecological purpose. In any case, once the overburden has been disposed of, to obtain a single barrel of bitumen, giant steam shovels must scoop two tons of sand into the world's largest trucks, which then carry the sand to a processing centre, where it's heated.

Enthusiasm for nonconventional resources such as this one began to grow in the lead-up to the Great Recession, when the world suddenly found itself facing triple-digit oil prices instead of the $20-per-barrel prices to which it had been accustomed. As oil soared to $100 a barrel and beyond, huge reserves of high-cost unconventional oil suddenly started to look economically attractive. In less than a decade, the oil sands leapt from commercial obscurity to become one of the most sought-after energy assets on the planet. Between 2000 and 2005, production in the region doubled, to almost a million barrels a day.

Getting all that bitumen out of the ground is difficult, and so too is moving it through a pipeline. Thanks to its hockey puck–like consistency—it also resembles asphalt, which explains the original "tar sands" moniker—the bitumen must be diluted with much lighter hydrocarbons, such as natural gas liquids, in order for it to flow. Dilutents, as they are referred to in the industry, make up about 30 percent of the mixture that allows bitumen to flow through a pipeline. And once the bitumen finally gets to a refinery, hydrogen must be added in a complex process to render the bitumen into a usable motor fuel like gasoline or diesel.

The process—already challenging and costly—is likely to get even more so in the future, as production shifts from strip-mining the close-to-the-surface bitumen to exploiting the deeper deposits through what is called in situ production.

Right now, a little over half of the 2 mbd that come out of the oil sands is extracted by in situ methods. But over 80 percent of the huge planned increase in oil sands output will come from this method. In situ involves injecting steam as hot as 538 degrees Celsius into the oil sands, which reduces the bitumen's viscosity, allowing it to pool and subsequently be pumped to the surface.

The process doesn't leave the moonscapes and toxic tailing ponds that lie in the wake of the mining projects that have scooped out the shallower bitumen deposits, but in situ production is not without its environmental challenges. The enormous amount of steam needed, usually created through the combustion of natural gas, means that more carbon is emitted per barrel of oil produced than in the strip-mining technique used on shallower deposits. That will raise the emissions intensity of what is already the most carbon-polluting oil in the world.

Moreover, when you start injecting massive amounts of high-pressurized steam into the ground, oil can start flowing in places where producers don't necessarily want it to flow. We know that other unconventional extraction methods, such as hydraulic fracturing, often have unintended seismic effects. The injection of waste water from the fracking process into deep wells has been connected to a ten-fold increase in the frequency of earthquakes in Texas and Oklahoma — both centres for production of gas and oil from shale reserves. Over-pressurization of a well can also fracture the surrounding cap-rock, allowing bitumen to escape to the surface. In situ production has already been associated with one of the largest accidental releases of oil in Alberta's history. Beginning in early 2013, an estimated twelve thousand barrels of bitumen have so far risen from football-field-length cracks that have emerged in the forest floor at Canadian Natural Resources Limited's Primrose oil sands site near Cold Lake, Alberta.

Environmental concerns aside, the in situ extraction process isn't cheap. The oil sands product already ranks as one of the most expensive fuels on the planet, according to a Citibank analysis of three hundred of the world's largest oil and gas projects.[11] Estimates for break-even oil prices on new Canadian oil sands projects range from $65 to $100 per barrel. Goldman Sachs claims most new projects require oil prices north of $80 per barrel, and some projects, according to estimates from analysts at energy consulting firms Wood Mackenzie and CERA, have break-even points as high as $100 per barrel or more.

Looking at the cost side of the equation, it's easy to see why no one was particularly interested in the oil sands before prices starting sky-rocketing toward $100 a barrel. But thanks to the leverage these prices provided, an obscure outpost of Canada's energy industry was suddenly being championed as the marquee project for the entire Canadian economy—and by the prime minister, no less. Capital flowed into the sector on a scale seldom seen before in this country. Labour flowed in as well, brought from all over Canada and around the world to fill the growing number of job vacancies in both the oil sands operations themselves and in the service sector and infrastructure needed to accommodate the resource boom.

Production quickly soared from a couple of hundred thousand barrels a day to over a million. Royalty revenues poured into the Alberta Treasury, so much so that the Alberta government thought nothing of spending millions on a public relations campaign to change the nomenclature of their treasured resource from the historic "tar sands" to the much more benign-sounding "oil sands." Meanwhile, share prices of oil sands producers soared, as did the number of new underwritings, making the sector the darling of investment banks and the stock market. For Canada's new-found ambition to become an energy superpower, things seemed to be moving full steam ahead—that is, if you were willing to ignore the environmental costs.

THE CARBON COST

Many, however, were not. The expected increase in oil sands emissions from 34 million tons in 2005 to 100 million tons by 2020 will more than offset all the emissions reductions that have occurred elsewhere in the Canadian economy—even the reduction generated by Ontario's decision to close or convert its remaining coal-fired power plants, including the giant Nanticoke plant, once the single-largest source of carbon emissions on the continent. These increases also preclude the country ever living up to the commitment Harper made at the Copenhagen climate summit in 2009, when he promised that Canada would reduce its emissions to 17 percent below 2005 levels by 2020. Documents filed by the Canadian government with the UN Framework Convention on Climate Change in late December 2013 show that Canada won't even come close. Instead of falling 17 percent from its 2005 level of 737 million tons, Canada's emissions in 2020 are projected to remain roughly the same, at 734 million tons.

If soaring emissions from the oil sands have already made Canada's troubling environmental performance conspicuous on the world stage—the country currently ranks tenth on a list of the world's top emitters[12]—they are nothing compared with what's scheduled to come down the pipe. The planned expansion of oil sands production from 2 mbd to 5 mbd will send Canada's emissions on a tear over the next decade. Figures submitted by the federal government to the UN show that the country's emissions are projected to rise by over 10 percent, to 815 million tons, by 2030. To put that number in perspective, it represents an almost 40 percent increase from emissions levels in 1990—the base year for the Kyoto accord that Canada originally signed.

Emissions from rapidly expanding oil sands production will quadruple between 2005 and 2030, and will continue to offset emissions declines in the rest of the Canadian economy. While Ontario, Quebec, Saskatchewan, Nova Scotia and New Brunswick will all have reduced their carbon emissions between 2005 and 2030, Alberta's emissions will have risen by 40 percent. All of the projected 76-million-ton increase in Canadian emissions between 2020 and 2030 (and then some) will come from oil sands production.

Until now, the Harper government has argued that its pathetic record on emissions is defensible on the basis that unilateral action by Canada would be hopelessly ineffective and costly without the cooperation of the United States and China, the world's two major carbon polluters. The prime minister has been supremely confident that an insatiable demand for cheap energy and economic growth would mean that neither country would take emissions reductions seriously—so much so that he went out of his way, in November 2013, to congratulate Australian prime minister Tony Abbott on scrapping that country's carbon tax.[13] Six months later, Harper used the occasion of Abbott's visit to Ottawa to expand on the topic: "No country is going to take actions [on climate change] that are going to deliberately destroy jobs and growth in their country."[14]

But betting the status quo isn't the sure thing it used to be. As we'll see, the United States and China have both recently changed course and are taking unprecedented steps to reduce their economies' emissions. Those moves not only leave Canada increasingly isolated, they also leave the more and more petro-dependent Canadian economy increasingly vulnerable to global reductions in fossil fuel combustion. High-cost and emissions-intensive bitumen is precisely the type of fuel that—along with coal—will be the most likely target of the coming carbon wars.

A MASTER SALESMAN

In the space of half a decade, Stephen Harper has taken an environmentally unpopular and economically dubious policy and turned it into what can only be described as a "motherhood" issue in Canadian politics. To question the exponential growth planned for the oil sands was to risk being publicly censured or described as an eco-terrorist, in the words of one federal cabinet minister.[15]

To his credit, Stephen Harper is a very skilful politician and a master strategist and tactician. After all, the dude has won three elections. But Harper also planted that vision of the country as an energy superpower in some very fertile ground. Canada's "rocks and trees" resource economy seemed downright anachronistic in the new age of information technology, especially as the dot-com boom hit in the late 1990s. While Americans had never felt richer (at least before that bubble burst), Canadians had never felt more backward — seemingly the same hewers of wood and drawers of water that their forefathers had once been.

But the world was changing, and in ways that made Harper's hopeful message of coming resource wealth resonate with new-found credence. The beginnings of a huge shift in what economists refer to as the "terms of trade" strongly favoured Canada. Information technology was now a commodity that could be moved from Silicon Valley to China in a nanosecond. Resources, on the other hand, have to be developed where they lie. And as growth in the BRIC nations shifted into overdrive, it was suddenly resources, not software programs, for which the global economy was willing to pay top dollar.

The price of gold, copper, zinc and, most of all, oil started to soar. So did the Canadian dollar (which had touched an all-time low of 61.79 cents against the US dollar on January 21, 2002) and the resource-laden Toronto Stock Exchange (TSX). Big global investment banks like Goldman Sachs started talking about a super cycle for commodities and, most of all, for oil. Canadians were starting to regain some of their lost self-confidence, and Harper's vision of a Canadian economy awash in billions of petrodollars looked appealing not only in Alberta but across the country.

And Harper didn't shy away from being the messenger. He had a messianic zeal for the oil sands, talking them up everywhere he went. In a speech to the Economic Club of New York, he pulled out the same "energy superpower" language he'd used in the UK a few months earlier.[16] Two years later, he would still be reciting the energy superpower theme, this time during the 2008 federal election campaign.

And just in case Canadians didn't get to hear one of those speeches, there were endless ad campaigns that played over the nation's airwaves. Sun-drenched wheat fields glistening under those big, bright-blue prairie skies. Earnest, hardworking engineers clad in safety helmets busily extracting the saviour bitumen from the ground. Elsewhere, a manufacturer, standing proudly in his plant somewhere in Quebec, would talk about how many jobs had been created in his factory thanks to machinery orders from the oil sands. Since 2009, the Harper government has spent more than $100 million of taxpayers' money on ads to convince Canadians that the oil sands are the way of the future. The Canadian Association of Petroleum Producers (CAPP) has spent hundreds of millions more doing exactly the same thing.

More recently, the message from Ottawa has been fine-tuned to address the pipeline disputes that Harper is having with the Obama administration. The fact that Obama and assorted American environmentalists have ganged up on Canada and withheld approval of the vital Keystone XL pipeline project has become an important part of the political narrative the Harper government is preaching. Not only is any criticism of the oil sands condemned as economically naive and wrongheaded, it has now come to be viewed as downright unpatriotic, since any domestic criticism can be used as ammunition by the pipeline's opponents in the United States.

After gaining his first majority in the 2011 federal election, Harper felt he had a mandate to do what was necessary to safeguard the nation's economic future. He took that and ran with it. Internally, he slashed federal funding for environmental studies, particularly anything related to climate change, and even forbade federal scientists from talking to the media.[17] Then, tucked into the 2012 federal budget, came a special $8-million allocation to fund Canada Revenue Agency (CRA) audits of basically every major environmental charity group in the country that opposed new pipeline construction (the David Suzuki Foundation, Environmental Defence, and Tides Canada among them), as well as other groups, such as PEN, with a fondness for free speech.[18] Even weather forecasters at the Meteorological Service of Canada are now under strict instructions never to even mention climate change.[19]

Harper has been vilified by the environmental movement for such Machiavellian tactics. But, to be fair, the Harper government isn't intrinsically against environmentalism. If groups like Environmental Defence devoted themselves to saving some toad from extinction in Yoho National Park, they no doubt wouldn't be subjected to such close scrutiny. But raising roadblocks to economic growth is another matter altogether. The government was not about to allow a posse of environmental groups to stand in the way of its vision of Canada's economic destiny. Producing 5 million barrels a day would catapult the country into the front ranks of world oil producers. The petro-wealth flowing from that production would be transformative not only for Alberta but for the whole country.

Some might consider the use of the national tax-collecting agency to harass political opposition as dirty pool. Even in the no-holds-barred tradition of American politics, President Obama was forced to admonish the Internal Revenue Service for its investigation of prominent Tea Party Republicans. Yet when the media reported on how the environmental groups had been targeted for audits, there was little public outcry. Instead, it looked as though the massive advertising campaign and the muzzling of environmental opposition groups was working. A Léger marketing poll conducted in late 2012 suggested that nearly three-quarters of Canadians supported oil sands development.[20]

All in all, the prime minister must have been pretty proud of himself. While he might not have been able to sell President Obama or the rest of the planet on the merits of developing Alberta's vast bitumen deposits, he'd done a masterful job of peddling the dream to his fellow Canadians.

CLOUDS ON THE HORIZON

For a while at least, it looked as if Harper's dream would turn into bright and sunny reality. Until the Great Recession of 2008–9, it was all blue skies for the development of the oil sands. Oil prices had been mostly on a one-way ride for the better part of a decade, and it seemed they could only go higher—world demand would always be growing, and supply was increasingly coming from high-cost unconventional sources like the oil sands. After bursting through the triple-digit threshold, oil prices soared to $147 a barrel in the summer of 2008. And the value of companies like Suncor, which held huge reserves of bitumen, started soaring as well. And it wasn't just Canadian investors who wanted in. Word was spreading around the world that Canada had enormous deposits of heavy oil—so enormous, in fact, that America soon wouldn't need to import oil from such trouble spots as Venezuela and the Middle East.

But investors in the oil sands were ignoring one essential fact: it was the torrid rates of global economic growth that had catapulted oil prices to those stratospheric heights, and those same high prices were undermining the very growth on which the development of these resources so critically depended.

Before the economic collapse in 2009, the juggernaut Chinese economy, whose level of oil imports was approaching America's, was expanding at over 10 percent annually. Economic growth in neighbouring India was clocking in around the 8 percent range. Growth in Brazil and Russia wasn't far behind.[21] In the developed world, the powerhouse US economy was still chugging along. Firing on all cylinders, global GDP was growing at close to an almost unprecedented 5 percent a year.

But scorching global economic growth is not sustainable in the face of record-high oil prices. As it was during the time of the OPEC (Organization of the Petroleum Exporting Countries) oil shocks in the 1970s, oil is still the single most important fuel for the world economy. And just as they did back then, soaring oil prices quickly led to deep global recessions. As economic growth faltered, so too did oil demand and oil prices. As output and spending contracted around the world, oil prices plunged from $147 a barrel to $40 a barrel—and those once-blue skies clouded over and rained down on the world's third-largest oil reserve.

Global demand changed what oil sands producers could get for their fuel, but it sure didn't alter the huge costs of getting the oil out of the ground. In a world of triple-digit oil prices, those costs can be absorbed; in a world of $40-per-barrel oil, they can't. In that world, it's not worth having a debate over environmentally contentious pipeline projects such as Keystone XL or Northern Gateway. In that world, Fort McMurray and its environs were well on their way to becoming another Oil Springs or Petrolia.

As one of the highest-cost sources of oil, the oil sands are particularly vulnerable to recessions and the crash in oil prices that they invariably bring. In the wake of the huge drop in oil prices, plans for as many as ten heavy-oil upgraders and refineries were suddenly cancelled in Alberta. Billions of dollars of planned capital expenditure was scrapped literally overnight.

Fortunately for the province's oil sands producers, massive fiscal stimulus efforts by governments around the world, together with record-low interest rates, eventually pulled the global economy out of its worst postwar recession. Global oil demand and oil prices were soon heading back up, reinforcing the fact that economic growth and burning oil are inextricably tied. In early 2011, world oil prices, benchmarked by the European standard Brent, once again moved into the triple-digit range. They reached as high as $125 per barrel during the Libyan revolt against Gadhafi, and for the better part of the next two years traded in the $105-to-$115 range.

With the recovery in global oil pries, the oil sands sector started to bounce back. Production climbed as billions of dollars from all over the world poured into Alberta to finance further expansion. Shares of oil sands companies, which had been absolutely hammered during the recession, began to recover.

It looked for a while as if things were finally getting back on track for the oil sands. But across the border, changes in the US energy market were about to turn Stephen Harper's dream into an economic nightmare.

PART
TWO

DANGER
AHEAD

WARNING SIGNS ARE ALL AROUND US: Don't Cross; Go Slow; Stop. As drivers and pedestrians, we learn to watch out for them, to heed them, to let them guide us safely on our path.

Warning signs aren't just handy on the road. If you know where to look, you can find them in your personal life (the blind date who seems off right from the start), your professional life (the co-worker who consistently takes credit for your work) or even your financial dealings (the house closing with one too many conditions). They can also alert you when a best-laid plan isn't all you thought it might be.

Right now, if you choose to look, there are plenty of warning signs on Canada's metaphorical road to becoming an energy superpower. Unfortunately, the Conservative government of Stephen Harper doesn't seem to be interested in looking. If it were, it would see that its best-laid plan isn't "best" at all. It's not best for the environment, for the economy or for your wallet. The price of oil is dropping, making it riskier to base the country's economic future on the high-cost, difficult-to-extract bitumen found in Alberta's oil sands. The shale revolution in the United States has dried up a once-certain market, and concerns over the environment have made reaching different markets through pipelines to the coast more and more difficult. And as all of this is playing out, the country's once-vibrant manufacturing sector (and the provinces that are its homes) are paying the price for an overinflated petrodollar. Is the bubble about to burst?

All of these warning signs, and others, are telling us to slow down, to proceed with caution. They are warning us, quite clearly, that there is danger ahead.

CHAPTER 4

THE FRACKERS

ON JULY 26, 2013, the city of Galveston, Texas, mourned the passing of one of its own. A businessman, real estate developer and oilman, George Mitchell may have been a local boy, but his death, at age ninety-four, made news around the world. Obituaries ran in the *Guardian*, the *New York Times*, the *Independent* and the *Economist*, among others. Most were lengthy pieces, describing Mitchell's birth to poor immigrant parents, his graduation from Texas A&M, his service on behalf of the United States during the Second World War and his early "wildcatting" days in the oil industry. Most also had a headline in common: they all recognized Mitchell as the "father" of fracking.

In the 1970s and early 1980s, as Americans were collectively wringing their hands over the idea that theirs might be a nation in decline—bound to soon run out of the oil that powered its economy—Mitchell was solving a puzzle. The oil industry had long known of the vast reserves of shale gas and oil trapped beneath Dallas and Fort Worth; it had even attempted to get at them. Since the 1940s, experiments in hydraulic fracturing—or fracking—had seen the dense shale rocks blasted with a solution of water, sand and a potent chemical cocktail. The idea was to create tiny cracks in the shale's surface, fissures that would release the microscopic bubbles of gas that had been trapped inside. But the gas was hard to capture, and even when it was captured, it had a tendency to leak away before it could be brought to the surface. In a cost-benefit analysis, the ends rarely justified the means.[1]

Mitchell was convinced that there had to be a better way, and in 1999, after two decades of experimentation, he figured out what it was: not just drilling down, but drilling sideways.[2] Vertical wells could bring only a small amount of gas to the surface, a situation that rendered the costs of drilling much higher than the potential profits. But horizontal wells—branching outward from a central "trunk"—were another story entirely. Now shale formations could be fracked again and again, increasing both productivity and profit.[3]

The results were nothing short of revolutionary. Fracking was dubbed the greatest industry discovery of the century by US energy guru Daniel Yergin, and credited with everything from spurring a renaissance in American manufacturing to bringing Iran's atomic ambitions to the negotiating table.[4] The IEA heralded it as a game changer, with the power to turn America, once the world's largest oil-importing country, into a major energy exporter and the world's largest producer of oil and natural gas.

As if scripted by the industry itself, Mitchell's drilling breakthrough occurred right in the backyard of America's oil and gas patch—in the Barnett Basin, not a stone's throw from downtown Dallas–Fort Worth. It didn't take long for news of Mitchell's success to make the rounds. The fracking of the Barnett Basin was followed in 2008 by drilling in the Haynesville Formation, which ranges through Texas, Arkansas and Louisiana, and the Marcellus Formation in the eastern United States. The practice quickly crossed over the border into Canada, and was applied to shale gas deposits in interior British Columbia, as well as Alberta, Saskatchewan and Manitoba.[5]

Fracking is contentious on both sides of the border. The environmental costs are huge. Anywhere from 3.8 to 30 million litres of water and 150,000 litres of chemicals are required for each fracturing job.

Once used for fracking, the water is so contaminated that it can't be used for anything else. Methane gas and toxic chemicals leak during the process, contaminating both the air and the drinking water around sites. And the process is even found to induce seismic activity in the surrounding areas. Several states and provinces have imposed moratoriums (including Vermont, New York, New Jersey, Nova Scotia, Quebec, and Newfoundland and Labrador), and in September 2014 the practice was a central issue in the New Brunswick provincial election. Liberal candidate Brian Gallant, who promised no fracking until the environmental risks could be studied and understood, was elected over David Alward, the Progressive Conservative candidate whose economic recovery plans for the province centred on shale gas development.

None of this, though, has stopped the rapid proliferation of fracking sites. At first, the frackers went after natural gas—the easiest of the buried resources to reach. As more and more gas wells were fracked, US production soared to record highs. In 2001, shale beds produced just 1 percent of America's natural gas.[6] By 2010, that number had risen to 10 percent; today, it's believed that anywhere from 30 to 40 percent of the gas flowing in the United States is coming from the country's own shale formations.[7]

THE SHALE REVOLUTION:
A BAD-NEWS STORY FOR CANADA

Prices are sensitive things. They react immediately to significant changes in supply. All of that fracking—and the resulting increase in gas supply—had a profound impact on natural gas prices. As shale gas flooded the market, the price in North America plummeted from over $9 per million British thermal units (mBtu) in 2008 to briefly below $2 in late 2012.[8] For most of the last five years, it has traded in a range from $2.75 to $4.75 per mBtu. All of a sudden, it became cheaper to produce power in North America by burning shale gas than by burning coal. With these prices, it wasn't necessary to legislate a carbon tax to shut down coal plants or even, for that matter, to raise emissions standards. On their own, power utilities across the continent are switching en masse from coal to gas. In 2011 and 2012, 14 gigawatts of coal-fired generating capacity was shut down. Another 60 gigawatts—a little over a fifth of America's entire coal-powered generating capacity—is expected to be shut down by 2017.[9] US coal consumption, over 90 percent of which is by power-generating utilities, fell by over a third, from a peak of 300 million metric tons just prior to the recession to below 200 million tons by the fourth quarter of 2013. The fuel's once-dominant 50 percent share of US power generation has shrunk by over ten percentage points, and is expected to claim an even smaller share of the US power market in the future.

Plunging natural gas prices not only put the kibosh on coal plants, they also began eating into the rate of return companies were getting from shale gas. To make up the difference, many fracking firms started going after the "tight oil" that was also trapped in shale formations. It turns out fracking is just as successful at unlocking trapped oil as it is at releasing trapped gas. Shale plays such as the Bakken in North Dakota and Eagle Ford and the Permian Basin in Texas are now each producing over a million barrels per day. Thanks to the contributions from these and other new fields, US oil production has posted all-time gains, close to doubling what it was a decade ago. The IEA expects that further increases from shale could catapult US production to the peak levels of the early 1970s, when the country produced over 10 million barrels a day. The agency is even forecasting that the US will become the world's largest oil producer by 2016, at least temporarily surpassing production in both Saudi Arabia and Russia, the current world leaders.

Considering that US oil production had fallen to as low as 5 million barrels a day in 2007, those numbers speak to a remarkable turn-around. Initially, fracking seemed to hold out only the more modest promise of American energy independence, but given how much new oil and gas it has produced, it's now on the verge of turning America into a major energy exporter.

Legislation is the only thing standing in the way of that happening. In 1975, shortly after the end of the Arab oil embargo that followed the Yom Kippur War, the US Congress approved the Energy Policy and Conservation Act, which banned the unlicensed export of crude oil—a move designed to safeguard the country's energy security. Those exports are still banned, with the exception of those to Canada. But there are no restrictions on the export of refined petroleum products such as gasoline or diesel, even if they are made from the domestic crude oil that otherwise cannot be exported. American refineries have been adept at exploiting that loophole. They are already exporting over 3 mbd of gasoline and diesel, and plan to export more if restrictions on crude exports aren't lifted. In a neat twist, American refineries are exporting their product to countries such as Nigeria and Venezuela, and some others in the Middle East, all of which the United States used to rely on for crude imports.[10]

The American Petroleum Association (APA), acting in the interests of domestic oil producers, is actively lobbying the White House and Congress to rescind the restrictions on crude oil—a step that would give producers more choice as to where they can sell their oil and better their chances of getting world prices for their product. Refiners, on the other hand, like the restrictions on crude exports just fine. If growing US (not to mention oil sands) production can't be exported, those fuels will more than likely trade at a discount in a captive North American market, giving American refineries a leg-up on international competitors who have to pay top dollar for their feedstock.

Who will ultimately win the political tug-of-war between producers and refiners is still unclear, although recent moves by the Obama administration suggest that the APA's efforts may be paying off. In 2014, the US Commerce Department permitted two energy companies to export a lightly refined product.[11] It's a long way from an overhaul of the original act, but many producers see the move as a step in the right direction. Either way, America plans to export more oil: either raw crude (if the export restrictions are lifted) or more refined petroleum like gasoline or diesel (if the restrictions remain in place)—provided, of course, that oil prices remain high enough to make the tight oil from fracking commercially viable.

The shale revolution was a great news story for the American oil industry, but north of the border, it has cast a pall over the oil sands' fortunes. Suddenly, America wasn't in such desperate need of Alberta's heavy oil. The shale-led turnaround in US domestic production shrunk oil imports to their smallest share of the US oil market in a quarter century.[12] By 2020, say some analysts, America's crude-oil dependency could decline by 32 percent.[13] For Canada, which currently sends 99 percent of its oil exports south, this was nothing but bad news.

From being a highly sought-after strategic reserve located in a friendly neighbouring country, Alberta bitumen suddenly became the odd man out in the US energy market. The light oil that flows from fracked shale formations like the Bakken is, on the whole, cheaper to produce and less emissions-intensive than bitumen from the oil sands. Most of all, it generates jobs, income and tax revenue in America, and not in another country.

On its own, this would be a difficult-enough challenge for oil sands producers to overcome, but the fracking revolution played out against the backdrop of steadily falling US oil demand. Prior to the recession, US oil consumption was running at around 20.5 million barrels per day. By 2012, it had fallen to 18 mbd. And all the recent driving trends in America point to it falling even more in the future.[14] Canada's oil producers now must face a difficult truth: their one and only market is steadily shrinking.

BLAME IT ON THE CAR

In 2009, *Merriam-Webster's Collegiate Dictionary* released an updated edition with nearly a hundred new words. Some hinted at the latest trends in healthy eating (*acai* and *goji*). Others (*waterboarding*) were ripped from the headlines. A number—such as *carbon footprint, green-collar* and *locavore*—represented our increasing concern with the environment.[15] And then there was *staycation*—a portmanteau (a lexicographer's word if ever there was one) of *stay* and *vacation*. According to the dictionary, the word means simply "a vacation spent at home or nearby."

Changes in our language and usage offer intriguing hints about changes in the world around us, and the appearance of *staycation* in the dictionary was no exception. While tamer economic growth following the last recession certainly played a role in curbing North America's oil appetite, an even bigger part was driven by a noticeable shift in the relationship between people and their cars.

While Detroit's automakers like to trumpet the strength of the largely taxpayer-financed recovery in auto production, what oil companies care about is gallons pumped, not cars sold. The bad news for them is that North Americans are driving their cars less. Per capita vehicle mileage in the US has fallen by almost 10 percent since 2004, and is now at its lowest level since the mid-1990s.[16]

When the price of oil hit triple digits a little over a decade ago, North Americans responded by driving less (just as Europeans did in response to their tax-laden fuel bills). Vacations gave way to staycations; online shopping for everything from groceries to birthday presents saved hours of driving from store to store; transit ridership increased, and for some workers, the long commute to the office was replaced by telecommuting. Some analysts suggest that even bigger changes may be coming. Census numbers parsed in 2012 show that, for the first time in twenty years, population growth in more developed areas has overtaken that in suburban areas.[17] More and more Americans, it would seem, are choosing to leave the suburbs for the bright lights of the big city, where efficient public transportation systems and a lack of parking can make owning a car less of a necessity and more of a nuisance.

This last trend in particular may be contributing to another: the growing number of North Americans who aren't even bothering to get their driver's licence. A University of Michigan study of driving habits in fifteen countries, including Canada, revealed a decrease in the number of younger drivers.[18] As aging baby boomers leave the road, there may be fewer and fewer new drivers to replace them.

How much of that 10 percent decline in miles driven per capita can be attributed to each of these factors is certainly open to debate. But the composite picture suggests that the North American automobile boom, which began in the 1950s, has run its course. Car ownership, along with buying a huge house in the far-flung suburbs, is a rapidly fading hallmark of the North American dream.

If declining miles driven and fewer drivers licensed aren't enough on their own to reduce future oil consumption, consider the impact of continual improvements in fuel efficiency mandated by ever more stringent Corporate Average Fuel Economy (CAFE) standards. Like the ban on exports of crude oil, the CAFE standards were enacted by the US government in 1975 in the wake of the Arab oil embargo. The goal was to improve the fuel efficiency of cars and light trucks sold in the States. In 2012—spurred on by increasingly catastrophic news on the environmental front—the Obama administration introduced new, more stringent rules that require the doubling of the average fuel economy of new cars and trucks—to 54.5 miles per gallon—by 2025.[19] (In 2013, the average US mileage was 23.6 miles per gallon.[20]) And unlike the past, when improved fuel efficiency often led to a "rebound effect" on gasoline consumption, that doesn't seem to be happening anymore, in light of other trends.

US oil consumption has already dropped over 2 mbd since the last recession. When you consider that over two-thirds of all the oil Americans combust is burned on the road, it's easy to see how changing driving habits, declining rates of vehicle ownership and ever more stringent CAFE fuel-mileage standards will drive further declines in US oil consumption. The IEA forecasts that if the world is to hold atmospheric carbon to 450 ppm, most of the decline in world oil consumption (roughly 12 mbd from 2014 levels) will have to come from the developed Organisation for Economic Co-operation and Development (OECD) economies. And no economy is expected to shed more of its oil demand over the next two decades than the world's still-largest oil consumer—the USA. Yet that is precisely the time frame in which Canadian oil sands production is expected to more than double, from 2 mbd to 5 mbd. And the demand is shrinking even more rapidly in Europe. European oil consumption has been falling every year since 2005, and is now at its lowest level in twenty years.[21]

IF NOT AMERICA, WHO?

All of a sudden, being adjacent to the world's largest oil market doesn't look quite like the panacea Alberta producers had been counting on. Between soaring US domestic production and shrinking domestic demand, America finds itself not needing Alberta bitumen at precisely the same time that bitumen producers have never needed the American market more. In fact, the Energy Information Administration (EIA)[22] recently released some startling data: in April 2014, Canada *imported* 263,000 barrels of crude oil per day from the USA—double the amount brought in during the same month in April 2013, and six and a half times as much as in April 2012.[23]

Canadians don't need to panic (at least not about this)—we still export far more to the Americans than we import from them—but the news is intriguing for what it reveals about possible future trends. In

July 2014, the *National Post*, one of Canada's two national newspapers, summed it up like this: "The dramatic rise of U.S. crude oil and natural gas production is disrupting even long-established trade flows inside Canada, as Alberta producers are increasingly finding themselves competing for—and losing—market share to American petroleum suppliers, even in their home province."[24]

It's a situation that not even the rabidly pro–oil sands Harper government can ignore. The newly appointed finance minister, Joe Oliver (who took over as Harper's right-hand man following the retirement of Jim Flaherty in March 2014), admitted that finding "new customers" is a key concern.[25] Canada doesn't need the oil itself—we already produce well over a million barrels a day more than we can use—so if not America, who is going to buy those 5 mbd of oil the industry is planning to produce from the oil sands?

There were, of course, other markets for Alberta's oil. While US demand has fallen, demand in other countries—particularly China—has risen. But without the infrastructure to reach these markets—without pipelines or rail routes—Alberta's producers found themselves no more able to deliver their fuel than the country's oil pioneers from southwestern Ontario were to able to deliver bitumen to Parisian street pavers 150 years ago.

CHAPTER 5

PIPE DREAMS

IF YOU'VE EVER FOUND yourself travelling in Maine, and had to stop and ask for directions, you may have been treated to a classic New England response: "Can't get they-ahh from he-yahhh." These days, the phrase could be adopted as a slogan by Canada's oil sands producers. For the moment at least, getting bitumen from Alberta to, well, anywhere is easier said than done.

Geography is certainly a big part of the problem. Landlocked in northern Alberta, the oil sands are an island of hydrocarbons surrounded by thousands of square kilometres of boreal forest. To reach world energy markets, oil sands producers require pipelines to take the fuel south to the United States or to a coastline where it can be loaded onto a supertanker and sent to a refinery. If Alberta bitumen can't get to either of those places, additional oil sands production will simply have nowhere to go.

This transportation dilemma—this "can't get there from here" conundrum—wasn't always an issue. Until quite recently, there was more than ample capacity in the North American pipeline system to handle the output from depleting fields in Texas and Alberta. But that's changed markedly over the last decade, as new unconventional sources of supply have driven record production increases on both sides of the border. Excess capacity quickly gave way to huge trans-port bottlenecks; for the first time, production started to exceed the takeaway capacity of the existing pipeline network. The result? Alberta oil producers, as well as those companies fracking North Dakota's Bakken shale formation, were at the mercy of the only refin-eries they could reach—those in the American Midwest.

It's interesting to consider that this geographical challenge (and the related problem of lack of pipeline capacity) might be far less of an issue had Canada's oil industry taken a different path in its early days. It has focused on the raw extraction of the resource, and not on processing it into more value-added refined products such as gaso-line, diesel or petrochemicals. In large measure, this direction was chosen because much of Canada's oil sector was foreign owned, his-torically by American interests.

The big integrated majors had their own refining capacity state-side, and saw it as redundant and uneconomical to build additional refineries north of the border. It made a lot more commercial sense (and still does) for those companies to ship the raw product from Canada to their American plants. As it turns out, most of these are concentrated in Texas and along the Gulf Coast, especially those with the capacity to refine heavy oil like Alberta's bitumen; only those already configured to handle similar heavy oils, like Mexico's Mayan crude and feedstock from Venezuela's massive Orinoco deposit, fit the bill.

The ownership problem is by no means unique to Canada's oil industry. It runs through much of Canada's resource sector, as has been graphically highlighted in recent years by the spate of takeovers in the country's mining industry. Unlike Australia or Brazil, which have used their natural resource base to support the development of their own international mining giants, such as BHP Billiton and Vale, Canada has watched as most of its major mining players— Alcan, Falconbridge and Inco—were sold to foreigners.

When it comes to oil, the issue isn't so much the selling off of assets as the underdevelopment of processing capacity. In the 1970s, Canada had forty refineries; today, the total is nineteen. For all the billions invested in soaring production, there hasn't been a single new refinery built in this country since 1984.[1] The province of Alberta has only four operating refineries, and one of them, the Imperial refinery in Edmonton, isn't even configured to handle bitumen. The three refineries that *are* designed for oil sands feedstock—the Suncor refinery, also in Edmonton, the Shell refinery in Scotford and the Husky refinery in Lloydminster—have a combined capacity of 270,300 barrels per day. When all three are running at peak capacity, only 13 percent of oil sands production can be refined in Alberta.[2]

So, if bitumen can't be refined here, it has to go elsewhere. The problem, of course, is where. Historically, the landlocked bitumen was typically held in bulging storage tanks at pipeline terminus points like Cushing, Oklahoma. Without access to world markets, and desperately needing to move their oil—and hence clear the way for increased production—Alberta producers were forced to give deep price discounts to Midwest US refineries.

Those discounts were punitive for producers, for the Alberta government and for the Canadian economy. At their peak, they made Western Canadian Select (WCS), the benchmark price for Alberta's heavy crude from the oil sands, the cheapest oil trading anywhere in the world. By November 2013, WCS was trading as much as $40 per barrel below the US oil benchmark, West Texas Intermediate, and as much as $50 per barrel below the world benchmark price, Brent.

For Alberta producers, those huge price discounts meant they didn't receive the returns they should have from triple-digit world oil prices, a situation that left their investors shortchanged. The Alberta government claims it lost $6 billion in revenues—and coined the term "bitumen bubble" to explain the havoc wreaked on the provincial Treasury by the deep discounts.[3] And the Canadian economy too was deprived of billions of dollars in export earnings, as the discounted price of WCS effectively paid a huge energy subsidy to US refineries. At one point, the discount on some 2 million barrels a day of oil exports to the States was running in the range of $30 to $40 billion a year.[4]

Selling the cheapest oil in the world is bad enough for any oil producer's bottom line, but it's even more dire when you marry that huge discount with some of the highest production costs for oil anywhere on the planet. All of a sudden, the economics of extracting bitumen from the oil sands start to look pretty grim, especially at a time when the industry's capital needs (to finance those huge expansion plans) have never been greater.

The problem is that without access to global markets—and the prices those markets bring—Canada's oil industry couldn't continue to grow. The oil will have no place to go, and investors won't be interested in financing any expansion of Alberta's production (they'd much rather finance new production that's going to get full world prices). Without growth to the tune of a projected 5 mbd by 2030, Harper's "energy superpower" plans would go up in smoke. For some—Harper, the Alberta government and oil sands producers, to name a few—the solution was glaringly simple: more pipelines. But not everyone has been quite so anxious to see all that oil flow.

THE KEYSTONE SAGA

Back in 2005, pipeline company TransCanada submitted a proposal to the Canadian government for a 3,456-kilometre pipeline—to be called Keystone—that would transport 435,000 barrels of oil a day from Alberta to Illinois, and then on to Cushing, Oklahoma.[5] The National Energy Board (NEB) gave the project the green light in September 2007, and the US State Department did its part six months later, securing a presidential permit for the cross-border work.

Looking back over the near decade that has passed since that initial proposal, it is interesting to wonder what would have happened had TransCanada built Keystone and left it at that. In hindsight, though, that was never likely to be the case, not with that 5-million-barrel-a-day target looming. In July 2008, with construction on Keystone under way, TransCanada announced plans for a much larger, high-capacity pipeline—Keystone XL. Like the original line, the planned new line would start in Hardisty, Alberta, but instead of veering east toward Illinois, it would head more directly south, stretching about 2,700 kilometres through Alberta, Montana, South Dakota and Nebraska, where it would link up with its sister line and then extend through Kansas, Oklahoma and Texas to the Gulf. The NEB approved this project in March 2010, noting in its announcement that it had found the proposed pipeline to be "in the public interest" and believed that the project would "connect a large, long-term and strategic market for Western Canadian crude oil with the US Gulf Coast in a manner that would bring economic and other benefits to Canadians."[6] Unlike with the original Keystone project, however, a similar approval from south of the border didn't come. It still hasn't.

For nearly seven years now, Alberta's oil sands players have been desperately counting on President Obama to finally approve TransCanada's Keystone XL pipeline. The additional throughput and the better pricing the pipeline would bring would immediately boost earnings and share values of producers (not to mention TransCanada stock). Every year, the pipeline company and the producers that signed up to fill it have been expecting approval, only to be told that they must await further findings from the US State Department or until a seemingly never-ending series of legal challenges in the state of Nebraska have been settled. On the surface at least, the delays have been attributed to environmental concerns. From the time he took office in 2009, Obama has been treated to a non-stop chorus of opposition to the project, based on both the environmental impact of burning all that oil (an act that would mean "game over for the climate," wrote NASA's James Hansen in a May 2012 op-ed piece for the *New York Times*[7]) and the potential destruction the pipeline itself would bring. As it turns out, the pipeline's proposed route runs straight through Nebraska's fragile Sandhills wetlands—the largest and most intricate wetlands ecosystem in the United States—and the massive Ogallala aquifer, one of the world's largest underground sources of fresh water, which supplies between a quarter and a third of the irrigation groundwater in the country.[8]

Faced with letters from business leaders, members of Congress and prominent climate scientists, and confronted with a two-week sit-in on the White House's front lawn (or as close as the Tar Sands Action protesters could get), Obama hedged. In December 2011, the administration announced yet another review of the pipeline's route, effectively pushing a decision on the project past the 2012 election and into the president's second term. In January 2012, Obama rejected a congressional deadline for a decision, claiming that the time frame didn't allow for a proper review (at the same time, he opened the door for TransCanada to resubmit its proposal with a modified route—an opportunity that TransCanada took, and with a route that the governor of Nebraska has since approved).[9] In 2013, the president upped the environmental ante for approving the pipeline project by tying it to Keystone's impact on future carbon emissions. And in November 2014, the US Senate rejected a proposal to fast-track approval of the pipeline by a vote of 59 to 41, one vote short of what would have been necessary to proceed.[10] In the meantime, TransCanada has acknowledged that the cost of building the pipeline has surged from $5.4 billion to $8 billion, while other industry estimates now peg it as high as $10 billion.[11]

Of course, beneath the Obama administration's new-found environmental concerns regarding oil sands emissions is the stark reality that Canadian bitumen has lost its once-strategic appeal in the US market. Insuring against future oil shocks from hostile governments in Latin America or the Middle East was always the resource's chief drawing card in the United States. But between soaring domestic production from booming shale plays and shrinking domestic demand, the United States doesn't need that energy insurance anymore. And if it doesn't need it, why suffer all the flak that comes with creating an 830,000-barrel-a-day pipeline that runs right down its spine to bring oil all the way from the Canadian border to refineries on the Gulf Coast? More than likely, Alberta's heavy oil wouldn't even be used in the US domestic market, but rather exported abroad — or turned into gasoline or diesel that would in turn be exported. The expansion plans for the oil sands require not just Keystone XL but multiple versions of the pipeline criss-crossing the continent. In fact, if the industry wants to pump 5 mbd from the oil sands, it's going to need not one Keystone XL but five or so similarly scaled projects.

Moving such a large quantity of any type of oil through a pipeline network is no small task, but it's even more of a challenge if it happens to be bitumen. Because bitumen is so viscous, and hence doesn't readily flow, it must be mixed with a diluent in order to be pumped. Adding diluent means increasing the pipeline's required capacity by 30 percent. According to the Canadian Association of Petroleum Producers (CAPP), the planned ramp-up in production would require a doubling of current takeaway capacity to 8 mbd.

In addition to Keystone XL, and President Obama approving a near doubling of the volume through the Alberta Clipper pipeline that would send 800,000 bpd from Hardisty, Alberta, to Superior, Wisconsin, CAPP estimates that oil sands producers would need a twinning of the existing Trans Mountain pipeline running from Alberta to Burnaby, BC, the 500,000 bpd Northern Gateway pipeline to Kitimat, BC, and the over 1 million bpd throughput of TransCanada's proposed Energy East pipeline, which would take diluted bitumen across Canada to export terminals in Cacouna, Quebec, and Saint John, New Brunswick. Even with all these additions, the industry would still be about a million barrels per day short of the required takeaway capacity.

That's an enormous amount of new pipeline to get approved through environmental assessment hearings and the like, even in the best of times. And these days, as any pipeline executive will tell you, are not the best of times. But without such infrastructure, investors will have good reason to fear that any expansion in oil sands production will leave Alberta's oil once again piling up in storage tanks in places like Cushing, and the spreads between Western Canadian Select and world oil prices will once again balloon. Or even worse, the ambitious gains planned for production will never materialize.

MOVING IT IN YOUR OWN BACKYARD

So where is all that oil to go? In September 2013, Stephen Harper told a group of business leaders in New York City that he wouldn't take no for an answer from Obama on Keystone XL,[12] but as early as 2012 he and members of his administration had already started publicly addressing the urgent need to find new markets.

In January 2012, the prime minister sat down for an interview with the CBC's Peter Mansbridge. After suggesting that some in the United States "would like to see Canada be one giant national park for the northern half of North America," he admitted that the Keystone delays had provided a "wakeup" call regarding "the degree to which we are dependent or possibly held hostage to decisions in the United States." He went on to emphasize the need to engage with Asia, saying that "selling our energy products to Asia is in the country's national interest."[13]

Harper's message has been echoed several times over by members of his inner circle. In April 2013, Joe Oliver, then minister of natural resources, told a news agency that demand for Canadian energy from south of the border was dropping. "To preserve and grow Canadian jobs," he said, "we must bring our resources to tidewater to diversify the market to the fastest growing economies in the world."[14] He delivered much the same message a year later, after he had become finance minister. Attending the International Economic Forum of the Americas meeting in Montreal, Oliver addressed questions about the markets for Canada's oil, and the challenges of reaching those markets. He conceded a couple of key points: first, Canada's energy projects are essentially landlocked; and second, almost 100 percent of the country's oil and 99 percent of its gas goes to one country—the United States. The changes in the US energy market were concerning, he admitted, because "they're not going to need us as much anymore," and might in fact become competition on world markets. The need to find new customers, he said, was "basic and simple," and pipelines were essential to meeting that need.[15]

Pipelines again—but this time with a difference (once burned, twice shy, after all). You need American approval only if you plan on building transborder pipelines. If, however, the new pipelines run only through Canada, it doesn't matter what a US president or Congress or state governor thinks about your carbon record. The only approval needed is from the National Energy Board, a creature of the Canadian federal government and the federal cabinet. And unlike authorities in the States, the National Energy Board doesn't even consider the issue of carbon emissions when making its environmental assessment.[16]

Given the drubbing oil sands producers have taken in the United States over the approval of Keystone XL, it shouldn't be surprising that all recently proposed pipeline routes run through Canada. That redirect sets the bar a lot lower. Instead of seeking approval from a US president who thinks climate change is the world's most pressing challenge (and is bolstered in his beliefs by a sudden supply of less emissions-intensive light oil from American shale formations), pipeline companies such as TransCanada and Enbridge now need the approval only of a prime minister who believes that climate change is a hoax.[17]

To no one's surprise, the National Energy Board dutifully approved Enbridge's environmentally contentious proposal for the Northern Gateway pipeline that would send over half a million barrels of oil sands product per day from Bruderheim, Alberta, through pristine BC rainforest to Kitimat on the Pacific Coast. There, the heavy oil would be loaded onto waiting supertankers, which in turn would navigate the treacherous waterways along the Inside Passage before heading out into open seas. The NEB's decision has subsequently been rubber-stamped by the Harper cabinet, the last step in the federal approval process.

NEB approval was given despite the fact that a provincial review board in British Columbia had rejected the Northern Gateway pipeline back in May 2013 on the grounds that the pipeline and the associated tanker traffic posed enormous environmental risks to wilderness areas in the province and to the coastline from potential spills. The idea of a massive spill really scares BC residents. A pipeline leak in the wilderness would be bad enough, but an *Exxon Valdez*–type accident involving one of those supertankers filled to the brim with millions of barrels of bitumen would be an environmental disaster on an epic scale. A University of British Columbia study estimates the cost of a major spill from one of today's super-large crude carriers (which can hold as much as 3 million barrels of bitumen) could be as high as $9 billion, dwarfing the economic benefits that the project would bring.[18]

Unfortunately for Enbridge, and the oil sands producers who have signed shipper agreements to supply it with feedstock, the federal government isn't the only player at the table. As they are quickly discovering, Native groups, the courts and provincial governments can all pose formidable roadblocks to proposed pipeline routes.

LAND CLAIMS AND COURT BATTLES

Constitutionally, the federal government has jurisdiction over the approval of interprovincial pipelines in Canada. But the reality is far more complex. If anyone doubts that, they just have to look at what happened to the proposed Mackenzie Valley natural gas pipeline in the 1970s. It was never built. Widespread Native opposition—based on fears over the negative environmental impacts on their traditional homelands—forced the federal government to appoint a commission, led by Justice Thomas Berger, to study the issue. After extensive dialogue with Native communities in the affected area, Berger recommended against the pipeline being built. At the time, the project was hyped by its supporters as having the same critical significance for the Canadian economy as today's pipeline supporters claim for projects like Northern Gateway.

Colonial-era treaties give Aboriginal communities say over land use in the territories in which they have land claims, but they also can enforce claims on areas where there are unsettled land claims. A recent unanimous landmark decision by the Supreme Court reaffirmed Native rights by granting the declaration of Aboriginal title to some 2,600 square kilometres of land in interior British Columbia to the Tsilhqot'in First Nation. The precedent-setting decision affirms Native jurisdiction in areas of unsettled land claims that have not been formally ceded by treaties.[19]

Unfortunately for Enbridge, the proposed Northern Gateway pipeline cuts through a number of such territories as it traverses the width of BC from the Alberta border to the coastal community of Kitimat, putting the company at loggerheads with multiple First Nation land claims. Enbridge's offer of a 10 percent ownership in the pipeline was flatly rejected by Native communities, which have vowed to file court challenges to stop pipeline construction. The NEB may have given the project the green light to begin construction in 2015, and for oil to flow by 2018, but no one at Enbridge is expecting anything other than an extended court battle whose outcome may turn Northern Gateway into another Mackenzie.

Also on the books is Kinder Morgan's proposal to twin its existing Trans Mountain pipeline—a move that would almost triple the pipeline's existing 300,000 bpd throughput to 890,000 bpd. Like Northern Gateway, the twinned pipeline would carry diluted bitumen, or *dilbit* as it is referred to in the industry, to the company's Westridge Marine terminal in Burnaby, BC, just outside Vancouver.

The citizens of Burnaby (and indeed the rest of the province's densely populated Lower Mainland) are about as enthusiastic about this project as the province's First Nations are about Northern Gateway. The city of Burnaby owns the land Kinder Morgan wants to build on, and it has vowed to do everything in its power to block the project. Undeterred, Kinder Morgan plans to go ahead with its application to the NEB, which is scheduled to rule on the $5.4-billion twinning project by early 2016. But as we are already seeing with Northern Gateway, NEB approval is not a guarantee that construction can begin.

BC'S ENERGY DREAMS

Native groups and municipalities weren't the only ones lining up to oppose a bitumen pipeline running through British Columbia; the BC provincial government was right there with them. Premier Christy Clark has already served notice that she is less than enthusiastic about her province being used as a conduit to get Alberta bitumen to oil markets in China, and polls in BC have shown a clear majority of British Columbians back her up on the issue. Even communities that would benefit from direct job creation from the pipeline seem against the project—and with good reason.

Bitumen is nasty stuff. As was discovered in 2010, when Enbridge's Line 6B ruptured and spilled 900,000 barrels of diluted Alberta bitumen into Michigan's Kalamazoo River—the worst inland oil spill in

US history—heavy oil is not biodegradable. Nor can it be skimmed off the surface of the water like regular crude. According to the US Environmental Protection Agency, which investigated the spill, the heavy oil sank to the bottom of the Kalamazoo and mixed with sediment, requiring the entire river bottom to be dredged in a process that took over three years to complete.

While BC's environmental concerns regarding Northern Gateway are undoubtedly very real, Christy Clark may share some common ground with Barack Obama when it comes to pipeline opposition. If Obama's fixation on carbon emissions has been strengthened by the results of the shale revolution, Clark's feelings about the Enbridge line are undoubtedly influenced by her own "energy superpower" plans. From her perspective, and the perspective of the majority of BC voters, it's not bitumen that should be exported to China but rather the province's abundant supplies of shale gas. Instead of a pipeline carrying Alberta's heavy oil through the province, Premier Clark wants natural gas pipelines that would take shale gas from the interior to Kitimat, where it would be converted into liquid natural gas and then sold to China. And instead of supertankers carrying Alberta bitumen down their coastline, BC residents would prefer supertankers filled with their own province's much cleaner natural gas.

Since liquid natural gas leaks simply dissipate into the atmosphere and don't threaten the local environment with lasting damage the way bitumen leaks do, a natural gas pipeline is also the preference of environmental and Native groups. Clark has even argued that moving gas is not only safer for the BC environment but better for China's environment as well. The natural gas that BC would be shipping to China would be used in place of coal and would hence contribute to that country's efforts to lower its own carbon emissions, which are now the largest in the world.

What Premier Clark hasn't mentioned in public, but is likely uppermost in her mind, is that the BC government receives both royalties and jobs from shale gas produced in the province; it receives none from Alberta's bitumen. All the BC government would get out of that deal is a bill for the cleanup costs associated with any leaks along the pipeline carrying the bitumen to Kitimat or, worse yet, for a spill from a grounded supertanker along its coastline. Clark has insisted that if the Northern Gateway pipeline gets built, BC must receive some economic benefits — in the form of shared oil revenues. That demand has been flatly rejected by the Alberta government, which has no intention of sharing any of its bitumen royalties with its neighbour.

As it turns out, though, Premier Clark's grand plans for turning Kitimat into a hub for natural gas exports are as unlikely to be fulfilled as Stephen Harper's plans to turn the remote northern coastal town into a hub for exporting bitumen. A lot of things can happen in the time it takes to approve and then construct pipelines. Often, the world changes in ways that suddenly leave multibillion-dollar pipeline projects making little if any economic sense.

A CAUTIONARY TALE

Just before the last recession, there were plans to build a regasification plant outside Quebec City to receive liquid natural gas from Russia. Back then, North American natural gas prices were well over double what they are today, and depleting supplies of conventional natural gas pointed to even higher prices in the future. Russia, at the same time, was gas-rich and looking for new markets. The shale gas revolution changed that outlook overnight. North American gas prices plunged, making the economics of importing LNG from Russia, or from anywhere else for that matter, nonsensical.

In fact, the price drop did more than just stymie Russian exports to North America. The huge decline in North American gas prices actually *reversed* the polarity of the liquid natural gas trade, turning North America from an importer into a potential exporter of the fuel.

With North American natural gas trading at anywhere from a third to a fifth of the price in Europe and Asia, there was suddenly a mad rush to build export terminals to ship gas to those high-priced markets. There are currently some thirty different proposals for such terminals in the United States, with Cheniere Energy's Sabine Pass project already under construction in Louisiana. Not wanting to be left out of the race to supply China with gas, British Columbia quickly planned as many as fourteen terminals and compressor plants along its coast, the majority clustered around the Kitimat–Prince Rupert area. The NEB has already approved seven of those projects for export licences.

But in today's energy markets, the goalposts can shift right when you are about to kick the ball. While potential North American suppliers were getting organized, China found a much closer and, more important, much cheaper source of gas. In June 2014, China and Russia signed a thirty-year, $400-billion accord that will serve as a springboard for Russia's national gas firm, OAO Gazprom, to develop its vast and largely untapped gas reserves in remote eastern Siberia. Some four thousand kilometres of new pipeline will be built, hooking up Siberian gas wells to Beijing and other parts of northeastern China, a region that holds the same population as all of western Europe. The supply of shale gas brought down North American gas prices and, likewise, the new supply of Russian gas from east Siberia will lower prices in China. It's thought that Gazprom will get just under $10 per thousand cubic feet for its gas exports to China, which undercuts current prices for imported LNG from British Columbia or Louisiana by 30 to 40 percent.

To add insult to injury, the Russia–China gas accord was in no small measure brought about in response to actions taken by the US and Canadian governments. By aggressively exhorting their European allies to wean themselves off their dependence on Russian gas, both Obama and Harper may have inadvertently quashed their countries' hopes of exporting LNG to China. What Obama and Harper failed to consider was that in a re-emerging cold war environment—tensions between Russia and Ukraine ratcheted up following the 2014 Olympics in Sochi to the point where Russia re-annexed Crimea, earning international condemnation—Russia's overwhelming reliance on western European markets is as strategically troublesome for it as it is for its customers. If a dispute compels Russia to turn off the gas, the lights may go out in Kiev or Berlin, but the cash flow in Moscow will dry up as well. Right now, Gazprom counts on European countries for about 80 percent of its revenue. Reorienting its sales to China is a natural hedge against any future conflict with western Europe that might imperil those vital cash flows. Unfortunately, it's a move that leaves would-be North American exporters—including those in British Columbia—out in the cold.[20]

IF THE WEST AND SOUTH ARE BLOCKED, GO EAST

With President Obama blocking new pipeline access to the Gulf Coast, and court challenges (including from Native groups) and a less than enthusiastic BC premier blocking access to the Pacific coast, the Canadian government and oil sands producers set their sights on the east. Moving oil from northern Alberta to Irving's large refinery and export terminal in Saint John, New Brunswick, may seem like a pretty circuitous route for Alberta bitumen to get to world markets, but it was the only direction left for the oil to flow.

Both TransCanada and Enbridge, the country's two largest pipeline companies, have proposals that together would move a lot more oil east than the proposed Keystone XL pipeline would deliver south to Gulf Coast refineries, or the Northern Gateway pipeline would deliver to the Pacific coast. TransCanada's proposed $12-billion Energy East pipeline would take 1.1 million barrels of bitumen a day from the oil sands to refineries and export terminals roughly

4,500 kilometres away on the east coast, compared with a little over 800,000 bpd that the Keystone XL would pipe or the half a million bpd that would flow through Northern Gateway. In addition to TransCanada's Energy East proposal, Enbridge has recently received National Energy Board approval to reverse the flow of oil and expand capacity in its little-used Line 9 pipeline, which originally took imported oil from Montreal to refineries and petrochemical plants in Sarnia, Ontario, adding another potential 300,000 barrels a day to the volume of bitumen flowing east.

But there may be just as many obstacles for an eastbound route as there are for those running west and south. While the NEB has approved the reversal of the forty-year-old Line 9 pipeline that runs between North Westford, Ontario, and Montreal to carry bitumen east, no oil is flowing. The regulator found the company failed to install safety shut-off valves on all the water crossings, a condition for pipeline approval. The importance of those shut-off valves was dramatically highlighted by the disastrous rupture of the Enbridge pipeline into the Kalamazoo River. More recently, the NEB has given permission to begin operating the pipeline in June 2015, overriding its original insistence that Enbridge install shut-off valves over as many as a hundred different water crossings.

Not surprisingly, the much-larger Energy East pipeline proposal is facing its fair share of opposition. The pipeline route travels through 180 different Aboriginal communities, each of which must have its concerns about the project heard and accommodated. Moreover, the provincial governments in both Ontario and Quebec have, like the BC government, good reason to be less than enthusiastic about the transit of over 1 million barrels of bitumen every day through densely populated areas of their province.

Ontario premier Kathleen Wynne has just as much reason to worry about a new pipeline passing through her province as Christy Clark does about seeing one head through hers. The move to convert

TransCanada's existing gas pipeline to a bitumen pipeline will cost Ontario. The province's supply of natural gas could be cut by as much as 25 percent, leaving some regions, such as eastern Ontario, with no obvious substitute.[21] The company's offer to build a new gas pipeline in the province is somewhat less than magnanimous when you consider it's asking for a huge increase in the rates it charges to customers in eastern Ontario. Why Ontario's natural gas consumers should subsidize the transit of Alberta bitumen through their backyards remains unclear.

And insofar as carbon emissions are concerned, the pipeline and the increased oil sands production that it facilitates would negate everything that Ontario has done to reduce such emissions. In November 2013, Premier Wynne shared the stage with Al Gore and received kudos from the one-time presidential contender and environmental evangelist for closing or converting all of the province's coal-fired plants, including Nanticoke, which was once the single-largest source of carbon pollution on the continent. But nationally, Ontario's efforts are more than offset by oil sands emissions that will triple from 34 million tons in 2005 to 100 million tons by 2020. Where Ontario's carbon emissions are expected to fall by 30 percent between 2005 and 2020, Alberta's emissions are expected to increase by over 60 percent. Alberta is the culprit behind Canada's pariah record on carbon emissions, but Ontario's acquiescence to the Energy East pipeline would make it a willing accomplice.

Both Premier Wynne of Ontario and Premier Couillard of Quebec might be asking what pipelines that are designed to fetch world oil prices for Alberta mean for pump prices in Toronto and Montreal. After all, gasoline is made from oil, and if the price of the feedstock (in this case bitumen) goes up, so does the price of refined products. To the extent that the gasoline we burn is made from Western Canadian Select, and the bigger the price discount between Alberta bitumen and world oil prices, the lower are pump prices in central Canada.

Lastly, TransCanada's plans to build a deepwater oil-shipping port in Cacouna, Quebec—one that would connect to the Energy East pipeline—has run into some major-league environmental opposition. The port, and the hundreds of oil tankers that would visit, is right in the calving grounds of the beluga whale, an endangered species. A Quebec court has slapped an injunction on the project until there can be a full-scale environmental assessment of its impact on the dwindling beluga population in the Gulf of St. Lawrence.

There is much that Ontario and Quebec could do to block TransCanada's and Enbridge's plans to pipe oil east across their territory. The Ontario Energy Board could deny TransCanada's request for a huge rate increase to finance the construction of a new gas pipeline to eastern Ontario. The province could also block permits for the new pumping stations that would be needed to move the bitumen, and ensure that the pipeline's multiple water crossings do not contravene its Clean Water Act. In Quebec, the provincial government could refuse to approve the construction of a brand-new pipeline from Montreal to the New Brunswick border to connect with TransCanada's existing natural gas pipeline that runs from Ontario to Alberta. And, of course, Premier Couillard can deny permission for the export terminal at Cacouna, a key feature of the whole Energy East project.

Court challenges to Northern Gateway and potential political opposition from provincial governments in Ontario and Quebec to Energy East demonstrate that even on their home turf, oil sands producers can't count on the speedy approval of new pipeline capacity. But producers in the oil sands, as well as in the neighbouring Bakken, weren't just going to sit on their hands waiting, Godot-like, for those desperately needed pipelines to be approved and built. Not when they can hear the clitter-clatter of thousands of tanker cars rolling down the track.

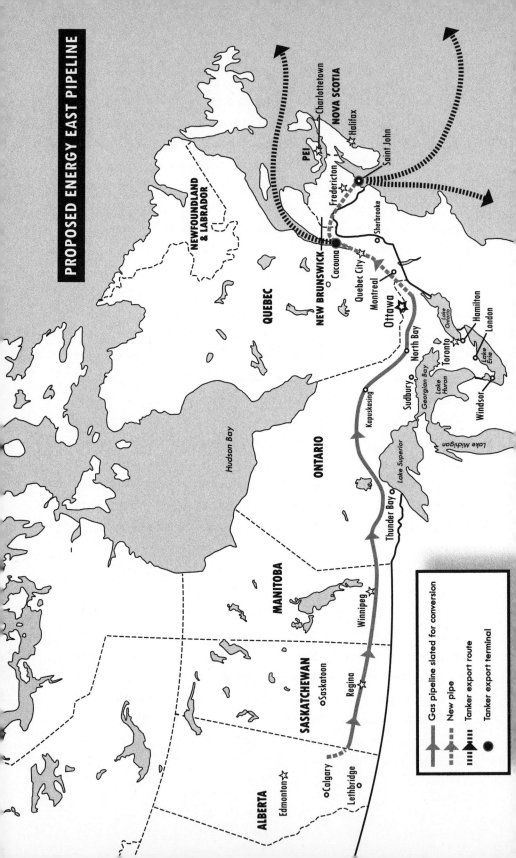

PROPOSED ENERGY EAST PIPELINE

ALBERTA
Edmonton☆
Calgary○
Lethbridge○

SASKATCHEWAN
Saskatoon○
Regina☆

MANITOBA
Winnipeg☆

ONTARIO
Thunder Bay○
Kapuskasing○
Sudbury○
North Bay○
Georgian Bay
Lake Superior
Lake Huron
Lake Michigan
Lake Erie
Lake Ontario
Windsor○
London○
Hamilton○
Toronto☆
Ottawa☆

QUEBEC
Montreal○
Quebec City○
Cacouna●
Sherbrooke○

NEW BRUNSWICK
Fredericton☆
Saint John◉

NEWFOUNDLAND & LABRADOR

NOVA SCOTIA
Halifax☆

PEI
Charlottetown☆

Hudson Bay

Legend
⟶ Gas pipeline slated for conversion
⟶ New pipe
▶▶▶ Tanker export route
● Tanker export terminal

CHAPTER 6

TICK, TICK, TICK

THE ORACLE OF OMAHA, as Warren Buffett is reverently referred to in investment circles, is a close economic advisor to the US president and has been a huge campaign contributor as well. More than most Americans, he has Obama's ear. What he's whispered in it about the Keystone XL pipeline is the subject of much media debate and controversy, if only because his investment firm, Berkshire Hathaway, has so greatly benefited from the president's refusal to approve the pipeline.

If Buffett did indeed counsel against approval, as is widely speculated, he was coming at the issue from a very different perspective than the pipeline's environmental opponents.[1] The fourth richest man in the world, according to *Forbes*, Buffett's holdings include some of the worst carbon-emitting utilities in the United States. In 2008, they spewed more than 65 million metric tonnes of CO_2 into the atmosphere[2], a feat that led *Rolling Stone* magazine to label Buffett a "climate killer" in a 2010 article identifying the world's worst climate offenders and climate-change deniers.[3]

While environmental opponents to Keystone XL were chaining themselves to the White House fence in protest, Mr. Buffett was busy buying the Burlington Northern Santa Fe (BNSF) railway. When Buffett acquired the company in November 2009, for $34 billion, he assumed control of one of the largest freight railroad networks in North America, with more than five thousand kilometres of track across the western two-thirds of the United States.[4] Buffett had made a related purchase the year before, when he picked up leasing companies Union Tank Car in the USA and Procor Ltd. in Canada. In case you're not familiar with them, those are the companies that provide the railways with the DOT-111 tanker cars used to haul oil from booming shale plays like the Bakken to refineries in New Jersey, Pennsylvania, the Gulf Coast and New Brunswick.

As information about Buffett's acquisitions bubbled to the surface in daily newspapers, blogs and financial reports, it became readily apparent that the billionaire was positioning his business interests to take advantage of the transport conundrum that would follow if Keystone XL did not proceed. If there was no pipeline construction, oil would instead have to be moved by trains—his trains, to be precise, supplied with tanker cars from his leasing companies.

As Keystone XL remains stuck in the mud—mired in a seemingly never-ending series of court battles, environmental assessments and political spats—Buffett's big bet is paying off. His tanker-car leasing companies are doing well, and his railway leads all North American railways in oil haulage, and had pledged to double its spending on oil-moving operations in 2014. Hauling oil around the continent has paid handsome returns to other railways as well. CN Rail chief executive Claude Mongeau cited booming oil business as playing a key role in the company's improved earnings, which beat analysts' expectations in 2013. The company has just built a new rail terminal in northwestern Alberta to increase oil shipments from the province, and has made other infrastructure improvement efforts as well, including numerous track upgrades.[5] CN doubled its oil haulage from 30,000 tankerloads in 2012 to 60,000 tankerloads in 2013.[6] Not to be outdone by its rival, CP Rail moved over 70,000 tanker cars of oil in 2013, up from only 13,000 loads the year before. The turnaround in the company's fortunes has been so dramatic, its board of directors saw fit to pay CEO Hunter Harrison a total compensation package of $49 million in 2013.[7]

Rail, it seems, is having a moment—or seizing one, as the case may be. With new pipelines blocked by widespread environmental opposition on both sides of the border, railways have been all too eager to fill the transport gap, suddenly regaining a prominence in the oil industry that they haven't enjoyed since the early days of John Rockefeller's Standard Oil monopoly well over a century ago. And is it any wonder? While new pipelines take years to build—and as long as a decade to approve (or not approve, as the case may be with Keystone XL)— trainloads of oil can be arranged in a matter of days. Overnight, it seems, hundred-car tanker trains have become pipelines on wheels.

For North American railways, at least, the upsurge in oil shipments couldn't have come at a better time—precisely as business from the railways' traditionally biggest carbon customer, coal, collapsed as many power utilities across the continent switched to cheaper natural gas from fracked shale formations. And in addition to the millions of barrels of oil that have been loaded into DOT-111 tanker cars, North America's shale revolution has brought a huge pickup in the volume of sand carried by rail. Once used primarily by glassmakers, silica sand is experiencing an unexpected boom. Sand is an essential component in the fracking process, needed to prop open cracks in the shale after the high-pressurized solution of water and chemicals fractures the surrounding rock. Union Pacific, America's largest railway, and Buffett's Burlington Northern Santa Fe now haul about 20 million tons of the stuff a year to drilling sites across the continent.[8]

With the exception of Buffett, the intention of Keystone's opponents was to keep oil in the ground, not to load it onto tanker cars. But when they started blocking new pipeline construction, their opposition opened up a whole new, or rather old, way of moving the fuel across the continent. With explosive results.

PLAYING WITH FIRE

On July 6, 2013, in Lac-Mégantic, Quebec, a seventy-two-car train carrying some fifty thousand barrels of explosive Bakken light crude rolled thirteen kilometres downhill from a parked position, derailed and exploded, destroying much of the town centre and claiming the lives of forty-seven people. There have been subsequent derailments and explosions near Plaster Rock, New Brunswick, in Aliceville, Alabama, in Casselton, North Dakota, and in Lynchburg, Virginia. Investigations into these disasters have revealed two separate but related problems with current practices around shipping oil by rail: the first is the nature of the tanker cars most commonly used, and the second is the type of oil being shipped.

Let's start with the tankers. DOT-111 tanker cars make up an estimated 85 percent of the ninety-two thousand fuel tanker cars in use on North American railways.[9] They have been the subject of repeated warnings from regulators since as early as 1994, when the US National Transportation Safety Board first began complaining about the tankers' thin metal skin, which is easily punctured in the event of a derailment. Some have likened the DOT-111 to Ford's infamous Pinto, subject of a massive recall in the early 1970s, when it was found that the car's fuel tank would ignite in a rear-end collision.

Not only are DOT-111 cars a particularly dangerous vessel in which to move oil, but the situation is exacerbated by the type of oil the cars are carrying. The train that derailed in Lac-Mégantic was shipping the most explosive oil ever railed across the continent. In fact, it's not even really oil, at least in the conventional sense. Oil from the Bakken shale formation is the exact opposite of bitumen, so light that it required a new name — ultra-light. And ultra-light oil, as it turns out, has the volatility of gasoline.

Ultra-light oil is actually oil mixed with a lot of explosive gas. When the gas comes out of the fracked ground along with the oil, it turns into natural gas liquids, or *condensate* as it's called in the industry.

Ninety-six percent of the increase in US oil production since 2011 is light or ultra-light oil. And all of the expected future increases are of the same variety.

The oil fracked from shale formations has so much gas that it often even bubbles, like popped champagne. But this is no bottle of Dom Pérignon. Those bubbling gases turn ultra-light oil into a ticking time bomb inside the poorly vented and thin-hulled DOT-111s. The fuel is even a handful for refineries, most of which bulked up for heavy oil from Venezuela and the oil sands and are now having to reinvest in new technology to deal with the polar opposite type of feedstock.

While the gaseous nature of oil fracked from shale formations was brought to light in the investigations that followed the Lac-Mégantic disaster—investigators were initially puzzled as to how normal crude could have been so explosive—subsequent investigations have found that the oil from other shale plays is just as gaseous, and hence just as unstable and explosive. High gas levels have been found in light oil from the Niobrara shale formation in Colorado and in oil from the Eagle Ford and Permian basins in Texas.

Following the explosion outside Casselton, North Dakota, in late December 2013, the US Department of Transportation issued a warning that shale oil from the Bakken was much more explosive than traditional oil and had to be treated as a hazardous material. The Transportation Safety Board investigation found that the flashpoint for Bakken crude was as low as for gasoline, making it a far more hazardous fuel for railways to carry than normal crude.

If the sheer amount of oil criss-crossing the continent in flimsy tanker cars—estimated to be over 2 million barrels a day by the end of 2014—isn't enough to make you nervous, there's yet another factor to consider.[10] The manner in which oil is moved by rail has changed in a way that dramatically increases the risk of explosion. Instead of being moved in "manifest" trains, where a few DOT-111 tanker cars would be interspersed with other cargo, today oil is being shipped in "unit" trains consisting of nothing but seventy to a hundred tanker cars carrying as much as eighty-one thousand barrels. The reason for these "virtual pipelines"—as the unit trains have been dubbed—comes down to cost: transport is about three dollars cheaper per barrel on unit trains than on manifest trains.

Warnings from transport regulators on both sides of the border are triggering alarm bells in communities across the continent that have or will soon have DOT-111 tanker cars rolling through their neighbourhoods—places such as Toronto and Chicago, Seattle and New Orleans, and thousands of other cities and towns, small and large. In Toronto, the old CPR line cuts across the populous midtown area, right past the courts where I play tennis each summer. That track now regularly sees hundred-car trains of DOT-111s rolling by, taking highly explosive light oil from the Bakken to refineries on the east coast.

Individual railways are tight-lipped about the amount of oil they are hauling through major North American cities,[11] but the general trends reported by both transportation ministries and rail associations suggest that there are many more of those DOT-111 unit trains to come. Some two-thirds of the rapidly expanding production from North Dakota, second only to Texas in production, is being hauled by tanker car. Thanks largely to the Bakken, rail haulage of oil has soared from almost nothing only a few years ago to represent over 10 percent of total US oil production.[12] According to the US Department of Transportation, rail haulage of crude oil increased from 9,500 tanker cars in 2008 to 415,000 tanker cars in 2013, with Bakken crude travelling, on average, more than 1,600 kilometres from its point of origin to refineries on the coasts.[13] Not surprisingly, the Association of American Railroads announced that petroleum products were the fastest-growing category of rail shipments in 2013. The statistics in Canada are no less spectacular, with shipments of oil by rail increasing from a paltry 500 tanker cars in 2009 to 140,000 in 2013.[14]

And this may be just the tip of the iceberg. While most of the oil currently railed across Canada is from the pipeline-deprived Bakken field, more is planned to come from the oil sands. With Keystone XL and other pipeline projects in limbo, and oil sands producers desperate to reach oil-hungry markets overseas, more and more are relying on rail to get their product where it needs to go. Three rail-loading terminals in western Canada are already being built, with a combined capacity of 350,000 barrels per day.[15] Exxon, meanwhile, is planning to build its own oil-loading rail terminal in Edmonton to handle production from its massive Kearl Lake project. Altogether, the planned construction of new oil-loading rail terminals could mean that within the next three to five years, as much as a million barrels of oil could be moved around Canada every day—a fivefold increase from the levels hauled in 2013.

While bitumen isn't nearly as explosive as ultra-light crude from the Bakken, it's much harder to clean up, and hence its environmental footprint is that much greater should the fuel be spilled.

BETTER SAFE THAN SORRY?

After Lac-Mégantic, the debate over the transport of oil by rail has become increasingly heated. While the public on both sides of the border engage in "not in my backyard" protests,[16] state and municipal governments are also getting in on the act. In Seattle, the municipal government has asked the Department of Transportation for a moratorium on the movement of oil trains through the city.[17] Some states—including Washington, Montana and Wisconsin— have refused to sign non-disclosure agreements with the railways, a clear sign that increasingly they view the public's "right to know" as more important than the railways' security concerns.[18] In Canada, Windsor, Ontario, is believed to be the only municipality to have refused to sign such an agreement.[19]

Essentially, advocacy groups and governments across North America (as well as worried citizens who have yet to join the protests) share a common concern: the more oil being hauled around by rail, the more oil can potentially be spilled in derailments. For its part, the rail industry has countered that more than 99 percent of all oil hauled by rail arrives at its destination without incident, and that far more oil is spilled by pipelines. But how confident can we be in those statistics when the volume of oil shipped by rail increases fortyfold over a five-year period, as it has done in the United States? And how robust are the industry's past safety statistics in the current situation, where instead of manifest trains hauling five or ten tankers each, hundred-car trains of nothing but DOT-111s filled to the brim with highly volatile light oil from fracked shale formations are coming down the tracks? And how relevant are past safety statistics when the oil now being shipped from places like the Bakken is far more explosive than normal crude?

According to data released by the US Pipeline and Hazardous Materials Safety Administration, there was more oil spilled in rail accidents in 2013 (1.15 million gallons) than during the last four decades put together (a total of 800,000 gallons). Moreover, the US numbers for 2013 don't include the 5.7 million litres of crude spilled in Lac-Mégantic. Nor do they include the spillage from the year-end derailment and subsequent explosion at Casselton, North Dakota, which is estimated to be north of 400,000 barrels. Obviously, a better than 99 percent safety record still leaves a lot of room for spillage when you are hauling the volumes of oil the rail industry is hauling today.

These thoughts seem to have crossed the minds of both American and Canadian regulators. Following the recent spate of derailment disasters, and the subsequent investigations into the causes, both the American and Canadian governments have proposed changes to the way crude oil is hauled by rail. The US plans, which were set out in July 2014, would require better cargo descriptions, lower speed limits, improved braking systems and a risk assessment for routes. Perhaps most important, the infamous DOT-111 tanker car would be phased out or rebuilt to new standards within two years (at least for the most volatile oil group; cars hauling less volatile oil would have five years to upgrade). In Canada, a three-year phase-out of DOT-111s ordered before October 2011 (when better safety standards were brought in) has been introduced, and cars built before the mid-1990s are now banned from carrying dangerous goods.[20]

The plans may sound good on paper, but they provide little assurance there won't be future oil-related rail accidents. Of the 98,000 tanker cars currently in use in the USA and Canada, only 18,000 were constructed after 2011, which leaves a lot of older DOT-111s to phase out.[21] And given that the new standards don't go into effect until October 2015—and the compliance date is October 2017—the phase-out is actually over three years. In the meantime, railways can go on using the outdated and dangerous tanker cars. And in the end, even the new and updated tanker cars come with risks. Although they offer improvements over the DOT-111s—including a thicker, explosion-resistant shell and better braking systems—they are far from foolproof. The train that derailed and exploded in Lynchburg, Virginia, in April 2014, dumping between 30,000 and 60,000 barrels of oil into the James River, was using newer cars.[22]

For the moment at least, shareholders in increasingly oil-dependent railways aren't unduly preoccupied with derailments and toxic spills; they are too busy enjoying what the huge boom in oil haulage is doing for the bottom line. But before investors get too comfortable with high rates of return, they should perhaps remember that Bakken oil is not the only thing that is explosive. Consider what would happen to railways' liabilities should the next disaster occur in a major urban area.

In the wake of the Lac-Mégantic disaster, the Canadian Transportation Agency began reviewing how it establishes the minimum insurance amounts for railways. When the accident occurred, the Montreal, Maine and Atlantic (MMA) Railway was carrying $25 million in third-party liability insurance—which turned out to be a fraction of the cost of cleanup. MMA filed documents with a Quebec court revealing that the environmental cleanup alone is expected to top $200 million; the railway is also facing a number of lawsuits from the families of those who died in the crash.[23]

And as bad as that derailment was, it's far from a "worst-case" scenario. What if the next disaster occurs in a densely populated urban setting? Six months after the accident, Hunter Harrison, CEO of Canadian Pacific, told the *Wall Street Journal* that his "worst nightmare" would be the sabotage of a train carrying a toxic substance in a heavily populated area: "The estimates of the lives and the damage—I don't even want to repeat what it would be."[24] What Mr. Harrison didn't mention was that with the amount of highly combustible extra-light Bakken crude his railway hauls in DOT-111 tanker cars through urban areas these days, his nightmare could come true without any help from saboteurs.

The train that derailed in Lac-Mégantic went through Toronto[25]; the one that derailed in Lynchburg, Virginia, travelled through Chicago. Both of these cities, and dozens of others across North America, see more than their share of DOT-111 tanker cars passing through their neighbourhoods. When you're hauling millions of barrels of oil by rail every day, it's only a matter of time before a derailment and explosion occurs in a major urban area.

And when that happens, the repercussions will send Alberta's bitumen producers, as well as those across the border in the Bakken, back to square one—at least where transportation is concerned.

SQUEEZED OUT AND LEFT TO HANG

The growing reliance on rail transport has fostered a symbiotic relationship between the oil industry and railways. The huge increase in oil freight volume has put a lot of money into a lot of pockets. The railways are enjoying the uptick in their business, while the oil companies are reaping the benefits of being able to get their fuel to a coast, and hence fetch world prices. But not everyone has benefited from this newly forged industrial alliance.

Railways, like all other transport systems, have a finite capacity. When the demand from one group of customers ramps up as rapidly as oil freight has of late, there is unavoidably that much less capacity to move the product of other customers. Some simply get left out in the cold. Those most inconvenienced by the recent boom in tanker-car shipments of oil have been farmers in the Canadian prairies and North Dakota. The current lack of railway service has left their bumper wheat crops sitting in near-bursting storage bins with no way of getting to hungry world grain markets.

Unfortunately for these farmers, the boom in oil shipments occurred just as favourable weather conditions in the 2013 growing season, combined with an increase in the area planted, produced a record wheat crop: 37.5 million tons, or 38 percent more than 2012 levels. Other crops benefited from the good weather too: an almost 30 percent bump in canola led to a record 18-million-ton harvest, while production of soybeans, barley and oats also increased.[26]

Imagine the response, then, when transport problems began to rear their heads. Grain piled up in barns and grain elevators as railcars failed to appear. Ships waiting to deliver crops to overseas markets waited some more. In May 2014, Wade Sobkowich of the Western Grain Elevator Association told the *Economist* that orders for sixty thousand railcars' worth of grain had not been filled, and that fifty-three ships were waiting in port on the west coast.[27]

The railways blame the weather. If 2013 was a record year for crops, it also featured a particularly bad winter—with temperatures cold enough to restrict the number of cars a train can carry (temperatures below minus-25 degrees Celsius make it hard to pump the air that keeps the train's brakes working) and the speed at which it can travel (tracks and switches are prone to freezing).[28] Farmers, on the other hand, blame oil—and the railways' desire to reap the rewards that come from shipping that industry's more lucrative product.

Regardless of who is to blame, the situation for farmers was dire. Planting costs run from $100 an acre for winter wheat to $250 an acre for canola. For a typical thousand-acre farm, those costs can run into several hundred thousand dollars. Farmers don't get paid until they deliver their product to an elevator, but when most elevators are full, that leaves no option but to store the grain on the farm. This, however, can lead to deterioration, which in turn can mean a lower price once the grain does reach market. Some experts estimated that the crisis cost farmers between $2 billion and $4 billion.[29] A cash crunch from an unsold harvest can threaten the next year's crop planting.

To make matters worse, Canadian farmers are extremely limited in their ability to switch rail carriers: historically, CN and CP have had an effective duopoly in the region.[30] Some farmers, desperate to get the cash flowing, resorted to hauling their grain by truck. But moving wheat by truck costs as much as $50 a ton more than moving it by rail, making it a very expensive option, and one that is beyond most farmers' means.

The lack of rail transport became so acute that even the oil-championing Harper government had to step in and intervene. Under enormous pressure from western farmers (normally a Conservative constituency), the government passed the Fair Rail for Grain Farmers Act in March 2014 and ordered both CN and CP to move a combined

1 million tons of wheat, corn and other grains a week—roughly equivalent to the volume of eleven thousand rail cars.[31] The legislation also allowed farmers far greater choice in switching rail carriers, challenging CN and CP's control.

PAST VERSUS FUTURE?

Those inclined to view the recent competition between oil companies and western farmers for rail service in Canada as a one-time anomaly should perhaps think twice. The conflict is indicative of a much broader divide. On one side is an oil industry desperate to get as much bitumen as it can to global export markets before tightening emissions constraints or falling oil prices threaten the commercial viability of the resource. On the other side are Canadian farmers who are finding themselves without any means of moving their grain.

In some ways, the battle can be described as a conflict between the country's past and its future. But understanding who is on which side is intriguing—and will be critical to the performance of the Canadian economy over the coming decades. Some, including Stephen Harper and his supporters, believe that the ultimate success of the Canadian economy, and the country's future prosperity, is tied to the growth and development of the oil sands. For these folk, the oil sands resource *is* the future: more oil equals more economic wealth. For others, though, that's far from clear. The boom in rail shipments is already losing steam as falling oil prices start to challenge the basic economics of transporting bitumen by rail. And for those who have paid attention to changes in climate, emissions standards and the global appetite for carbon, oil is increasingly looking like the past. While it's true that the recent grain transportation bottleneck stemmed from a freakish bumper crop in 2013, it's entirely possible that climate change on the Canadian prairies could make bumper crops tomorrow's norm.

Railways might want to be more mindful of the bad blood they are creating with the farm community. Coming restrictions on carbon emissions and the lower oil prices that they must ultimately mandate will put much of the railways' new-found oil business at risk. Mr. Mongeau and Mr. Harrison, along with their boards, may want to stop and reconsider who—in a world of warming prairies and longer growing seasons—will be their most important customers.

[CHAPTER 7]

HOLLOWED OUT

FOR MOST OF THE LAST DECADE, Alberta's booming oil sands was a powerful engine of economic growth. While the US economy struggled with the fallout from the sub-prime mortgage fiasco and the European Union wrestled with the potential default of the nearly insolvent PIIGS (Portugal, Ireland, Italy, Greece and Spain), the petro-driven Canadian economy just seemed to be sailing along. And in the heart of that petro economy—Alberta—things had never been as good.

Back in the early years of Stephen Harper's government, when the potential of the province's bitumen reserves was a hot topic and investment was rolling in from Canada and abroad, Albertans were living the high life. Fort McMurray grew from a small, remote outpost to the centre of the country's booming oil industry, buoyed on a stream of labour and capital that flooded the province from the rest of the country and around the world. Despite a few cyclical booms and busts, the upward trajectory continued. In June 2012, the average household income in "the Mac" (or Fort McMoney, as it's also known) was about $180,000, and the unemployment rate was an enviable 4 percent. The population was sitting somewhere in the region of 104,000—a figure that had doubled since 2002, and was predicted to continue growing by more than 10 percent annually for the foreseeable future.[1] By June 2013, the average price of a home in Fort McMurray had soared to just shy of $785,000, significantly higher than in Calgary and Edmonton,[2] and almost $200,000 higher than Toronto.[3] Nearly 1.3 million passengers made their way through the Fort McMurray airport in 2013—almost a quarter of them flown in on oil sands company charters.[4]

Fuelled by the boom in its oil sands development, Alberta led the country in growth for more than a decade. It cut itself an increasingly larger slice of the national economic pie, and now sits at 17 percent of Canada's GDP—a four-percentage-point increase over 2002 figures[5] and its greatest share of the Canadian economy in the postwar period.[6]

A four-percentage-point swing in the province's share of Canada's GDP may not seem like a big deal, but considering that Alberta has only 11.4 percent of the nation's population, it's huge in per capita terms.[7] During the nineties, Alberta's per capita GDP was roughly comparable to Ontario's ($33,000 versus $30,500), but by 2012 Alberta's had swelled to over $80,000—almost 60 percent higher than Ontario's.[8]

Through the exploitation of the oil sands, the province became the new hub of the Canadian economy, and Albertans should certainly thank the federal government for doing everything in its power to sponsor and promote the rapid development of their province's key economic resource. But other regions of the country weren't feeling so grateful.

THE OTHER SIDE OF THE BOOM

The Fort McMurray–based boom shone a spotlight on Alberta, but it cast a long shadow in less oily parts of the Canadian economy. Much of the capital and labour that poured into the flourishing Alberta economy flowed out of other provinces.[9] While the free movement of labour and capital across provincial borders is vital to the health of any national economy, the scale at which this shift occurred in Canada over the last decade was both unprecedented and unsettling. In 2013, there were approximately 105,000 interprovincial employees earning their living in Alberta.[10] Since 2002, Ontario alone has sent more than 206,000 workers to the province—including 34,000 in 2013.[11] Meanwhile, Alberta's share of international migration doubled.[12]

As the Canadian economy started to morph to fit the mould of an energy superpower, oil and gas quickly became the mark that delineated the have regions from the have-nots. Those provinces that didn't have huge deposits of fossil fuels fell by the wayside. Newfoundland, which developed a thriving offshore oil industry, began to prosper. And Alberta, the province that held the lion's share of the nation's hydrocarbons, surged way ahead of the pack. Saskatchewan, which is also an oil-producing province, did likewise.

No province felt the crunch more than Ontario—centre of the country's manufacturing sector and once the leading auto producer in North America. Manufacturing and the financial services industry had historically made Ontario the country's economic powerhouse, but in recent years the province had been in a persistent slump that left it looking like a rust-belt state (drive through areas of London, Kitchener and Oshawa and you might think you've mistakenly ended up in Detroit).[13] Per capita GDP in the province had fallen well below the national average, a distinction that since 2009 has permitted Ontario, for the first time, to draw from the federal equalization fund—a roughly $17-billion pot designed to help poorer provinces provide basic services such as health care and education at a national standards level.

Unfortunately for Ontario taxpayers, drawing from the federal government's equalization fund doesn't mean the rest of the country is subsidizing the province. Far from it. Ontario's tax base continued to be a cash cow for the federal government. In the same year that Ontario first qualified for equalization, it sent the federal government around $11 billion more in tax revenue than it received in federal spending. And that $11 billion was a multiple of what the province drew in equalization payments.[14]

While Alberta's growth significantly outpaced the rest of the country, Ontario's lagged well behind. Year after year of subpar growth shrunk the province's once-dominant share of national GDP to its lowest level since the depths of the 1981 recession.[15] And to compound matters, the lack of economic growth, and hence growth in tax revenues, left the provincial government with huge budget deficits that may require it to bring down significant tax increases in the future.

If you compare Alberta's economic performance with Ontario's, it turns out there's more at play than nature's roll of the dice. The major culprit behind the last decade's stagnation in Ontario's trade-oriented and manufacturing-based provincial economy wasn't the absence of oil deposits, but rather the meteoric rise in the value of the Canadian dollar.

THE RISE OF A PETRO CURRENCY

The oil sands may account for only 2 percent of Canada's GDP, but the sector dominates where it counts for the currency—in the country's trade and capital flows.[16]

Canada's foreign trade has always been resource-based, and so has its currency. In the past, "resource-based trade" encompassed a broad array of commodities including lumber, minerals and wheat. Today, it means mostly bitumen. Back in 1977, energy accounted for less than 20 percent of the resource sector. By 2012, it had more than doubled its share, to just under 50 percent. During the same time period, oil's share of Canada's exports almost doubled, to more than 25 percent. This certainly wasn't the "rocks and trees" currency that foreign exchange markets had always known, and the change left its mark: the increasingly oily nature of Canada's exports was quickly turning the loonie into a bona fide petro currency.[17]

It is the capital flows that finance the exploitation of the oil sands, and the export earnings that flow from the hundreds of millions of barrels of bitumen sent to the United States every year, that cemented the strong bonds between the Canadian dollar and the price of oil. The higher oil prices moved, the more bitumen could be scooped out of the oil sands and exported to the USA, and the more oil dominated the country's exports.

Not only did rising oil prices encourage rising production and exports, but they also served as a beacon, attracting international capital into what had suddenly become recognized as the third-largest oil reserve in the world—and the largest one open to private investment (unlike the bigger deposits in Venezuela and Saudi Arabia). The bigger those oil-linked trade and capital flows, the more leveraged the Canadian dollar became to the price of oil.

Hitched to the fortunes of the booming oil sands sector, the value of the Canadian dollar soared on a trajectory the likes of which it had never before experienced. From a trough of 61 cents in 2002, the loonie rose to a record peak of $1.10 by 2007—an astonishing 80 percent appreciation against the US dollar, the currency of the country that had absorbed more than three-quarters of Canada's merchandise exports.

Back in 2002, oil was trading at a skimpy $20 per barrel, and the oil sands were a quaint little sideshow in Alberta's energy industry. For some time, the Bank of Canada had been keeping interest rates lower than the Federal Reserve Board to try to compensate for all the fiscal pain the Canadian economy had had to endure from years of deficit-slashing, growth-killing Paul Martin federal budgets. Keen to generate all the economic stimulus it could, the Bank of Canada watched from the sidelines as the Canadian dollar plunged. Before long, economists on Bay Street were talking about the currency's demise and some even suggested the advisability of a monetary union with the United States.[18]

Then things started to change. First, the bursting of the dot-com bubble ended the world's love affair with the greenback. All of a sudden those huge inflows of foreign capital wanting to buy NASDAQ's hottest new tech issue dried up. Worldcom collapsed, as did Broadcast.com, Pets.com, Webvan.com and a host of other promising start-ups. According to the *Los Angeles Times*, the bubble took out $5 trillion in tech company market value, and hundreds of thousands of jobs.[19] The NASDAQ dropped from a peak of 5048.62 to 1114.11 — a loss of 78 percent[20] — and without a steady diet of tech-inspired cash flow, the US dollar ceded ground against most of the world's major currencies.

But no major currency would come close to matching the Canadian dollar's appreciation over the next half decade. With dot-com stocks in the economic doghouse, global investors were searching for the next big thing — and natural resources began to look awfully sexy. The economies of China, India and the other BRICs were booming, and they suddenly had a voracious appetite for everything from coal to steel to copper. Most of all, though, they developed a raging thirst for oil. And when it came to that most important fuel, Canada had some pretty grand plans. Investment poured in and oil sands production grew by leaps and bounds. So too did the currency.

By 2004, the loonie had climbed all the way back to 80 cents. Most Canadians were relieved — after all, their assets, including their homes and pensions, were likely denominated in their native currency. With an 80-cent loonie, snowbirds could once again afford to fly south during the winter, and small-market Canadian NHL clubs didn't have to ask the league for subsidies to stay in business. For a while, everything looked good. If the loonie's rise had topped out there, the Canadian economy, particularly in Ontario and Quebec, would look very different today.

That 80-cent mark is a bit of a magic number for the Canadian dollar, perhaps its "ideal weight." That's roughly where both a Bank of Canada study back in 2002 and an OECD report in 2011 pegged the purchasing power parity (PPP) value of the Canadian dollar.[21] PPP is an economic concept that tries to determine the true underlying value of a currency by measuring what it can buy relative to the purchasing power of other currencies. One of the most popular versions of the concept is the Big Mac Index that appears every year in the *Economist*, comparing the price of a Big Mac at McDonald's restaurants around the world.[22] The OECD purchasing power parity calculation goes a little further, looking at hundreds of prices to compare what a dollar buys in Canada compared with what a dollar buys in the USA.

Theoretical calculations like this can be informative (and amusing), but by 2007 there was far more compelling evidence to suggest the loonie had become egregiously overvalued.

A SILENT KILLER

If the true economic value of the Canadian dollar is around 80 cents, the loonie has been overvalued by between 20 and 25 percent for most of the last decade. For an economy like Canada's, where exports used to account for almost half of GDP, and with the bulk of those heading to the United States, this scale of overvaluation applies a huge brake to economic growth.

Unfortunately, there was no such brake on the Canadian dollar. For years, Canada was one of the most trade-oriented economies in the world, with exports carrying four times more weight in the country's GDP than the same sector carried in the States.[23] But in the shadow of the oil boom, the trade sector collapsed. As the loonie soared to ever-higher oil-driven heights, exports of everything but bitumen suffered. In recent years, the country has posted its worst trade performance in decades. Exports have plunged from 44 percent of GDP to just 30 percent.[24]

There was an equally dramatic change in the country's once-sizable trade surplus. Canada recorded a merchandise trade surplus every year from 1988 to 2006. But since then, the balance has turned negative. From a peak of a nearly $70-billion surplus in 2001, the trade balance fell to a deficit of over $7 billion in 2013.[25] For much of that period, the exchange rate of our dollar against the US dollar skyrocketed.

The soaring value of the loonie didn't hurt the oil sands—like all grades of crude, bitumen exports are priced in US dollars—but elsewhere, the rising Canadian dollar made most of the country's other exports uncompetitive in world markets. While the trade surplus in energy products moved ever upward, driven by huge increases in largely unprocessed bitumen exports from rapidly expanding oil sands production, the country started racking up trade deficits everywhere else. By 2013, the energy trade surplus had grown to almost $70 billion, but that was more than offset by a nearly $77-billion trade deficit in non-energy products. Hit worst was the auto trade—once a pillar of Canada's traditional merchandise trade surpluses, and the industrial backbone of the Ontario economy. Between 2003 and 2013, an $11-billion surplus morphed into a nearly $17-billion deficit, with the sector posting persistent deficits since 2009.[26] In short, the more bitumen the country exported, the less of everything else it sold abroad.

If the rising Canadian dollar was wreaking havoc on the national economy, you wouldn't have known it in Alberta. With oil dominating the economy, that province went merrily on its way, paying Starbucks baristas exorbitant wages to make half-caff-no-whip coffee concoctions and playing host to bus lines from down east that specialized in luxury rides between Edmonton and Fort McMurray.[27] But elsewhere in Canada, the soaring value of the loonie was silently killing over half a million manufacturing jobs across the country. Everything from food processing plants to steel plants to auto assembly plants were suddenly shutting down.

The food processing industry that had grown up in the rich agricultural land of southwestern Ontario was particularly hard hit. Kellogg closed its 500-worker plant in London while Heinz, which had been in the region for a century, shuttered its 740-employee food processing plant in Leamington.[28] Bick's Pickles closed its southwestern Ontario plant and relocated 150 jobs to the States.[29]

The axe swung through other manufacturing industries too. Heavy-equipment manufacturer Caterpillar shut down its Ontario operation. Crane Valves closed its Brantford, Ontario, plant while auto parts maker Collins & Aikman packed up in Guelph. Sonoco Products shuttered its Cambridge operation, and German computer giant Siemens pulled out of Hamilton. CCL Industries and Novartis also left Ontario. The workers laid off in this mass exodus were just a percentage of the 33,000 manufacturing job losses that Ontario experienced in 2013. And they in turn were part of an even greater trend: 300,000 factory jobs lost in the province over the last decade, and nearly 600,000 manufacturing jobs gone from the Canadian economy during the same period.[30]

The production numbers told the same grim story. Between 2000 and 2010, manufacturing GDP fell by 33 percent in Ontario and by 26 percent in Quebec.[31] Just as a shrinking manufacturing sector was the flip side of the oil sands boom, stagnating Ontario and Quebec economies were the flip side of a red-hot Alberta one.

While billions poured into the oil sands, less and less capital was invested in the manufacturing sector, and a vicious cycle got under way. As production shrank and plants were closed, investors shied away from putting new money into what they saw as a terminally ill sector. In 2000, manufacturing accounted for 14 percent of total investment in the Canadian economy. By 2012, it had fallen by almost half, to 8 percent.[32]

In theory, the higher Canadian dollar should have made it cheaper for manufacturers to invest in high-precision equipment from abroad, where roughly 40 percent of the machinery and equipment in the sector originates. But in practice, a ballooning exchange rate had quite the opposite effect: instead of investing in new machinery and equipment, firms closed their Canadian factories and invested in new production capacity elsewhere. And more frequently than not, elsewhere wasn't on the other side of the Pacific Ocean but right across the border, in the United States.

Before the loonie's meteoric ascent, investment and productivity in the manufacturing sector had both been growing at a healthy pace in Canada. Since productivity gains are for the most part driven by continually upgrading production machinery, they are closely linked to capital spending. So, as the high dollar choked off new investment in machinery and equipment, it choked off productivity growth as well. Over the last decade, productivity has stagnated in the investment-deprived factory sector, which grew at a third of the US sector's pace.[33] And if that wasn't enough to close the doors on your Canadian plant, the huge rise in exchange rate–adjusted Canadian wage costs put the last nail in the coffin.

When your currency goes up as much as 80 percent against that of your trading rival, as the Canadian dollar did between 2002 and 2007, it means your wage costs rise by the same amount. Canadian factory workers weren't seeing that increase in their paycheques, but their employers were certainly seeing it in their costs. Every cent that the loonie gained against the greenback meant that their wage costs were that much more expensive relative to what competitors were paying their workers in a US manufacturing plant.

In its 2012 Annual Monetary Policy Report,[34] the Bank of Canada estimated that the country's manufacturing sector had suffered a 40 percent loss in unit labour cost competitiveness against the United States between 2005 and 2011, with most of the lost ground caused by the huge appreciation in the Canadian dollar. Considering that the USA accounts for over three-quarters of Canada's trade in manufactured goods, the deterioration in cost competitiveness was nothing short of a death sentence for the country's distressed factory sector.

BANKING ON BITUMEN

Notwithstanding what the Bank of Canada's own research department had found, the head of the institution—Governor Mark Carney—had a very different story to tell Canadians. As it turns out, Canada's monetary chief, while officially independent from the Harper government, was one of its strongest allies in supporting the massive expansion of the oil sands.

In a number of headline-making speeches in western Canada in 2012, Carney argued that the Canadian economy's growing reliance on the rapid expansion of the oil sands was "unambiguously good for the whole country."[35] Notwithstanding all the evidence in the currency markets, Carney argued against tying the record-high value of the Canadian dollar to the oil boom, suggesting that the petro-currency view was too simplistic and that there were other important factors at play.

The governor would have had to be blind not to see the correlation between the trade and capital flows generated by the oil sands and the huge lift in the value of the Canadian dollar. But he certainly was right about one thing: there were other factors at play. He was one of the most important of them.

While his counterpart, Ben Bernanke at the US Federal Reserve Board, was doing everything possible to reassure recession-wary Americans that record-low interest rates would remain in place for the foreseeable future, Governor Carney was admonishing Canadians for their growing reliance on debt and threatening interest rate increases. Juxtaposed against what other central bankers were doing around the world—many of them were deliberately devaluing their currencies to prop up faltering growth—Carney's constant warnings of pending rate increases made a very favourable impression in foreign exchange markets, only adding to our dollar's strength.

That didn't seem to bother Carney too much. He wore the loonie's brawn in international banking circles as a badge of honour. Nor did it ever seem to occur to him that the Canadian economy's overreliance on debt-financed household spending was perhaps fuelled by the complete collapse in exports and investment in every sector other than energy—sectors that were making little contribution to growth. When the governor packed his bags in June 2013 and headed off to become the head of the Bank of England, the country's surviving manufacturers likely heaved a collective sigh of relief. From their perspective, Carney was the country's most welcome export.

WHY CANADA IS NO NETHERLANDS

Although Carney's speeches in western Canada ignored the negative impact the oil sands were having on the rest of Canada, they didn't come completely out of left field. Carney was reacting to the assertion—levelled by both then Ontario premier Dalton McGuinty and federal NDP leader Thomas Mulcair—that the Canadian economy was falling prey to the dreaded Dutch disease. The disease, not to be confused with the one that kills elm trees, was first diagnosed by the *Economist* in the 1970s, following the Netherlands' discovery and production of offshore natural gas. The flow pushed up the value of the Dutch gilder against the currencies of its European trading partners, suddenly rendering huge swaths of the country's manufacturing sector uncompetitive. Once the wells depleted and the natural gas revenues dried up, all the Netherlands was left with were the gutted remains of a once-vibrant manufacturing sector.

While Canada's situation did seem to be mimicking earlier events in the Netherlands, there was one crucial difference: the Netherlands' story played out on a tiny land mass in which different industries all lived cozily next door to each other. Canada, on the other hand, is a vast country with provinces lined up across an entire continent. Each province has very different resource endowments, and as a result each has a very distinct industrial makeup.

Home to almost three-quarters of all factory jobs in the country, Ontario and Quebec rely on manufacturing almost as much as Alberta relies on oil and gas extraction. The implications are clear: any huge shift in economic activity away from manufacturing and toward the oil industry would have dramatic regional impacts in Canada, the likes of which the Netherlands had never seen. For the experience of the two countries to be truly comparable, Ontario would need an oil industry, and the west would have to make a lot of cars.

Once upon a time, that was almost the case. As we saw in chapter 3, Canada's oil industry was actually born in southwestern Ontario. But cars made out west? Yup. Back in 1927, in anticipation of strong auto demand by wealthy farmers in western Canada, General Motors put down roots in the Prairies, building a full-scale assembly operation in Regina. At its peak, the plant, which produced Chevrolets, churned out 150 cars a day and employed 850 workers. Unfortunately, the timing of GM's foray into the Canadian prairies couldn't have been worse. A year after the Regina plant began production, the stock market crashed and the Great Depression followed. The plant closed in 1930, just two years after opening. In reopened briefly in 1931— GM started producing Oldsmobiles there—but the ongoing depressed economic conditions led GM to close it again, this time for good. By 1941, the plant was being used by the federal government to produce war materials for the Canadian armed forces fighting overseas. It was later converted into a warehouse complex that bore little hint of its auto-making past.[36]

How different the Canadian economy would look today if, instead of closing its one western Canadian assembly plant, GM had decided, along with its competitors Ford and Chrysler, to expand production there. Imagine car plants in places like Edmonton or Red Deer, instead of clustered in southern Ontario.

At the same time, let us suppose that, instead of the modest oil deposits that were quickly depleted in and around Petrolia, vast deposits of oil sands were discovered. Instead of all those billions of dollars being spent on oil projects in northern Alberta, some of that money would have found its way to southwestern Ontario's bitumen deposits. Think of the boost to Ontario's petrochemical industry, right next door in Sarnia. Think of the billions of dollars of bitumen royalties flowing to a cash-starved Queen's Park. And, most of all, think about the income and jobs that would be generated in Ontario as a result of scooping, say, a million barrels of bitumen out of the ground every day.

That, in a nutshell, would have been the Canadian version of Dutch disease. The massive development of the oil sands would still have led to the rise of a Canadian petrodollar. And the soaring value of that petrodollar would still have gutted the country's manufacturing sector. But regionally, it would have been much more of a wash. Some of the thousands of manufacturing jobs killed by the soaring exchange rate would have been lost in western Canadian auto plants. And some of the billions of dollars invested in developing oil sands would have been spent in southwestern Ontario.

Of course, there is no mention of Dutch disease in the splashy ads that the Canadian Association of Petroleum Producers continually runs, reminding Canadians of the spinoff benefits that accrue to every region of the country from oil sands development. But contrary to the message you might see while watching a hockey game or the nightly news, those spinoffs are remarkably small. The Conference Board of Canada found that three-quarters of all jobs created from the expansion of the oil sands stayed in Alberta. Similarly, the Canadian Energy Research Institute (CERI) estimated that over

90 percent of the increase in GDP from the oil sands stayed in the province. Moreover, CERI estimates that to the extent that there are external economic benefits outside Alberta, the United States reaps twice as much of those benefits as the rest of Canada.[37] These hardly seem like the attributes of a project so vital to the national economic interest that its development needed to be fast-tracked by the federal government.

HEADING SOUTH

Of course, not every manufacturing job lost in central Canada over the last decade can be laid at the feet of a soaring petrodollar. China, more often then not, is invoked as the bogeyman by those who prefer not to see any connection between the oil sands boom, the appreciation of the Canadian dollar and the subsequent hemorrhaging of factory jobs. But even studies funded by the Harper government—such as the one commissioned by Industry Canada—as well as studies by the International Monetary Fund and the Organisation for Economic Co-operation and Development, suggest otherwise.[38] They've found that the appreciation of the loonie played a critical role in the factory sector's demise, accounting for as many as 60 percent of the job losses in Canadian manufacturing—or some 350,000 jobs.

A look at where all those lost jobs have turned up supports that finding. Many of the manufacturing jobs in central Canada didn't move overseas to China; instead, as I've already mentioned, they took a much shorter journey—across the border to the United States. Some Canadian manufacturing jobs did cross the ocean in search of rock-bottom wages, but the ones that headed south were driven there by the soaring Canadian dollar.

Comparing the performance of the manufacturing sectors in the two countries during this period drives that point home. Cheap Chinese wages posed every bit as much of a threat to the US manufacturing sector as they did to the Canadian factory sector. Yet between 2002 and 2011, manufacturing output in the USA grew by over 20 percent, while Canadian manufacturing output shrank by more than 10 percent.[39] Obviously, there was more at work in the Canadian decline than cheap overseas labour.

Nowhere are these contrasting fortunes more apparent than in the auto industry. Ontario used to be North America's largest motor vehicle producer, and Canada used to be the fourth-largest auto assembler in the world. Today, Canada has dropped to tenth place globally, and its share of North American vehicle production has shrunk to its lowest level since 1987, now trailing well behind Mexico. In 2013, Michigan surpassed Ontario as the state or province producing the most motor vehicles in North America, a position Ontario had enjoyed for nearly a decade (since 2004).[40]

And the future didn't look any brighter. As we've seen, tomorrow's production levels are determined by today's investment. Of some $17.6 billion spent around the world in new vehicle production capacity in 2013, not a dime was spent in Canada. Despite healthy auto sales across North America, Canadian vehicle output fell 4 percent in 2013. The next year wasn't much better. Of some 7 billion invested in the global auto industry in 2014, only $750 million found its way to Ontario, roughly a fifth of the $3.6 billion invested in the booming Mexican industry. Meanwhile, Canadian auto production fell to 14 percent of the North American total, its lowest level since 1987.[41] Given the lack of new investment, bigger production declines are likely to follow.

General Motors — North America's largest auto producer — provides an illuminating case study. An analyst looking at US operations and then at Canadian ones might be convinced that she was in fact investigating two different companies. North of the border, a soaring Canadian dollar encouraged General Motors to shut down one of its huge Oshawa-based truck plants in 2009, following the recession. While it still has a two-assembly-line operation at its Oshawa car plant, one line has been scaled back from three shifts to one and there is widespread speculation that the line might be shut down altogether when production of the Camaro is moved back to the States (the sixth generation of the popular car is set to roll off the line in the fall of 2015).[42] By 2012, GM's production at its Oshawa plant had shrunk to 378,000 cars, a little over half its peak level of 671,000 cars back in 2003.[43]

South of the border, it's a totally different story. Production has soared since the recession, and General Motors has announced over $12 billion in new investment in its US operations, much of it in its home base in Michigan, including investments in assembly plants in Flint and Detroit–Hamtramck, and in a powertrain operation in Romulus. The company has also made significant investments in its Ohio plants.

It's not just in the auto industry that you see the manufacturing activity in the two countries moving in very different directions. Energy-intensive industries such as chemicals and steel have had a renaissance south of the border while contracting up north. Ironically, it's the US energy sector that's directly responsible. Whereas soaring oil sands production has driven up the Canadian dollar to the point where it's jeopardizing the very existence of much of the country's factory sector, the stateside shale revolution has lowered natural gas prices so much that it is actually bringing energy-intensive manufacturing jobs back home. Thanks to the fracking boom, the USA is once again looking good to a whole range of energy- and capital-intensive manufacturing industries — industries in which the cost of power is far more important than the cost of labour. "Reshoring," as it is now called, has suddenly replaced "offshoring" in the American business lexicon.

Chemical producers, for example, win doubly with cheap natural gas: both as a means of powering their energy-sucking plants and as a cheap and plentiful feedstock from which petrochemicals are manufactured. For energy-guzzling industries such as chemicals or steel, cheap power from shale gas encourages the moving of production back to North America from places like Asia, where natural gas can cost five times as much. Canada can also provide cheap natural gas (compared with Asia and Europe), but the elevated Canadian dollar ensured that footloose energy-intensive manufacturing jobs settled on the American side of the border.

While manufacturing is certainly the most newsworthy (or at least the most covered) sector to feel the pain wrought by a hugely over-valued Canadian petrodollar, the loonie has claimed other casual-ties in the economy too. Few sectors are more sensitive to the value of the Canadian dollar than the tourism industry. There have been almost as many fishing camps and resorts closed across the country in the last decade as there have been factories shut down. The reason behind the business failures is the same. When the Canadian dollar averaged 63 cents US in 2002, a $200-a-night room at a Whistler ski resort would have cost an American tourist $126. Fast-forward to 2007, with the Canadian dollar trading at a premium to the green-back, and the same hotel room cost over $200. If you ever wondered why the waits at ski lifts had become a lot shorter, it was because there were a lot fewer Americans skiing at Whistler. In fact, there were many fewer American tourists coming to Canada in general. The USA had become one of Canada's poorest-performing tour-ism markets, so much so that the Canadian Tourism Commission decided, in 2012, to stop marketing south of the border.[44]

THE STAPLES MODEL

It's quite possible that Prime Minister Harper didn't mind a drop in tourism revenues, or even the hollowing out of the manufacturing sector. After all, he's had his eye on the energy-superpower prize. In some ways, Harper's economic vision for the country is a throwback to the old "staples model" of the economy, based on the extraction of a single resource and its export to world markets. Three hundred years ago, the model involved trapping as many beaver, martin, mink and fox as possible and exporting their valuable pelts to a fur-hungry Europe. Today, the staple is unprocessed bitumen—extracted from the oil sands and transported, via tanker car or pipeline, to some coastal export terminal. But the staples model's blueprint for one-dimensional economic growth is as problematic today as it was in the past. Then as now, the economy becomes hostage to factors over which the country has no control—including world demand for whatever your chosen staple happens to be. Suncor can no more control world oil prices than the Hudson's Bay Company could set prices for the pelts it sold at an 18th-century London auction house.

Canadians should have found that troubling for a few reasons. On the one hand, the laser-like focus on oil sands production was clearly having a negative effect on the rest of Canada's economy. How many more manufacturing jobs would be lost, and how many more central Ontario towns would come to resemble the ghost towns of Michigan? On the other hand, and perhaps more important in the long run, is the fact that Ottawa was betting the country's growth on a fuel that was not only considered an environmental pariah by the rest of the world but requires sky-high oil prices to be economically viable—attributes that render the oil sands highly vulnerable to either slower economic growth or much greener growth in a carbon-constrained future. Just look at what changing public attitudes about wearing fur have done to the fur trade. Changing public attitudes toward emitting carbon promise to do the same to the bitumen trade.

What would happen to Harper's vision of bitumen-bred prosperity if oil prices ever plunged? If that happened, the oil sands wouldn't just be a low-value-added resource play that caused negative distortions in the rest of the Canadian economy. In a world of sinking oil prices, Alberta's massively developed oil sands turn into the home of stranded assets and abandoned dreams.

PART THREE

THE
BEST-LAID
PLANS . . .

IN 1785, famed Scottish poet Robbie Burns penned "To a Mouse, on Turning Her Up in Her Nest with the Plough." The speaker, initially distraught at having ruined the rodent's home, reflects on the nature of life and fairness and whether the mouse has a right to be upset at the unfortunate turn of events. In what is surely one of poetry's most quoted lines, he concludes that happenings like this are simply a fact of life, and that "the best-laid plans of mice and men / often go awry."

It's a sentiment that Stephen Harper may be grappling with these days. In 2006, when he became prime minister of Canada, betting the house on an oil-hungry future seemed like a decent-enough plan. But as we've seen over the last several chapters, this plan has indeed gone awry—and the implications are being felt across all sectors of the Canadian economy.

They are also being felt by investors. An investment in fossil fuels once seemed like a no-lose proposition, a way to sit back and watch your portfolio grow as the world burned ever-greater quantities of the stuff. These days, however, the game is changing—and in ways we might never have predicted. The players have aligned in unexpected ways, and the rules have been rewritten. In order to protect our economy and our investments—to play on this new field—we're going to need to make some changes. We're going to have to wrap our heads around these new circumstances and adjust. We're going to have to be willing to change the plan. If we can't, our failure to do so will prove costly.

[CHAPTER 8]

SHIFTING GOALPOSTS

ONLY THREE YEARS AGO, investors in coal stocks went to sleep every night confident that rapid coal-fired economic growth would continue forever and that seriously reducing carbon emissions would be so prohibitively expensive to our economies that no country could afford to take action. Those were the same sentiments Prime Minister Harper had expressed when he boldly asserted that no country would take action to reduce carbon emissions because those actions would hurt the economy. Recently, however, those investors woke up to a nightmare.

Thermal coal prices have fallen from over US$140 a metric ton in 2011 to below US$70 a ton.[1] That price decline, in turn, has closed coal mines from Australia to British Columbia, and pummelled share values of publicly traded coal companies. The largest such companies in North America, like Peabody Energy or Arch Coal, have lost between 85 and 90 percent of their share values over the last three years. The benchmark for the world coal industry, the KOL index — an exchange-traded fund that holds all the largest coal companies in the world, as well as major coal terminal operators — has lost two-thirds of its share value. Whatever coal stock investors might have bought, if they held on to it, they have lost most of their investment.

What happened?

THE DEMISE OF COAL

It's not that investors didn't realize that coal, as the principal source of global carbon emissions, is on the front lines of any war on carbon. Coal investors knew they were in for a hard landing in a carbon-constrained world, but most of them just didn't believe those constraints would show up in the here and now; it was a problem for the long run, and any meaningful response to it would be far off in the distant future.

To some degree, their thinking was understandable. It's certainly easy to be skeptical, if not downright cynical, about international climate change conferences that seek binding global agreements on carbon emissions. Beginning with the Kyoto accord, the agreements signed at these conferences have had little practical effect. And while world leaders can be expected to say all the right things at the upcoming United Nations Climate Change Conference in Paris, it's by no means certain that an agreement with real penalties for non-compliance will emerge.

So it might seem as though it's business as usual. Fossil fuel producers will keep on producing as much as they can, households and businesses can keep on combusting as much as they want, and investors can fall back on governments' failure to take real action on controlling emissions. Or can they?

The fatal mistake coal investors made was equating the absence of any global agreement on carbon emissions with a lack of action around the world. While it's true that we haven't seen a meaningful globally encompassing agreement with real teeth, it is not at all true to say that individual governments have been sitting on their hands. Many have acted unilaterally, and in ways that have been as punitive (if not more so) to the valuation of coal stocks as any elusive international agreement would be. Billions of dollars of market capitalization have gone up in smoke during the last couple of years — and not because of a document signed at Copenhagen or Durban.

Instead, individual countries are getting the job done—and some surprising countries at that.

UNLIKELY ALLIES

Neither China nor the United States signed the Kyoto accord—a pretty large omission considering they're the world's largest users of coal and emitters of CO_2; together, they account for 42 percent of global emissions from the combustion of fossil fuels.[2] Nevertheless, no other two countries have had a greater impact on the global coal industry. If coal consumption had continued to grow at the same pace in these countries after the recession as it did before, investors in companies such as Peabody Energy and Arch Coal would be a lot richer than they are today. In both countries, however, the playing field has changed dramatically. While the USA and China may not see eye to eye on all matters carbon, the world's two biggest emitters realize they have to engage each other and are now negotiating directly to limit their future emissions. More important, both have taken, for very different reasons, unilateral actions that have decimated the value of coal stocks.

In the States, as we've seen, technological and policy changes have combined to crush coal consumption during the last three years. US consumption in the electric power sector dropped by almost 20 percent between 2008 and 2013. And the outlook for future American coal demand is even bleaker. Over 90 percent of coal burned in the US economy is used by power stations, and that's precisely where the greatest changes are occurring.[3] The huge deposits of shale gas accessible through hydraulic fracking have reduced American natural gas prices to the point where it is now cheaper to generate power by burning natural gas than by burning coal. Recognizing coal's vulnerability, an opportunistic President Obama has used his executive powers (hence bypassing a Republican-controlled Congress) to mandate emissions controls through the

Environmental Protection Agency that effectively preclude new coal-fired plants from being built (at least not without pricey carbon capture and sequestration technology that no one can afford).[4] More recently, he has targeted a 30 percent reduction in emissions from power plants over the next decade and a half. If you're still investing in US coal stocks, not only are you facing the competitive challenge of shale gas, you're also investing in a sector that the White House has targeted for obsolescence.

But if investors in coal stocks were shocked by what has happened in the US market, they've been downright horrified by the events that have unfolded in China, by far the world's largest coal market, accounting for almost half of all the coal burned in the world.[5]

China has never shown a willingness to do much on the climate change front. From Beijing's perspective, carbon emissions were a global problem best left to the world's richest countries to tackle—the same countries that have been responsible for the lion's share of global emissions since the Industrial Revolution.[6] But all of that started to change in 2013, when stories about the country's worsening "airpocalypse" began to hit the front pages of the world's newspapers. "Air Pollution Linked to 1.2 Million Premature Deaths in China," read a *New York Times* headline on April 1, 2013. The article featured a picture of Shanghai's distinctive skyline, barely recognizable through the smog. Other images followed: famous landmarks shrouded in haze; people wearing masks as they went about their daily lives; smokestacks belching.

Most of China's smog is coming from carbon emissions. It seems that when you become the world's factory, you also become the world's carbon toilet. According to the World Health Organization (WHO), the air pollution levels in China's cities can be a stunning eight to thirty times higher than what the organization considers acceptable.[7]

Citizens of Beijing and Shanghai routinely wear masks outside. Record levels of smog in December 2013 forced Shanghai to close

Pudong International Airport, one of the world's busiest, due to a total lack of visibility. In March 2014, parents were warned to keep their children indoors in Shanghai because of air pollution levels that were so high they could cause respiratory distress. China's air quality has become a national health problem, while 16 percent of the country's land is so badly polluted it is now unfit for human use.[8]

These environmental horror stories aren't happening in some far-flung rural region like Inner Mongolia. Instead, they are there for all to see—and, more importantly, breathe—in the country's premier cities, including its seat of government and its financial capital. More and more, the people living in those centres of economic and political power are demanding action.

And the Chinese government is listening. In March 2013, Premier Li Keqiang vowed to use an "iron fist" to tackle the country's pollution problem.[9] Three months later, the premier announced ten air pollution control measures, including the reduction of emissions through the renovation of key industries, consumption controls, the development of renewables, and improvements in public transport and clean energy production.[10] The Chinese legislature has since passed the first amendments to the country's environmental laws in a quarter century, giving authorities greater power to enforce laws and inflict harsher penalties on polluters,[11] and has also announced plans to ban the use of coal in Beijing by the end of 2020.[12] In addition, the Chinese government has mandated reductions in coal use in key industrial areas, including the region surrounding Beijing, as well as in the Yangtze and Pearl delta regions.

But perhaps the most telling signs of just how far the goalposts have moved for these unlikely carbon collaborators are their recent bilateral agreements on emissions. In July 2013, the two countries agreed to five initiatives aimed at cutting carbon output from heavy-duty vehicles, manufacturing, and coal-fired plants.[13] And in late 2014, President Obama and Chinese president Xi Jinping jointly announced a carbon pact that pledged both countries to new emissions targets. Beijing residents were immediate beneficiaries. As during the 2012 Olympics, they got a few days of better air quality as many of the city's factories were shut down prior to Obama's visit. Obama, for his part, promised that economy-wide US greenhouse gas emissions would fall by 26 percent by 2025; Xi Jinping announced China's emissions would peak by 2030 and that the country's reliance on nuclear, wind and solar would jump from less than 10 percent to 20 percent of the nation's energy mix over that time period.[14] The country already leads the world in investment in solar power.

While there is skepticism in some quarters about what a lame-duck president's pledge means in practice, and over Beijing's real commitment to improved air quality, the fact that the world's two largest emitters have entered into direct bilateral discussions on carbon management is a game-changer. Without their involvement, no global treaty on emissions is even worth pursuing. Perhaps more important is the fact that, for the first time ever, China's authoritarian, growth-hungry government is putting the environment ahead of carbon-fuelled economic growth. While the country's environmental track record may not inspire much confidence that real change is at hand, when China's leadership defines an issue as its new national priority, it has the means to turn talk into action in ways that would simply be impossible in Western democracies. If you doubt that, just remember the country's one-child policy.

The potential impact of China's changing approach to emissions cannot be overstated. Keeping coal in the ground is vital in our war on carbon emissions. China's double-digit growth in coal consumption may have meant good times for the world's biggest coal producers, but it undermined any global progress at managing carbon emissions. Over the last decade, the country's voracious appetite for coal has singlehandedly accounted for more than half of the increase in global CO_2 emissions.[15] Year after year, ever-greater emissions from China simply overwhelmed the progress made by other countries on reducing their own coal combustion, often discouraging those countries from making further efforts. By putting the brakes on its consumption, not only is China making a direct contribution to halting the growth in global emissions, but for the first time its actions will complement, as opposed to cancel, the efforts made by other countries.

AN EVEN BIGGER THREAT

But this newly declared war on air pollution isn't the only threat to coal production and prices coming from far and away the world's largest coal-burning country. Coal producers have to look forward not only to a greener Chinese economy but to a much slower-growing one as well. In the end, that constraint may pose a more lethal threat to a global coal industry that has hitched its fortunes to supplying the huge Chinese market.

China's spectacular economic growth over the last four decades was driven by one fuel—coal. The transformation of the Chinese economy from a backward agrarian one in the early 1970s to today's industrial powerhouse increased the country's coal consumption over tenfold, from a modest 300 million tons a year to roughly 4 billion tons.[16]

But China's economic growth, which for three decades averaged double-digit annual rates, decelerated to barely over 7 percent in 2014, and is likely to decelerate further as unsustainable increases in exports and associated investment spending have led to a massive overbuild of factories and even new cities. Just as Japan's spectacular economic boom decades earlier suddenly fizzled out in the 1990s, Chinese growth is also decelerating rapidly. The Conference Board business research group expects the Chinese economy to grow at less than a 5 percent annual rate between 2015 and 2020, and below 4 percent annually between 2020 and 2025.[17] Coal accounts for roughly three-quarters of all the power produced in China, so when GDP growth shifts into a lower gear, so does coal demand, even without any changes in environmental policy.

China's coal consumption is already reflecting that slowdown in economic growth. Until recently, consumption was routinely growing at 10 percent or more every year. For the first time this century, however, it looks — on the basis of data from the first three-quarters of the year — as if China's coal consumption will drop by 1 percent in 2014.[18] Not a huge decline, to be sure, but if you are a coal company banking on exports to China, it's a huge adjustment from previous double-digit growth rates. And if the Chinese government meets its stated goal of reining in future growth in the country's carbon emissions, falling coal consumption will soon become the norm, as it already is in the United States.

That's a very troubling prospect for the world coal industry, given China's oversized share of world coal consumption. When China puts its foot down regarding what's pouring out of the country's smokestacks — regardless of what's driving the change — it leaves a pretty heavy footprint on world coal markets. All the more so when that Chinese footstep follows on the heels of a reduction of nearly a third in the size of the once-huge American coal market.

As coal prices tumble, operational losses mount for producers.[19] And those losses are shutting down coal mines all around the world. In Australia, mining giant Glencore Xstrata is closing its Ravensworth coal mine. BHP, another mining colossus, recently shuttered its Norwich Park and Gregory coal operations in Australia as well. Across the ocean, Walter Energy is closing its Wolverine coal mine near Tumbler Ridge, British Columbia, and Canadian mining giant Teck Resources has put on hold earlier plans to reopen its nearby Quintette coal mine. In all cases, the companies have suggested that operating the mines is no longer economically viable at today's coal prices. Nor are many coal infrastructure projects viable in today's market, like the once planned expansion of the Ridley Coal Terminal in Prince Rupert, British Columbia. With global coal demand suddenly hitting the skids, a week can go by without any ships waiting in harbour to take BC coal to once-energy-hungry Chinese markets.

As bad as things look for coal stocks today, it's only going to get worse in an emissions-restrained future. Imagine where coal prices will be in a world required to cut its coal consumption by almost a third over the next two decades. Back in 2000, thermal coal prices were $40 a ton, little more than half of today's price. As Chinese coal consumption follows in the footsteps of US coal consumption, we may soon see those prices again.

PUTTING A MAN ON THE MOON

So the goalposts have clearly moved on coal. They are now moving just as decisively on the world's other great fossil fuel: oil. After a triumphant return to the triple-digit range by early 2011, world oil prices plunged by 60 percent over the second half of 2014, falling to levels not seen since the last recession. And to make matters worse, that huge price decline came on the heels of soaring costs in the industry.

Even before the recent collapse in oil prices, investors had growing cause for concern. Oil companies were spending about five times as much on finding new reserves as they were returning to shareholders through dividends. And despite those triple-digit prices, earnings weren't growing at nearly the pace that investors had come to expect. The problem wasn't the price the oil was fetching; the problem was the cost of getting it out of the ground.

In 2013, three majors, Exxon, Shell and Chevron, collectively spent $120 billion on capital expenditures to find and develop new reserves.[20] In inflation-adjusted dollars, that's the same amount of money it cost NASA to put the first man on the moon. While that was a landmark achievement for the US space program, all that a similar amount of cap ex spending has brought fossil fuel companies are huge writeoffs. Despite spending over half a trillion dollars in exploration and development over the last five years, combined production for the three oil giants is down over the period.[21] The same holds for other majors such as BP, Total, ConocoPhillips and Eni.

The tandem of soaring costs and stagnating production has flowed through to the bottom line. Shell, the Anglo-Dutch colossus, doubled its cap ex spending to over $40 billion in 2013 — including billions poured into its Athabasca oil sands project and its troubled Kashagan oil field in Kazakhstan's Caspian Sea. In return, it saw its 2013 earnings cut in half compared with the previous year. It even had to write off some $4 billion of its Arctic drilling program as Kullag, its supposedly state-of-the-art drilling platform, was crushed in stormy seas off the Alaskan coast. Exxon, Chevron and a host of other major oil companies had all posted disappointing financial results as well.

Bloomberg estimates that the costs of finding and developing new reserves for European majors like Shell have risen almost threefold over the last decade. And to compound matters, huge cost overruns have often been accompanied by lengthy and at times interminable production delays. For example, the giant Kashagan development is still not producing any oil, despite an expenditure of $50 billion that was supposed to see oil flow by 2008.[22]

Investors began to query what kind of return they were getting on these huge exploration budgets. While exploration spending by oil companies globally has increased 180 percent since 2000, global oil supplies rose by only 14 percent during the same period. In baseball terms, that's like giving somebody who has only a .140 batting average (the 14 percent increase in supply) almost three times as many at-bats (the 180 percent rise in spending). The Mendoza Line of a .200 batting average is said to separate true major-leaguers from incompetent bums. The comparison isn't particularly flattering to oil companies' bottom line or to shareholder returns. How much longer would disappointed investors tolerate this type of unproductive spending?

The only justification for it was rich, triple-digit oil prices. New reserves were much harder to find than they used to be, but sky-high prices made those that were found that much more valuable. Once prices start to drop, however, the whole picture changes.

DÉJÀ VU

If crude prices were high enough, oil companies could paper over many of the problems confronting the industry: huge cost overruns, Mendoza Line–like batting averages on discovery rates, and growing global concern over mounting carbon emissions and their link to ever more apparent climate change. But by the second half of 2014, triple-digit world oil prices were a rapidly fading memory. All of a sudden, the goalposts had shifted. Brent, the world oil price, dropped over 50 percent to five-year lows, plunging all the way to $50. But for Canadian bitumen producers it was even worse: their oil price dropped to recession-level lows. Western Canadian Select was trading under $40 a barrel. For the second time in over half a decade, oil prices had collapsed, leaving an industry that was spending hundreds of billions of dollars around the world developing new high-cost sources of unconventional oil in financial jeopardy.

Conspiracy theories abound in the business pages these days, attempting to explain the demise of oil prices, but if you're looking for a villain, you can blame good old Adam Smith's invisible hand and the time-tested laws of demand and supply. The supply curve is upward-sloping, meaning the higher the price of a good, the more of it will be offered for sale. When Brent quickly rebounded to the triple-digit range following the 2008–9 recession, it incented a flood of new supply onto the market. Only it wasn't the low-cost conventional oil that OPEC produced. OPEC production hasn't grown, nor has conventional oil production, which hit a global peak back in 2005 and has been declining over the last decade. Instead, it was a torrent of high-cost unconventional supply that suddenly flooded the market.

Most of that supply came from North America, principally tight oil from fracked shale formations like the Bakken, Eagle Ford and the Permian Basin in the United States, and bitumen from Alberta's oil sands. US production rose by nearly 50 percent between 2008 and 2013, adding almost 5 million barrels a day to world supply, thanks largely to the shale boom. Canadian production, principally from the oil sands, rose by around 25 percent, adding another million barrels a day to world supply.[23]

While headlines in the *Wall Street Journal*, *New York Times* and *Globe and Mail* trumpeted these gains as the achievement of our long-sought energy independence from OPEC, they could just as easily have trumpeted our new-found dependence on sky-high oil prices. Because without those sky-high prices, the rapid production growth from these new sources of high-cost supply wouldn't have been commercially viable.

The problem facing high-cost North American oil producers was this: while the supply curve is upward-sloping, the demand curve slopes the other way. Yes, higher prices are sure to raise supply, but they are just as sure to kill demand. And that's particularly true for oil, still the world economy's mainstay fuel. Not only do higher oil prices ration demand, as would be the case for any good, but the rising price of the world's most important fuel has a huge impact on the rate of economic growth, which, along with oil prices, determines the demand for the fuel. Every major global recession in the last forty years was caused by soaring oil prices, including the last financial market–centred recession, which began when the inflationary impact of rising oil prices forced a reluctant Alan Greenspan–chaired Federal Reserve Board to hike interest rates and prick the subprime mortgage bubble.[24] During a recession, the economy stops growing, and so does demand for its primary energy source—oil.

While another global recession is not yet on the horizon, economic growth in most places around the world has been a shadow of what it was before the last recession. The global economy that was once clocking 5 percent annual growth is now barely doing 3 percent. And since oil is the world economy's most important fuel, it only stood to reason that slower economic growth would translate into slower demand growth for oil. In 2014, the IEA cut its demand forecast for oil no fewer than four times.

But just as world oil demand was slowing, world oil supply was gushing. More and more oil was sloshing around world markets, weighing on crude prices. And despite growing signs of a saturated market, shale and oil sand producers were in a mad rush to produce even more. Something had to give. And it did—at a much-anticipated OPEC meeting in November 2014.

Ironically, North American producers were desperately hoping that OPEC would announce plans to crank the spigot a few turns and, hence, boost prices. I say ironically because the whole motivation for energy independence in North America was to insulate our economies from OPEC's ability to manufacture the very same high prices upon which shale producers in the USA and oil sand producers in Canada had now become so critically dependent.

Of course, the onus wasn't on Saudi Arabia and the rest of OPEC— the lowest-cost producers in the world—to curtail production, no matter how urgently North American producers wanted them to. Even with the huge decline in prices, they were still making more than a healthy profit on every barrel they sold. The same, however, couldn't be said for either shale or oil sands producers in North America. Their costs are a multiple of OPEC's. In an oversupplied market, it's incumbent on these high-cost producers to take excess supply out of the marketplace. If they don't cut back their production, the oil glut will only get bigger, and oil prices will drop even further, making oil sands and shale operations even less viable.

Sounds like another boom-bust oil cycle—the same kind that has always been an intrinsic feature of the industry. But coming on the heels of coal's demise, and with increasing restrictions on carbon emissions looming in the future—not to mention the possibility of carbon taxes to prevent demand from creeping back up, as we discussed in chapter 2—this downturn in oil prices could be a lot more permanent than the one that occurred during the last recession.

If nothing else, the collapse in oil prices calls into question the sustainability of the very triple-digit oil prices upon which so much of the recent gains in production outside OPEC are dependent. After seeing prices rebound quickly following the devastating 2008–9 recession, oil producers bought into triple-digit oil prices as an anchor for their forecasts and business plans. But having seen prices collapse twice in the last six years, just how confident can producers be that they will ever realize the cash flows from those prices in the future? And yet without them, the new reserves that oil companies spend billions trying to find and develop aren't worth finding, even if we ignore—to our peril—the emissions trail they would create. Just as soaring costs made NASA ultimately abandon its manned moon shots, falling oil prices will force the likes of Exxon and Shell to abandon their similarly sized cap ex spending programs.

The oil industry, of course, will try to reassure investors that this is a cyclical downturn and that prices will inevitably move back up. They will cite history, and argue that oil demand will continue to rise indefinitely. In fact, this is the response that Exxon gave when faced with queries about stranded assets from a group of global investors, including the California Public Employees Retirement System, the biggest pension fund in the United States.[25]

The company confidently predicted that most of the expected 35 percent rise in world energy demand over the next two and a half decades must come from oil and other hydrocarbon fuels, rendering impossible the roughly 12-million-barrel-a-day drop in world oil consumption that the IEA has calculated will be required to stabilize atmospheric carbon at the 450-ppm threshold.

But three years ago, Peabody Energy would have reassured its investors about the health of future coal demand. And like Exxon's forecast for future oil demand, Peabody was pinning its hopes on China. Unfortunately, China's seemingly insatiable demand for oil may be no more lasting than its once-insatiable demand for coal. That will be as lethal to oil markets as it has already been to coal markets. The IEA, for example, is expecting that China will single-handedly account for half of the increases in world oil demand over the next two decades. So if China's oil demand turns out to be less than predicted, overall world demand, too, is likely to be less robust than forecast.

Just as the environmental goalposts have shifted radically for coal producers, they may soon shift just as decisively for oil. The smog-shrouded cities of China can't handle the emissions from the nearly 300 million cars already on their roads any more than they can handle the emissions belching from surrounding coal-fired power plants. Yet it's precisely further robust growth in China's oil consumption— and, by implication, vehicle sales—that is driving Exxon's projections for demand growth and, hence, the price of oil. What the Exxons of the world are not recognizing is that if public pressure has forced Beijing to clamp down on what's been belching out of the country's coal stacks, it could do the same for what's spewing from the nation's tailpipes. In an attempt to deal with the toxic smog that frequently engulfs the city, Beijing has already implemented vehicle emissions standards that match the strictest European guidelines and has ordered 6 million of its worst emitting vehicles off the road. It's only a matter of time before the authorities move to limit vehicle registrations there and in other major smog-choked cities as well.

PEAK DEMAND

The explosive growth of high-cost non-conventional oil has debunked earlier fears of a looming supply peak. But concerns over depletion have given way to even greater concerns—about peak demand. Oil consumption has been falling in the OECD economies of North America, Europe and Japan for some time now. If what is happening to coal is any guide, oil demand may soon be peaking in countries like China as well.

If that's the case, the world won't need the output from the Bakken or from Alberta's oil sands. In a world of shrinking demand, OPEC, the world's lowest-cost producer, will be the last man standing in whatever is left of the world's petroleum industry. As for Exxon, it may soon be following in the path of Peabody Energy and the other fallen angels of a decimated coal industry.

But from an environmental perspective, peak demand and plunging prices are seen differently. Rising commodity prices, like a surgeon's scalpel, slice open the earth's resource veins and bleed them to markets. Low prices suture those wounds and keep resources in the ground.

CHAPTER 9

MEAN REVERSION

HAVE YOU EVER PLAYED WITH AN ELASTIC BAND? Maybe you've picked one up from your desk and fidgeted with it while on a long phone call. Stretch and snap, stretch and snap: once the force you're exerting no longer holds all those jumbled molecules apart, the band immediately snaps back to its original state. That snap back demonstrates the principle of mean reversion—a financial theory based on the belief that fluctuating values will over time return to an underlying average value. Really, mean reversion is just a technical way of saying that when things get wildly out of whack—one way or the other—they have a tendency to right themselves by swinging just as wildly in the other direction before finding a happy medium. In Alberta, that process of mean reversion is known as a resource cycle—and the bigger the boom, the meaner the bust.

These days, there is much to go bust. The oil and gas sector makes up a quarter of the province's GDP[1]—a hefty percentage that would get even bigger over the next two decades if oil sands producers can more than double production, as they intend to do.

If you think that ramped-up production is going to leave a big carbon footprint on Alberta's economy, you're right. But it's already left a significant a mark on the province's finances. Resource royalties accrue to the provinces, not the federal government. That little feature in Canada's constitutional division of powers provides a direct-drive relationship between oil and gas production and provincial revenues. It also sets the stage for some very unequal sharing of the country's resource wealth, and in particular the economic and fiscal benefits that flow from oil production.

THE ALBERTA ADVANTAGE

Royalties from oil and natural gas have been the cornerstone for what is known in the province as the "Alberta advantage." What that refers to is the tax advantage Alberta residents enjoy relative to other Canadians. Most notably, Alberta is the only province that does not impose its own provincial sales tax.

High energy prices also leave the Alberta government sitting pretty. Royalties, land lease sales, and other oil and gas revenues now account for almost as much government revenue as the sector's weight in the provincial GDP. These non-renewable revenues, as they are called, are currently running at over $9 billion a year, or just over 20 percent of the province's total revenue take of $45 billion in fiscal year 2014–15.[2] And that doesn't include either the personal or the corporate income tax revenue that the province collects from those who earn their livelihoods in the energy sector.

More and more of these non-renewable revenues were expected to come from the oil sands. According to the fiscal plan set out in the province's 2014 budget, revenues from the oil sands were expected to account for 70 percent of all non-renewable resource revenue by 2016. Only a decade ago, bitumen royalties accounted for less than 3 percent of the same revenue stream. But the oil price assumptions behind those projections are no longer tenable. Even the revised lower estimate of $75 a barrel in the fall 2014 fiscal update from Alberta was $20 above the price of Western Canadian Select at the time. A month later, those estimates were almost twice what oil sands producers were getting for their heavy oil.[3] Premier Prentice confessed that every dollar decrease in the price of oil chops over $200 million from the provincial coffers.[4] With WTI trading below $50 a barrel and WCS below $40 a barrel, Prentice acknowledged in January 2015 that the province would no longer be running the $1.5-billion surplus forecast in the last budget, but would instead be incurring a $500-million deficit (more recent statements from the premier suggest the province is now facing a deficit in the billions). He further warned that the province will likely remain in a deficit position until at least 2018.[5] And if oil prices fall further and more and more new projects are cancelled, those deficits are likely to grow over time.

It's a stunning shift in fortunes, one that underlines the fickle nature of revenues from resource extraction. They come, and then they go—and it's worth remembering that when they're gone, they're really gone (hence *non-renewable*). In theory, resource wealth should be shared by successive generations of Albertans. After all, the more oil that is extracted for the benefit of today's Albertans, the less oil will be available to extract for tomorrow's. Once upon a time (in 1976), the provincial government recognized this principle—and established the Alberta Heritage Savings Fund with the goal of socking away some of those pennies for a later day. The plan was to deposit 30 percent of the province's royalty revenue into the fund, and for a very short while that is exactly what happened. But when oil prices tanked in the eighties and nineties, provincial revenues felt the hit. In 1987, Alberta stopped depositing money into the fund, and in the mid-1990s it actually began to withdraw investment income for use in general revenue.[6]

The amount actually put away for future Albertans to date—a little shy of $17 billion[7]—exposes the province's lack of commitment to the fund, and pales in comparison with what other oil-producing jurisdictions have set aside. Alaska, which set up a similar program at roughly the same time, has saved three times as much. Norway, which didn't even establish a fund until the mid-1990s, has saved more than any other oil-producing nation, and now has over $900 billion warming the coffers. The United Arab Emirates' (UAE) Abu Dhabi Investment Authority (one of many funds to which the country contributes) is number two on the list, with $773 billion, while Saudi Arabia is third, with $737 billion. And Alberta's $17 billion? That ranks twenty-third, behind East Timor and Russia, among others.[8]

Unlike Norway, the UAE and Saudi Arabia, Alberta chose to use the vast majority of its non-renewable revenues to fund current budgets.[9] And that funding has afforded those who live in Alberta today a few juicy perks (tomorrow's Albertans may not be so lucky), including that lack of a provincial sales tax. There can be little doubt these advantages have spurred economic activity.

Little wonder, then, that the province has bent over backwards to accommodate the producers who keep the oil sands royalties flowing into government coffers. It's also clear why Alberta is so desperate to see new pipelines built. As we learned in chapter 5, more pipelines means ramped-up production and higher prices for Alberta producers, both of which in turn translate into more resource royalties for the provincial treasury. These days, oil sands royalties and taxes pay for everything from schools to hospitals. In fact, bitumen royalties have become so critical to the province's budget that the state of affairs in the oil sands dwarfs in importance anything else going on in the Alberta economy.

When oil prices are high, this seems like a pretty good deal: lots of money, lots of spending, lots of growth. But think for a moment about the long-term prospects for the relationship between Alberta's economy and its favourite non-renewable resource. It's not even as if we have to imagine the future; we can just look to the past. Albertans have already had a taste of what this type of fiscal dependency can bring. They've seen economic busts several times in recent memory. And now, given the massive development of the oil sands, they're facing what could be the biggest bust ever.

WAKE-UP CALLS

The OPEC oil shocks may have been bad news for the rest of the country, but the subsequent rise in oil prices was good news for Albertans. Resource revenues from oil production were steadily increasing and were expected to continue to grow. But in 1987, it all came to a screeching halt. The stock market crashed with the savings and loans debacle in the USA, and took energy prices along with it. Seemingly overnight, Alberta was in the midst of a full-fledged oil bust. The province lost more than 60 percent of its non-renewable resource revenue and nearly a quarter of its total revenue. Premier Donald Getty waited patiently for a price rebound that never came. Deficits persisted and the provincial debt grew.

Determined to stop the downward spiral, Getty's successor, Ralph Klein, slashed spending on social services by 30 percent and cut the education budget by 16 percent in his first term in office, from 1993 to 1997. He also took the knife to health expenditures, which in real terms were slashed by almost 20 percent per capita. By the time Klein left, a decade or so later, the province was once again awash in cash, helped along by—you guessed it—rising world oil prices.

This was the boom-bust cycle playing out in real time, and it would take only another few years for the whole thing to start again. In 2008-9, oil prices fell from almost $150 a barrel to briefly below $40. The hit to oil royalties quickly turned a huge $8.5-billion budget surplus into a $1.4-billion deficit, prompting former Alberta finance minister Ron Liepert to declare that "riding the roller coaster of non-renewable resource revenues is not workable going forward into the future."[10]

Yet that is exactly what the province has done ever since. And it was tossed around by that roller coaster again in 2013, when revenue shortfalls from the so-called bitumen bubble—caused by that double whammy of increased US production and pipeline delays that left heavy oil from the oil sands trading as much as $50 a barrel below world oil prices—left the province shy a purported $6 billion in revenue, forcing the government into painful spending cuts in its 2013 budget.[11] President Obama and the environmental movement shouldered much of the blame (at least in Alberta, where Keystone XL approval is considered critical), but Alberta taxpayers' time might have been better spent questioning why their government continued to be so singularly dependent on one resource to fund the provincial budget.

If the 1987 crash and the 2008 recession seem like ancient history, the 2013 bitumen bubble scare should have been a recent-enough wake-up call to the Alberta government—a flashing neon light exposing the province's vulnerability to oil sands–generated disappointments. Instead, the same government that had just lived through yet another resource revenue shortfall tabled a 2014 budget with a fiscal plan that doubled down on the sector by making the province's financial position even more dependent on growth in bitumen royalties. Those royalty increases, of course, were dependent upon projected increases in production and, most of all, on high oil prices.

THE CHEAPEST OIL IN THE WORLD, WITH THE HIGHEST COSTS

Before his death in September 2012, Peter Lougheed made an interesting and unexpected return to the public eye. In his day, Lougheed was a force to be reckoned with—as premier of Alberta from 1971 to 1985; as the founder of Canada's longest-running political dynasty (Conservatives have ruled the province for more than forty years and counting); and as the "voice of the new West," willing and eager to butt heads with Pierre Trudeau over the controversial National Energy Program in the 1980s.

But by 2008, Lougheed was a distant memory for most Albertans— at least until he started talking publicly about the province's resources.

The eighty-year-old former premier was questioning the torrid pace of oil sands development, foreign ownership of the resource and the outsourcing of refinery jobs. His overarching message was blunt: "I . . . feel strongly that the public policy of Alberta is wrong, and that they're trying to do too much, too quickly . . . We should have a more orderly development."[12]

Lougheed's public plea was a poignant reminder that those who have lived through the province's resource cycles worry most about its oil sands–dependent future. And with very good reason. Few if any of the world's oil resources are as dependent on sky-high oil prices as Alberta's oil sands. Given the size of the resource—an estimated 170 billion barrels of bitumen—the growth potential is enormous. Unlike the tight oil fracked from shale formations in the Bakken or Eagle Ford, the oil sands are so vast that producers don't have to worry about rapid depletion rates. Add Alberta's modest royalty rates and industry-friendly regulatory environment to the region's geological endowments and you have an ideal location for the global oil industry to invest its money.[13]

Alberta was expecting to attract the lion's share of global industry spending to its reserves. Of the $1.1 trillion in planned capital spending on high-cost oil projects over the next decade, nearly 40 percent was slated for the oil sands. The nearly $400 billion to be spent in Alberta was twice what the runner-up, the US Gulf Coast, would be getting, and roughly four times what's earmarked for offshore Brazil.[14]

But there's a catch. Every single cent of that planned capital spending is dependent on high oil prices. As noted in chapter 3, oil sands success needs oil prices higher than $80 a barrel—anything less and the investment just doesn't make economic sense. The same holds true for other unconventional oil sources around the world, but thanks to Alberta's overreliance on oil for its long-term growth, the province will feel any pullback more than most. Capital spending won't go ahead, the huge planned production increases won't materialize—and the royalty revenues that the Alberta government is counting on, if not already spending, will never accrue.

This scenario was, in fact, playing out even well before that fateful OPEC meeting in November 2014. Total E&P Canada, the Canadian arm of French oil giant Total SA, along with its partners Suncor Energy and Occidental Petroleum, had already walked away from the $11-billion Joslyn North sand mine project, saying it no longer made economic sense.[15] Similarly, Royal Dutch Shell halted work on its Pierre River mine, a project that was supposed to produce 200,000 barrels a day, also citing unfavourable economics.[16] Norway's Statoil shelved its multi-billion-dollar Corner steam-drive oil sands project, intended to produce 40,000 barrels a day.[17] And once OPEC made it clear it had no intention of cutting its production to bolster world oil prices, the onus suddenly shifted to high-cost producers like the oil sands to cut back their production or face the prospect of even lower oil prices. Cenovus, one of the largest players in the sector, announced a 15 percent cut in capital expenditures, lopping off $700 million in planned investment for 2015, while Canadian Natural Resources, another oil sands heavyweight, signalled that it might shelve as much as $2 billion in planned investment.[18] Suncor followed suit, announcing a billion-dollar cut in capital spending for 2015 and the elimination of a thousand jobs from its payroll.[19]

Mounting project cancellations in the wake of plunging oil prices suddenly changed the conversation that oil sands producers are having with their investors and the rest of the country about the urgent need for new pipelines. After oil prices plunged 60 percent over the second half of 2014, there was no longer an economic context for the huge expansion planned for oil sands production. At today's prices, the oil sands look more like a contracting sector rather than one about to undertake a rapid expansion. Instead of how to double production, the more pressing issue facing the world's highest-cost oil producers is how much of their current 2-mbd output is sustainable.

And if the current global economic slowdown and the oil glut it's created isn't troubling enough for oil sands producers, consider how much more precarious their position will be as climate change forces the rest of the world to rein in carbon emissions.

If I were Jim Prentice—former Harper environment minister, former CIBC vice-chairman, and now the sixteenth premier of Alberta—I'd be giving some serious thought to Plan B. Once and for all, the province must wean itself off its dependence on oil and start to diversify its economy and tax base. While there is no question that the royalties from producing 5 million barrels of bitumen every day would fund a lot of school and hospitals, those production targets are no longer credible in today's market—and they will be even less credible in tomorrow's emission-constrained world.

As much as he might like to, Premier Prentice cannot force OPEC to cut its production and artificially raise oil prices to bail out his province's imploding high-cost oil industry. Nor can he revive flagging global demand for the fuel, any more than he can revive flagging global economic growth. Lastly, Premier Prentice can't dictate the carbon standard for the rest of the world. And he knows full well that when that standard is raised, as it ultimately must be in order for the world to address climate change, the value of his province's primary resource can only go down even more.

To his credit, Premier Prentice has acknowledged that neither the province's tax advantages nor spending regimes are sustainable. He even briefly floated the idea of introducing a provincial sales tax, a brave suggestion for something that has been anathema to most Albertans. But he might also consider the revenues that the British Columbia government next door raises every year from its carbon tax. BC's $30-a-ton carbon tax raised more than $1.2 billion for the province in 2014. Instead of relying on royalties from the extraction of carbon fuels produced in the province, why not tax the emissions that come from the combustion of that fuel? In a world of low oil prices and increasing emission constraints, carbon taxes stand a significantly better chance of generating much-needed government revenues than do royalties accrued while producing high-cost bitumen that the rest of the world doesn't need or want.

If the Alberta government is facing huge fiscal adjustments, it's only because the province is also facing no less formidable economic challenges. Where does a burst carbon bubble leave the Albert economy? With new announcements of project cancellations and layoffs making the news virtually every day, Alberta's giant oil boom is turning into a no-less-giant oil bust. Billions of dollars in investment was cancelled when oil prices plunged during the last recession, but given how much has been planned for the sector in recent years, expect to see a multiple of those cuts this time around. The energy research firm Wood McKenzie already estimates that almost $60 billion of cap ex is likely to be cancelled over the next three years, in the wake of the decline in oil prices. The scope of the cancelled projects could readily curtail the planned 650,000-barrel-a-day increase in oil sands production by 2017. As prices continue to languish at low levels, we can expect more project cancellations reverberating through the Alberta economy. But elsewhere in the country, fallen oil prices will bring a more favourable tide.[20]

FROM PETRO CURRENCY TO FALLEN ANGEL

Just as the oil boom affected the rest of the Canadian economy, so too will its bust. As the centre of economic growth once again shifts, it will be evident in a whole range of economic indicators, from interprovincial migration to the shifting fortunes of provincial budget balances. But the two impacts that will likely be dominant in the minds of Canadians relate to the value of their property and of their currency.

Calgary's once red-hot housing market has turned cold. Home sales plunged in January 2015, sinking to their lowest level in more than seven years.[21] With more and more massive expansion plans for the oil sands being cancelled, don't bet on the average house in Fort Mac selling for $200,000 more than a house in Toronto for very much longer. Those migrant workers from the Maritimes will be staying home or looking elsewhere for a high-paying job. And the cutbacks in the oil patch won't be limited to production workers up north; they will also beat a path to the office towers of Calgary, as producers find themselves under all kinds of pressure to cut costs everywhere they can. Sounds like a good time to lighten up on Alberta real estate.

On the other hand, the bursting of the carbon bubble doesn't just imply the workings of mean reversion in Alberta. It also implies mean reversion for other regions of the economy, and for a province like Ontario, that is a welcome adjustment—it's already leading the country in economic growth and prospects for the provincial economy look brighter than at any time during the last decade. Just as the carbon bubble shifted the focal point of economic growth in the country to the oil-laden west, the deflation of that bubble will see it return to the centre. Plunging oil prices are a major depressant to the bitumen-leveraged Alberta economy. But they play very differently in Ontario, not only because the province is oil consuming instead of oil producing, but because its major trading partner, the United States, will benefit even more. And that trade relationship will be all the more leveraged by the sinking loonie that has gone hand in hand with falling oil prices. Both will breathe new life into the long-depressed factory sectors in Ontario and Quebec.

The same trade and investment ties to oil that shot the Canadian dollar to record strength are now pulling the currency in the other direction—a change that most of the players in the Canadian economy, with the exception of those in the petroleum industry, have desperately wanted (and needed) for a long time. The Canadian dollar has already dropped below 80 cents, a stunning 20 percent depreciation from January 2013, when it was trading just under parity with the greenback. But given how mean reversion usually works, the loonie may still have a long way to fall, especially now that it's lost the support of what was once its most important ally—the Bank of Canada.

Stephen Poloz, the new governor of the Bank of Canada, is the polar opposite of his investment bank–bred predecessor, Mark Carney. As the former chief economist and then president of the Export Development Corporation, Poloz doesn't need anyone to school him about the symptoms of Dutch disease. He has first-hand experience of the carnage wrought on exporters, particularly manufacturers, and preventing an encore performance has been at the front and centre of the bank's recent actions.

Whereas Carney was always talking the dollar up, his successor has done everything in his power to talk the currency down, publicly lamenting the weakness of exports from the auto sector and other manufacturing industries, and effectively ruling out any interest rate increases until that situation changes. And just in case there was any doubt in foreign exchange markets where the Bank of Canada wanted the loonie to trade, Governor Poloz sprung a surprise interest rate *cut* in January 2015 that saw the Canadian dollar drop 3 cents in a week and crash below the 80-cent threshold. The message to foreign exchange markets could not be clearer: the Bank of Canada wants to see the loonie continue to fall in value. How low will it go? It's already broken through 80 cents, its supposed underlying purchasing power parity value. But the very principle of mean reversion strongly suggests that after an extended period of extreme overvaluation, the Canadian dollar is likely to experience an opposite movement now that the pendulum is swinging the other way. With the help of the Bank of Canada, and perhaps even more rate cuts, don't be surprised if the once-mighty Canadian petrodollar is back trading at 70 cents in the not too distant future.

To be sure, not everyone will be such a fan of a falling Canadian dollar. The price of American imports will rise (although they never seemed to fall proportionately when the loonie was trading at a premium to the greenback). More Canadians will choose to stay home in the winter, and we may be drinking more wine from Ontario and BC and less from California. Our big protected telecom service providers such as Rogers and Bell will have to use more of their cable, phone and Internet subscriber revenues to fund the huge US-dollar payrolls of their billion-dollar sports franchises.

But at the same time, a 70-cent dollar will start to breathe new life into the hollowed-out remains of manufacturing industries in southern Ontario and Quebec, and across the country. The same currency advantage that allowed Ontario to have an oversized auto industry will once again start guiding investment north of the border, where Canadian dollar–denominated wage costs will once again be affordable, as they were for so much of the postwar period. And with new investment will come the productivity gains that have been so sorely lacking over the last decade. Slowly but surely, the Canadian economy's centre of gravity will start to move back to the centre of the country. And the manufacturing sector will rise again.

There are already some signs of this shift. As we've seen, the once-beleaguered Ontario economy has recently led the nation in growth as a tumbling dollar has breathed some new life into exports. If it continues to do so, it will be the first time since 2002 that the Ontario economy will have grown faster than the national average. In July 2014, the country's merchandise trade balance recorded its largest surplus since 2008 (though still puny by prerecession standards). And finally, after six hard years, manufacturing sales have inched above the levels they'd reached prior to the last recession. Although there is still scant evidence of the much-awaited recovery in manufacturing employment, the tide may be turning as the currency keeps falling from those oil-fed highs. In November 2014, Honda announced plans to invest $857 million in its Alliston, Ontario, plant, where the next generation of the perennially popular Civic will be built.[22] In

February 2015, General Motors announced a $450 million invest-
ment in its Ingersoll assembly plant to expand production of its
Chevrolet Equinox and GMC Terrain crossover utility vehicle.[23]
Ford also announced that month a $700 million investment in its
vehicle assembly plant in Oakville to produce a redesigned Edge
crossover vehicle. The company will add four hundred jobs. If the
currency keeps dropping, we will be hearing a lot more of those
announcements throughout the manufacturing sector.

And it won't just be manufacturers who will benefit. Canada's
beleaguered tourist industry will also get a huge lift. In fact, in
February 2015, the Canadian Tourism Commission resumed
advertising in the United States, a practice it had stopped during
the loonie's meteoric rise. Judging by the chair line up that my
kids—Jack and Margot—and I contended with at Whistler this
Christmas, it looks like a sinking loonie is already doing wonders
to bring tourists back.

Contrary to what some believe, there need not be anything permanent about Canada's strain of Dutch disease. It was brought about by
a huge distortion in the exchange rate, and as such, it can be cured by
a good case of mean reversion in the value of the loonie. The bursting of Alberta's oil sands bubble will be the catalyst that triggers that
sell-off. If soaring oil prices sent the loonie sky-high, falling oil prices
will bring it back down to the ground. And as the bubble bursts, it's
not just the value of the Canadian dollar that's come crashing down.

CHAPTER 10

SAVE YOUR PORTFOLIO BEFORE YOU SAVE THE WORLD

WE'RE OFTEN TOLD that change is a good thing—that when life gets a little too boring, a change of scenery or a change of pace can do wonders. And sometimes that's true. Sometimes we do need to shake things up and get out of our comfort zone. But what card-carrying members of the Change Is Good school don't often mention is that it can also be deeply unsettling.

Investors in carbon stocks would undoubtedly agree. Right about now, they're probably longing for a return to the good old days when runaway carbon-fuelled global economic growth was pushing oil and coal prices to record highs, when evidence of climate change could be ignored, and when no one cared how much CO_2 we spewed into the atmosphere. Back in those days, carbon stocks were driving the value of their portfolios ever higher. Unfortunately, those days are gone—and like it or not, they aren't coming back.

When China's leadership declares air quality in its smog-choked cities to be more important than brute coal-fired economic growth, you know things have changed. All the more so when—even before the trade-offs for a cleaner environment can be made—the Chinese economy is struggling to grow at 7 percent a year, whereas it used to routinely clock double-digit growth. When you're talking about a country that accounts for nearly half of the coal burned every year on the entire planet, and over half of the annual increase in world oil consumption, that type of slowdown leaves a big imprint on the demand for, and price of, fossil fuels. When the US president mandates emissions standards that will make it almost impossible to build new coal-fired generating capacity without installing pricey carbon capture and sequester technology that no coal-burning utility can afford, change is definitely in the air. And when that same president targets a 30 percent reduction in emissions from power plants over the next decade and a half, well, things are changing even more.

As we saw in the last chapter, the failure to anticipate these changes has cost investors in coal stocks dearly; the same thing is now happening to investors in oil stocks. Not only are oil prices a casualty of faltering global economic growth and a torrent of new high-cost supply, but the oil market will soon face the same environmental challenges that have been so lethal to the coal industry. Just as the United States and China, among others, have recently targeted coal-fired emissions, climate change will compel them to likewise target oil-fired emissions.

Instead of a future characterized by ever-rising global demand, the oil industry faces the prospect of demand peak within the next decade, and declining demand thereafter. In most OECD economies, including the United States and the European Union, that has already happened. And between China's rapidly decelerating rate of economic growth and its urgent need to improve air quality in its cities, it's only a matter of time before the same thing happens in that country—the economy that the oil industry is counting on to account for half of the growth in future world oil demand.

So, as you can see, contrary to what investors in coal mines and oil sands operations would like to think, business as usual is no longer an option. Between stumbling global economic growth today and the policies dictated by climate change tomorrow, the outlook for carbon stocks is grim. If today's strategic energy reserves are about to become tomorrow's stranded assets, what happens to the value of the energy companies that own them? What happens to the stock markets that these companies are listed on? And, perhaps most important, what happens to you as an investor?

BIG FOOT

If you're thinking you don't have to worry about that last question because you don't own any coal or oil stocks, think again. Just because your portfolio doesn't hold these stocks directly doesn't mean it is not exposed to them. If you own an index fund, as many investors today do, you're more heavily into carbon than you think—and probably more than you want—particularly if that index happens to be the Toronto Stock Exchange (TSX). It's one of the most carbon-intensive indexes in the world.

Just how much carbon is embedded in the Canadian stock market? By one estimate, the TSX holds no less than 33 GT of carbon: 25 in oil, largely in the form of bitumen deposits; 5 in coal; and 3 in natural gas.[1] At least in relative terms, the TSX has one of the heaviest carbon footprints of any stock exchange in the world. While major indices such as the S&P 500 in New York or London's FTSE hold far more carbon reserves among their listed firms, they are much larger indices overall, with market capitalizations many times that of the TSX. But when it comes to how much of an index's is in oil and gas, few of the major stock exchanges can top Toronto. The TSX's Energy sector (oil and gas) has two and a half times the weighting of the equivalent sector in the S&P 500.[2]

Carbon casts an even longer shadow over the TSX if you count firms that receive all of their revenue (or a disproportionate share of it) from transporting fossil fuels. Aside from the country's two largest pipeline companies, TransCanada Pipelines and Enbridge, which are included in the Energy sector, there are railways whose earnings growth have become increasingly reliant on hauling oil. CN and CP together represent another 5.5 percent of the TSX Composite. While falling fuel costs would normally be bullish for railway stocks, the loss of potential oil business has more than outweighed the impact of fuel savings. And what about Teck Resources, the huge mining firm in the TSX, with roughly 40 percent of its business in badly slumping metallurgical coal? In addition, Teck has a 20 percent share in the Fort Hill Oil Sands Project, slated to go into production in 2017.

Add it all up—oil and gas producers, pipelines and railways, and Teck—and you are talking almost 30 percent of the market capitalization of the entire TSX Composite. That suddenly makes a seemingly sector-neutral investment in a TSX exchange-traded fund a much bigger bet on the future of carbon fuels than perhaps most investors would want to make. The question, then, is what to do about it.

THE PASSIVE APPROACH
(LESSONS FROM NORTEL)

One option, I suppose, is to take the long view. That is what many stockbrokers tell their clients: ride out the bumps and stay in there for the long haul because the stock market has proven over time to provide superior returns to competing investments in bonds or short-term money market funds. They look as if they have a point. Even with the loss of nearly half of its value during the recession, the return from the TSX Composite over the last decade, including dividend payments, is 8.5 percent.

But one of the key reasons the stock market has been able to outperform other asset classes is its ability to shed losers and make room for new winners. In that respect, the stock market, in this case the TSX Composite, may be more resilient than the economy. It takes a long time to change the industrial structure of an economy (all those billions in cap ex spending in the oil sands can't be transformed over-night into new manufacturing plants in Ontario); but it takes no time for the TSX to change its sectoral weightings, and hence its exposure to what goes on in any one of those sectors. Compared with the pace of change in the bricks-and-mortar economy, stock portfolio shifts can happen in a heartbeat—or in the time it takes for carbon stocks to shrink in value relative to the rest of the index. That transition can certainly be unnerving for investors, especially if you happen to be long what the market is shorting, but it is precisely this ability to shift sector weighting that gives the stock market resiliency in the face of economic adversity and change.

If you doubt the TSX's resilience, consider that over a decade ago roughly a third of the entire market capitalization of the index was held not in the weighting of a single sector like Energy but in the weighting of a *single firm*—Nortel, the former telecommunications equipment giant. Like the latter-day BlackBerry, Nortel had its moment in the sun before being crushed by global competition. The company's capitalization fell from a peak of $398 billion in September 2000 to less than $5 billion by August 2002, while its share price collapsed from $124 to a pitiful 47 cents.

Prior to the company's collapse, the TSX Composite was trading at around 6,600. The following August, a year after Nortel's demise, the index traded at over 7,500—an almost 14 percent gain. If the TSX index was able to digest the bankruptcy of a firm that held, at its peak, almost a third of its total market cap, and within a year post a double-digit gain, it shouldn't be a stretch to believe that the TSX can survive a massive loss of share value of its carbon stocks and still go on to post new highs.

Oil and gas stocks are already a noticeably smaller slice of the TSX index. Before the last recession, the Energy sector accounted for nearly a third of the market cap of the entire TSX Composite. At the time of writing, that figure has fallen to 22 percent. In the future, they will account for much less as falling oil prices strand more and more of Alberta's bitumen in the ground. As the sector's weighting continues to shrink over time, broad index-wide returns from the stock market will become less sensitive to the write-downs of stranded carbon assets. That process may provide little solace to anyone who has invested directly in oil sands companies; investors who held on to their Nortel shares to the bitter end got nothing for their trouble. But as Nortel's shares plunged, so too did its weighting in the index, and hence its impact on index returns. Index investors can look forward to the same protection over time from a steadily shrinking weighting in carbon stocks.

All of that being said, telling nervous TSX index investors to "wait it out" as the index's carbon stocks implode is probably akin to telling air travellers to breathe normally when those oxygen masks drop. When faced with an impending crisis—physical, mental, financial—most people are lousy at staying calm, and even worse at doing nothing. So, if you're not turned on by the notion of allowing index rebalancing to soothe the pain of holding a tanking sector, the good news is that there may be another option—one that a growing number of investors are already exercising.

DUMPING CARBON STOCKS WILL MAKE YOU MONEY

Ethical investing has been around since the 18th century, when the Religious Society of Friends (a.k.a. the Quakers) forbade its members from participating in the slave trade. Around the same time, John Wesley, the founder of Methodism, offered a sermon on "The Use of Money," in which he cautioned against hurting one's neighbour through business practices; he suggested avoiding industries, such as tanning and distilling, that could cause harm.[3]

The landscape of ethical investing has broadened considerably since then. Guns, booze and tobacco have been and still are hot-button issues for those looking to invest in a socially responsible way, but they've been joined by everything from political boycotts to executive compensation to the environment. Unfortunately, ethical funds have generally performed poorly—at least when benchmarked to broad stock market performance—and that less than stellar reputation has reinforced the stereotype that letting your conscience be your portfolio manager will come at the expense of your return.

And yet, despite this commonly held belief, the last few years have seen a growing movement toward what appears to be some ethically motivated investment practices on the fossil fuel front. Clearly, some investors are unhappy about letting their hard-earned savings underwrite more and more emissions, and are beginning to take steps to rid their portfolios of carbon. And it's not just individuals who are choosing to walk away. In May 2014, Stanford University—holder of a very healthy $18-billion endowment fund—announced that it would sell its stake in publicly traded coal companies and make no future investments in the coal sector. That decision followed moves by a number of smaller US colleges to divest their endowment funds of two hundred leading fossil fuel companies.[4] And student- and faculty-led efforts to push the divestment agenda are under way at other prominent institutions in both North America and Europe, including the University of British Columbia, Harvard and Oxford.[5]

The movement is also growing off campus. More than 180 pension funds, cities, foundations, charities and financial institutions have made commitments to divest.[6] Massachusetts, Vermont and Maine are looking at ridding their state pension funds of carbon, as are the cities of Seattle, San Francisco and Boulder.[7] The Rockefeller Brothers Fund—an $860-million philanthropic organization bankrolled by the descendants of American oil pioneer John D. Rockefeller—has followed suit.[8] Across the Atlantic, Sweden and Norway have already removed fossil

fuels from their national pension plans, and financial services companies such as Rabobank and Storebrand have done the same.[9]

Given the historically poor performance of ethically motivated
investments, the mass exodus is—at least at first glance—surprising.
Until recently, fossil fuel divestment has been pitched as a way to save
the world from potentially cataclysmic emissions-induced climate
change. The financial performance of fossil fuel–free holdings was
rarely if ever mentioned. That's because, in the past, the exclusion of
such an important component of the stock market would have hurt
your rate of return. But today, the opposite is true.

Morgan Stanley Capital International (MSCI), provider of widely
followed benchmarks for global stock markets, estimates that you
would have been better off not owning carbon stocks of late. Excluding
all companies owning carbon reserves from the MSCI All Country
World Index actually improved returns over a recent five-year period.
And in 2014, plunging oil prices made oil stocks one of the worst-
performing sectors in stock markets around the world. These days,
then, divestment from carbon has become a win-win scenario, and a
somewhat easy move for institutional investors to make. On the one
hand, divesting from oil, coal or natural gas looks good in an increasingly enviro-conscientious world. On the other, the financial "risks"
traditionally associated with ethical investing aren't what they used
to be. As it turns out, many publicly traded coal stocks no longer
even qualify as "investment grade," a benchmark requirement for
their inclusion in institutional portfolios such as pension plans and
endowment funds. For example, Peabody Energy, the largest US coal
producer, which posted a $787-million loss in 2014, was downgraded
by Standard & Poor's rating agency to three notches below investment grade.[10] Peabody has lost almost 80 percent of its value on the
stock market since April 2011.[11] Arch Coal, the second-largest US coal
producer, has lost over 90 percent of its value since the recession.
Alpha Natural Resources, another US coal giant, has had a similar

stock performance. According to Fitch rating service and Bloomberg, at least a dozen US coal firms have declared bankruptcy recently. And as we've noted, it's not just US coal producers that are taking it on the chin: the entire KOL (world coal stocks) exchange-traded fund is down more than 60 percent over the same time period. The trustees of Stanford's now coal-free endowment fund cited social responsibility as the reason behind disinvestment, but given the performance of coal stocks over the last several years, they could just as easily have cited fiduciary responsibility.

Earlier, we explored the trade-off between the environment and the economy that politicians have traditionally wrestled with when debating the costs of dealing with climate change. We saw that when we place a carbon budget into the economic equation, going green actually does the opposite of what we have been schooled to believe: instead of stunting growth, it opens up room for it. The same will hold true for investors who have wrestled with the trade-off between doing what's right for the world's well-being and doing what's right for their portfolio. As countries around the world increasingly take measures to clamp down on their own carbon emissions, your investment portfolio will yield higher returns if it doesn't hold any coal, oil or gas stocks.

And in this new world—where time-honoured investment beliefs are turned on their head—Stanford's decision to jettison coal from its portfolio will no doubt prove prescient. If coal stocks are already taking a beating as coal prices plunge, how are they likely to fare over the next two decades, when world coal consumption must fall by about a third in order to keep atmospheric carbon from rising above the critical 450-ppm threshold? Can oil do much better?

Just as the world must combust less coal in the future, so too must it combust less oil. Countries banking on developing their oil reserves need to reassess their economic strategies in light of this constraint. In September 2014, the UN's Global Commission on the Economy and Climate released a report warning that countries and companies that rely on investments in high-carbon fossil fuels are at a tremendous risk as the world adjusts to a low-carbon future.[12] Individual investors should also take heed. Instead of trailing index returns, a portfolio divested of fossil fuels is far more likely to beat the overall performance of the stock market, particularly if that stock market happens to be as oily as the TSX Composite. So, if you want to save the world, you might just want to save your portfolio first.

THE FUTURE IS NOW

The University of Toronto's endowment fund is about one-tenth the size of Stanford's, but it's the largest of any Canadian university. The $1.9-billion fund—to which I make a very modest annual contribution through my alma mater, Innis College (which my son, Jack, currently attends)—holds a number of oil sands heavyweights: Suncor, Canadian Natural Resources and Imperial Oil, as well as global oil giants Exxon and Chevron and the coal-laden Teck Resources. As we embark on an age of emissions restraint, fund trustees might wish to consider the contribution of those carbon holdings to the endowment fund's performance and follow Stanford's lead.

The performance of oil sands stocks may not be quite as bad as that of American coal stocks, but they aren't much better. Next to coal, oil sands stocks have been the worst performing in the entire carbon sector of the stock market. And, looking forward, the oil sands' emissions intensity and high production costs make them especially vulnerable to falling oil prices and the global task of holding atmospheric carbon in check.

Like the rest of the stock market, oil sands stocks initially bounced back after the recession. World oil prices, benchmarked by the price of oil from the Brent field in the North Sea, quickly rebounded to triple-digit range, providing huge cash flows to petroleum producers around the world. But as we've seen, it soon became apparent to investors that oil sands producers were missing the party. Their land-locked fuel started to trade at ever-widening discounts not only to Brent but to West Texas Intermediate, the North American oil price benchmark. At one point, the oil sands' Western Canadian Select was trading as much as $50 a barrel less than Brent. And to make matters worse, oil sands producers kept ramping up their daily output, only adding to the glut of heavy oil with no place to go, other than bulging storage tanks in places like Cushing, Oklahoma. In other words, the more oil Alberta shipped to the USA, the lower the price that oil received. Not surprisingly, investors were less than enthusiastic about financing that business model.

NO MORE WHITE KNIGHTS FROM CHINA

Faced with this bleak vision, it's no surprise that pensions and other big institutional investors pulled back on their faltering position in oil sands stocks. And it didn't take long before individual investors followed suit. But while all of that was going on, there was a small group of very large potential investors who were not discouraged by the sector's poor financial performance, and their continuing interest injected the markets, at least for a while, with a false sense of hope for the future of the oil sands.

For years, a handful of foreign, state-owned oil companies had been scouring the world for its last remaining reserves of untapped oil. To them, the oil sands looked good—very good. Given its voracious appetite for fuel, it stands to reason that most of these asset-shopping state energy companies hailed from China. At first, these companies made relatively small investments, either buying junior firms in the sector or taking a minority ownership in oil sands projects. PetroChina Co. Ltd. completed a deal for Athabasca Oil Sands for around $2.5 billion, and in 2010 Sinopec paid $4.65 billion for a 9 percent share in Syncrude, which runs Alberta's largest oil sands mine. But in 2012, China's National Offshore Oil Company (CNOOC) dramatically upped the ante, making a huge $15.1-billion offer to buy Nexen, one of the larger Canadian oil sands producers, lock, stock and barrel.

Before the recession and the subsequent crash in oil sands stocks, the notion that a state-owned Chinese company could buy one of Canada's best-known and homegrown oil sands producers would have been politically unthinkable. Back in those days, Prime Minister Harper was still hammering the Chinese government on its human rights record, not trying to engineer huge investment and trade deals with them. In any event, such an arrangement would have been flatly turned down by the federal Foreign Investment Review Agency, with the ringing endorsement of the Alberta government.

But by 2012, that had all changed. The pickings for attractive buyout candidates among oil sands properties had got pretty slim, and despite its earlier hostility to China, the Harper government gave its blessing to the controversial sale. Nationalists perceived the CNOOC buyout as a surrendering of sovereignty over a key resource to a foreign, and not necessarily friendly, power. But from a Nexen shareholder perspective, it was a pretty sweet deal; in fact, it was precisely the kind of deal that shareholders in Suncor or any of the other major oil sands operators can only dream of these days—just three years later. Unfortunately, no white knight in shining armour is going to ride to their rescue as CNOOC did when it opened its wallet and generously paid Nexen shareholders a huge 40-percent-plus premium over the market price for shares of a company that had struggled since its inception with chronic production problems and crippling cost overruns. Those days are well and truly over.

Since the Nexen deal, the Harper government has put in place tighter rules for foreign takeovers of oil sands properties in an effort to appease concerns that the country was selling its oil wealth to unfriendly foreign powers. Those measures have drawn criticism in Alberta for scaring off potential foreign suitors, but it's unlikely that those tougher regulations will really be tested in the future. Even China's reserve-hungry state-owned oil companies have cooled considerably on the challenging economics of the resource.

You see, the Nexen acquisition hasn't exactly turned out to be a home run for CNOOC. Nexen is one of CNOOC's worst-performing assets.[13] Continuing problems at the company's troubled Long Lake operation (near Fort McMurray) together with the lingering price discount on Alberta crude resulted in CNOOC's massive investment returning about a third of what the company got on its other assets around the world. CNOOC acknowledged that a 7 percent increase in firm-wide operating costs over the first half of 2014 was largely due to operational problems at Nexen.[14] To top it all off, without more pipeline capacity to the west coast, CNOOC has no way of getting its Canadian oil to China.

It's worth noting that CNOOC's experience is hardly a one-off. Sinopec's 9 percent share of Syncrude, a firm recently plagued by technical problems, is estimated by analysts to be worth well below the $4.65 billion it paid in 2010.

What originally attracted companies (state-owned or otherwise) to the resource was the vast amount of bitumen contained in the oil sands and Alberta's friendly operating environment, including the low royalty rates the province has historically charged for its share of resource revenue. There are even bigger reserves in Saudi Arabia and Venezuela, but they aren't open to private investment. After the late Hugo Chávez expropriated Exxon's oil upgrader in Venezuela's Orinoco heavy oil belt, it's not too hard to see why the world oil industry decided to put its money into Alberta. But what investors in the oil sands have come to focus on these days is not Alberta's oil-friendly operating environment or the low royalty rates it charges on its hydrocarbon resources. Even the need to build new pipelines to connect to world oil prices has suddenly taken a back seat to a far more pressing problem—one that threatens the very commercial viability of their industry.

LIFE AFTER THE FALL

Until the summer of 2014, the number one problem for oil sands producers was getting their land-locked bitumen to tidewater, which would allow them to capture those triple-digit world oil prices— hence the need for more pipelines and the explosive growth of rail transport.

And there was some progress on that front. The building of the southern leg of the Keystone XL pipeline—as well as other pipelines connecting the bulging inventories at Cushing, Oklahoma, to refineries along the Gulf Coast—helped oil sands producers get pricing closer to world oil benchmarks. So did the record amount of oil being moved to the coast by rail. But just as the huge discount on Alberta bitumen began to shrink, oil sands producers had to grapple with a much more lethal problem: world oil prices themselves began to plunge. By the end of 2014, they had fallen over 50 percent, leaving Brent and West Texas Intermediate, the benchmarks Alberta bitumen producers so desperately sought, trading at levels that made most of their grandiose expansion plans uneconomic. Even if the oil sands had sufficient pipeline connections to capture world oil prices, those prices were no longer high enough to pay the freight.

When it comes to low prices keeping oil in the ground, the oil sands rank at the top of the "most vulnerable" list; as we've seen, Alberta bitumen is one of the most expensive oils in the world to extract. Of the $1.1 trillion in planned global spending on the development of high-cost oil over the next decade, almost $400 billion is slated for oil sands projects.[15] Just one project, such as the planned expansion of production from 100,000 barrels a day to 500,000 barrels a day at Exxon's Kearl Lake operation, could ultimately cost in the neighbourhood of $22 billion. But that project, like so many planned for the oil sands, isn't going to make much economic sense in an emissions-constrained world of falling oil prices. Most of these projects require a minimum oil price of $80 to $90 per barrel in order to be worth the expense. By the end of 2014, Western Canadian Select was trading at less than $40 a barrel.

As we saw in chapter 9, some companies had already cancelled major projects that were part of the sector's huge planned expansion. Given where world oil prices are trading, it seems a safe bet that these won't be the only projects cancelled. The IEA estimates that with oil trading below $80 a barrel, more projects will be cancelled in the oil sands than in any other oil-producing region of the world.[16]

SHOW ME THE MONEY

So how has this all played out for you as an investor? Taken as a group, the share performance of the oil sands stocks is best captured by BlackRock's iShares Oil Sands Index exchange-traded fund (ETF), which is listed on the TSX. Exchange-traded funds, which are now all the rage in the wealth management business, allow investors to buy either a sector of the market or an entire index as opposed to making investments in individual company stocks. The iShares Oil Sands Index ETF includes all the oil sands producers that are publicly listed on the Toronto Stock Exchange, including Suncor, Cenovus, Imperial Oil, Canadian Natural Resources and others.

Unlike mutual funds, whose stock holdings are at the discretion of a portfolio manager, the stock composition of an exchange-traded fund is determined by the exact weighting of the index or sector that it proxies. So, for example, if Suncor represents 13.38 percent of the value of all TSX-listed oil sands producers, then its weight in the oil sands exchange-traded fund will be the same 13.38 percent. In this way, the performance of an ETF effectively mirrors the performance of the sector (in this case oil sands stocks) or the index (TSX Composite) that it proxies.

As it turns out, the oil sands haven't just tarnished Canada's international image, they've also badly diminished the returns of investors. They may be the crown jewels of the Canadian economy in Prime Minister Harper's eyes, but that's certainly not the way the stock market has viewed them. Industry leaders like Suncor that once traded north of $70 per share are now trading at little over half that amount. Canadian Oil Sands, a co-owner of the huge Syncrude operation, has fared even worse. It's off almost 80 percent from its prerecession peak value. The entire sector, as measured by the valuation of the BlackRock iShares Oil Sands Index exchange-traded fund, is trading at the same levels seen during the lows of the last recession, some 70 percent below its prerecession peak of $30 a unit (see chart on page 170). By comparison, the broad TSX Composite has regained all the ground ceded during the recession. The iShares Oil Sands ETF has posted negative annual returns in each of the last four years (2011, 2012, 2013 and 2014). In 2014, it underperformed the broad TSX index by more than a third. That kind of performance comparison makes morally motivated divestment a lot easier to stomach.

BLACKROCK ISHARES OIL SANDS INDEX ETF 2007–15

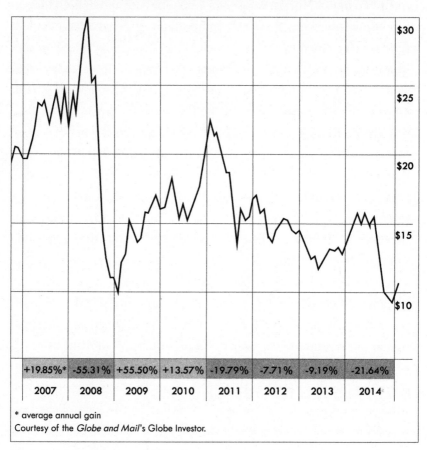

+19.85%*	-55.31%	+55.50%	+13.57%	-19.79%	-7.71%	-9.19%	-21.64%
2007	2008	2009	2010	2011	2012	2013	2014

* average annual gain
Courtesy of the *Globe and Mail*'s Globe Investor.

INCOME TRUSTS 2.0?

So this is the world we are heading toward: a world of carbon constraints (whether internationally or nationally motivated); a world of
higher production costs and low oil prices; a world in which the oil
sands aren't the attractive source of new oil supply they were once
considered to be, at home or abroad; a world in which your investment in the bitumen-laden TSX is suddenly very much at risk.

It's a very different world from the one for which Alberta's oil
sands industry had been planning. That industry—once a model of
dynamic growth—is now clearly in retreat. In place of doubled

production numbers, we are more likely to hear a doubling in announcements of project cancellations. And that changes the ground rules for investors.

Shareholders look for different things in mature sunset industries than they do when investing in growth industries. With the latter, shareholders are typically willing to forgo dividends so a company can reinvest all its earnings. In return, investors hope to be rewarded with the huge share-price gains that often come with explosive growth. But investors in sunset industries are looking for a rich stream of dividend payments—something to compensate them for the lack of the big upside in share prices investors in growth stocks can achieve. Since sunset industries have limited need for new investment, they can afford to pay out much of their earnings in the form of dividends.

If oil sands producers are now a sunset industry, there will be no need to spend billions of dollars developing new production sites, new pipelines or new rail-loading terminals. Instead, investors will want to see those companies' cut costs sufficiently to produce earnings at today's oil prices, and to the extent that earnings are possible, investors will want them to be paid out instead of squandered on unprofitable and hence unsustainable increases in production. In other words, shareholders will want to be treated much the same as they were in the old income trust model. Remember income trusts?

Before the late finance minister Jim Flaherty nuked them in 2006, income trusts were the hottest things going in Alberta's oil and gas patch. Income trusts were the latest version of what was known in the financial world as flow-through shares. Instead of companies retaining their earnings and paying corporate tax on them, they would instead distribute them to their unitholders, who in turn would pay personal income tax on the distributions received from the trust. In theory, income trusts were designed for mature industries that did not have major capital expenditures. Otherwise, the financing model wouldn't have room to distribute earnings to unitholders, since much of it would be needed for reinvestment. Mind you, companies could still borrow to finance investment in new capacity, and many did. While the trust model would not be an ideal form of financing for an oil sands sector in a mad rush to invest hundreds of billions of dollars in a massive expansion of production, its principle of paying out earnings would work just fine for a sunset industry that wants to offer its shareholders reasonably attractive dividends from what over time will be declining revenues.

Of course, as was the case with income trusts, the ability of oil sands companies to pay out earnings is dependent on making them in the first place, and that, in turn, depends on costs, production levels and oil prices. Today, oil sands firms are cutting dividends almost as fast as they are cutting investment. What is particularly challenging in today's glutted oil market is that the onus is on oil sands producers, and other high-cost supply sources like shale producers, to cut back production in order to restore prices. The more they keep increasing production, the more downward pressure they create on prices.

Will oil sands companies be able to reduce costs enough to survive in a world of falling oil prices? If they can't, it won't matter what their dividend policy is; there won't be any earnings to distribute. Given the new reality of low oil prices, the need to expand has very quickly given way to the struggle to stay alive. Without any pricing power to speak of, the only way to do that is to dramatically cut costs. And still looming out on the horizon is the almost-certain (and not too distant) prospect that the world will need to limit how much oil and other fossil fuels it can burn.

BEYOND BITUMEN

All of this amounts to a whole lot of bad news—at least if you happen to live in a country that has chosen to put all its economic eggs into one oil sands basket, or if you happen to be an investor in that same

country's oil-laden stock market. But while opportunities in one sector disappear, opportunities in other sectors may suddenly appear.
Climate change and its link to carbon emissions clearly threatens
to deliver a fatal blow to Canada's energy ambitions—to extract 5 million barrels of bitumen a day from Alberta's vast oil sands and
become the energy superpower envisioned in its federal government's economic dreams. Instead of leaving a huge emissions trail
in the atmosphere, most of the carbon in that resource is going to
stay exactly where nature put it—in a carbon sink made of billions
of tons of sand.

At the same time, however, the very climate change that stands in
the way of exploiting the country's considerable carbon assets could
make some of Canada's other resources that much more valuable.
Identifying them and the emerging opportunities to exploit them has
been difficult in recent years. Backing a losing horse like the oil sands
isn't the only consequence of the Harper government's denial of climate change. It has also resulted in a failure to identify the commercial opportunities that a profoundly changing climate might bring. In
the end, that may be more costly to the Canadian economy than the
stranded assets left behind in the Alberta sands.

The good news is that Canadian investors need not be blinded by
the same ideological blinkers that distort their government's percep-
tion of our economic future. Knowing what economic opportunities
a changing climate will bring to the Canadian economy will go a long
way toward helping you find a place to move your bitumen-tarnished
investment dollars.

PART
FOUR

OPPORTUNITY
KNOCKS

WHEN THE FIFTH SEASON of the wildly popular show *The Walking Dead* premiered in mid-October 2014, a mind-boggling 22.4 million viewers tuned in. The numbers dropped slightly the following week, but even so, the chances are pretty good that at least some of the people currently reading this book were watching. If you happen to be one of them, you would have seen Rick and his crew trudging through the woods, away from the smoking ruins of Terminus. To pass the time, Bob is playing a game with his girlfriend, Sasha. The game, called Good Out of the Bad, might not seem an obvious choice for entertainment during a zombie apocalypse, but there they were—Sasha naming bad things about their current situation ("Danger around every corner") while Bob gamely tried to provide a positive spin ("Never a dull moment").

Bob's optimism, while endearing, is a little out of place. And it seems similarly inappropriate in a discussion of climate change. After decades of dire warnings about the impending end of the world as we know it, we can perhaps be forgiven for not immediately seeing that there might be a few tiny pieces of good news amid all the bad. Perhaps "good news" is a bit of an overstatement. Left unchecked, climate change will be catastrophic. We'll also have to adjust (we already are adjusting) to the havoc unleashed by the carbon we've been emitting since the Industrial Revolution, even as we figure out how a carbon-constrained world will work. And it's there, in that adjustment, that opportunity may lie.

If the world is changing, those willing and able to change with it will be rewarded. For a high-latitude country like Canada, whose average temperature is expected to rise a multiple of the global average, that change points to a fundamental rethink of our national economic priorities.

CHAPTER 11

BREADBASKET

THE SCENE WAS UNUSUAL: four hundred local farmers packed into an auditorium in the small agricultural community of Morris, Manitoba, listening to a lecture by an Ohio farmer brought in by DuPont Pioneer (the chemical giant's seed division). The talk was called "Ear Count 101," and it was, not surprisingly, about corn—both how to grow it and the attractive returns the crop yielded. At the other end of the crowded hall was a John Deere exhibit. In addition to the usual harvesters and planters, corn dryers were on display.[1]

Corn is the most important grain when it comes to feeding the world's 7-billion-plus population. We consume it in thousands of different ways—straight off the cob, certainly, but also as corn oil, corn flour, corn starch, corn sweeteners (including the ubiquitous high-fructose corn syrup), and corn thickeners and additives (check labels for maltodextrin, diglycerides and monoglycerides). Our livestock also have a taste for the stuff; it's used as a feedstock for everything from cows to chickens to salmon. Today, the United States is the world's biggest corn producer by a country mile. From the Ohio Valley to Nebraska, corn is America's most common grain and principal cash crop. Not only is the United States the world's largest corn producer, accounting for over 40 percent of world production, it is also the world's largest exporter (a fact that underlines the importance of American harvests on world corn prices).

Unfortunately for western Canadian farmers, corn has been nearly impossible to grow during the fertile prairies' short growing seasons. But our changing climate is quickly altering the length of growing seasons, which is what brought those four hundred farmers out to hear DuPont's presentation. In a move that could have a far-reaching and lucrative impact on the country's economy, many prairie growers have already started to experiment with the new cash crop.

A NEW DAY DOWN ON THE FARM

It's a little-discussed fact that, up to a point, carbon emissions are actually good for agricultural production. All other things being equal, CO_2 is vital to photosynthesis; it acts a bit like a fertilizer, encouraging plant growth and improving crop yields. Since the Industrial Revolution, carbon fertilization has actually improved global agricultural production, helping the world feed its ever-growing population.

The problem going forward is that all things will not remain equal. Thanks to unchecked emissions, the rising CO_2 levels that encourage plant growth are now changing the climate in ways that tip the scale against food production. Heat waves and droughts—natural by-products of rising global temperatures—can be devastating for agricultural production, as can torrential rains that flood fields and wash away vital topsoils. Consider:

- In Australia, a drought that began in 2002 and lasted until 2009 reduced the water available for agriculture to a tenth of its normal level in the Murray–Darling watershed, the country's breadbasket. At one point, the water supply for the entire region—which covers approximately a million square kilometres—shrank

to one-tenth its average over the last century. As
water was rationed, wheat and rice production in
the region was cut in half.[2]

- A record heat wave in Europe in 2003 resulted in an
estimated 35,000 human casualties and reduced the
continent's corn, wheat and barley harvests by up to
15 percent. Production of animal feed collapsed by
an astonishing 60 percent.[3]

- In the summer of 2010, record-high temperatures and
drought set Russia's vast forests ablaze, blanketing
Moscow in smoke. So much wheat shrivelled on the
stalk that the country banned wheat exports, eliminat-
ing about 10 percent of global supply. Within a month,
soaring wheat prices had sent the UN's Food and
Agriculture Organization (FAO) Food Price Index
up 50 percent.[4]

American farmers got a look into the crystal ball in 2012, when
the worst drought in over half a century affected 70 percent of the
Midwest's Corn Belt and sent grain prices to record highs. The blis-
tering heat that baked breadbasket states such as Iowa and Illinois,
which together produce about a third of US corn and soybeans, followed on the heels of the warmest January-to-June period on record.
The hit to US corn production not only boosted corn prices, which
rose by almost 50 percent, but through soaring feedlot costs it
impacted prices along the whole food chain, including dairy, poultry,
pork and beef. To make matters worse, in the following year the
region was deluged by record rains that washed away topsoil. And
then, just as farmers began to consider switching to wheat, nature
rewarded them with a bumper corn crop in 2014.

What farmers in America and the rest of the world are quickly discovering is that a "normal" growing season is a thing of the past.

Thanks to our rapidly changing climate, the "new normal" features unpredictable year-to-year swings in temperature and precipitation. Just imagine what "normal" will look like with at least one more degree of global warming coming down the pipe, and possibly as much as four degrees if we don't rein in global carbon emissions in a big hurry.

MOVING ON UP

You don't have to be an agricultural expert to figure out that an out-of-whack climate is going to have devastating repercussions for world food production and supply, though the experts certainly have been paying attention. Scientific evidence presented in the latest IPCC assessment report shows that yields of the world's major crops are sensitive to rising temperatures.[5] While global warming is likely to see temperatures in higher-latitude areas rise much more dramatically than in lower-latitude areas (where a good portion of the world's food is currently produced), the fact that temperatures in tropical regions are already near threshold levels means that even small increases will have significant adverse effects on agricultural production.

Researchers at Stanford and Columbia, looking at the period from 1980 to 2008, estimated that rising temperatures have already reduced theoretical global wheat yields by more than 5 percent (relative to what had been expected in a stable climate) and corn yields by almost 4 percent. The impact on harvests was estimated to have increased crop prices by as much as 20 percent during the period. In turn, those higher wheat and corn prices induced farmers to switch to these suddenly more lucrative crops (from other staples such as soybeans), with the resulting supply-and-demand shift pushing up soybean prices as well.

The IPCC's assessment suggests that actual global crop yields will start declining by 2030. While the report recognized that the world's northern regions, most of which are now marginal for food production, could contribute in much more meaningful ways to future crop supply, the loss of production in lower-latitude regions is expected to reduce global crop yields by about 2 percent per decade over the rest of the century. A 2-percent-per-decade decline may not seem huge in its own right, but as we shall soon see, it's enormous when compared with the grain production needed to keep pace with current population and dietary trends.

Given all of this, it's certainly not hard to understand why basic grain prices have been on a steady upward march over the last ten years or so. The US Department of Agriculture estimates that world crop production fell short of world consumption in eight of the twelve years between 2000 and 2012, requiring drawdowns of global food inventories. In part, that situation was the result of weather-related supply shocks. But it was also brought about by demand growth that seemed almost as inexorable as climate change itself.

NINE BILLION CHEESEBURGERS TO GO, PLEASE

Over the last thirty years, world population has doubled to 7 billion, and the United Nations is now projecting that it will hit more than 9 billion by the midpoint of this century. On its own, the prospect of another 2 billion mouths to feed might be enough to drive food prices higher, but a look at what those mouths are being fed really tips the scales. Around the world, more and more people—particularly in emerging economies—are trading rice bowls for cheeseburgers. Recent data suggests that the meat sector in China and India (the world's two most populous nations) could experience as much as an 80 percent boom by 2022, thanks largely to a growing middle class that can now afford to choose meat over more traditional grain- and vegetable-based meals.[6] Between 2008 and 2011, per capita protein consumption in India rose by 21 percent; in

China, by 7 percent.[7] Driven by this new-found demand, global meat consumption has grown at twice the rate of the population over the last two decades.[8]

Not getting the cheeseburger/grain price connection? Consider, then, that it takes an average of seven pounds of grain to produce a single pound of beef. If the current trend in rising protein consumption per capita in the developing world continues, the shift to richer diets and the projected increase in world population will require a *doubling* in world crop production by 2050. Line up those requirements against that 2-percent-per-decade drop in crop yields and it shouldn't be too hard to figure out which direction food prices will be heading.

It's a dead-simple equation: rising grain prices spell rising food prices. The cost of a basic grain like corn has a ripple effect on the food system, impacting the dollar figure stamped on everything from meat and poultry (for which it is used as a feedstock) to processed food (in which corn syrup and corn starch are common additives). At the same time, however, rising prices mean higher returns to the farmers able to produce those grains, and higher farmland values in areas where those grains can be grown. Those economic incentives could soon be a powerful force in spurring new agricultural production in higher-latitude countries like Canada.

Facing an almost-certain decline in crop yields in tropical countries, world food production will depend on the emergence of new breadbaskets. In higher-latitude regions—where, remember, average temperatures are expected to increase at a multiple of the global average—production could benefit not only from longer growing seasons but also from a potential expansion of the area under cultivation as farmland creeps farther north.

To what extent increased supply from northern countries will compensate for the loss of agricultural production in tropical areas remains to be seen. A key factor will be how quickly production can shift from one region to another. Another scenario, of course, is that the inevitable rise in grain prices will halt or even reverse the trend toward higher-protein diets in developing countries, lowering the bar for world grain production needs. More ominously, declining crop yields and the resulting price spikes could start to affect population growth itself.

Malthusian-type demand adjustments aside, there are likely to be massive amounts of effort and capital invested in adapting global agriculture to a changing climate. You can bet that the attention of seed companies such as Monsanto, DuPont and Syngenta is already trained in that direction.[9] Seed varieties that either are drought resistant, are tolerant of higher growing temperatures or require shortened growing seasons will soon be in very high demand, if they aren't already.[10] You can also bet that those same companies are busy trying to figure out just where their new genetically modified seeds, tailored to tomorrow's climate, will be planted. US-based firms such as Monsanto and DuPont Pioneer don't have to look too far. The country's national space agency, NASA, has already identified a prime potential market right next door.

THE CANADIAN PRAIRIES:
A CLIMATE CHANGE HOT SPOT

NASA has long been involved in studying global climate change. In 2012, it released a study mapping out how a 2-to-4-degree-Celsius rise in average global temperatures would affect the planet's surface. NASA found that 37 percent of the planet will undergo profound changes by the end of the century, with entire ecosystems — deserts, plains and forests — moving in response to the coming changes in temperature and precipitation.[11]

Of course, not all areas will be affected in the same way. Some parts of the world won't be affected at all. But others — places NASA labels climate hot spots—will experience as much as a 100 percent change in their ecosystems. The Canadian prairies, along with much of Russia's Siberia, glow bright red on the map shown in the NASA report, designating maximum change. Much of Alberta, Saskatchewan and Manitoba will see major ecological changes, particularly in what are now the transition zones between the prairie and the boreal forest. Grasslands will extend much farther north. At the same time, the boreal forest will push northward, encroaching on territory that is currently tundra.[12]

What lies behind the NASA projections is a rapidly warming Canadian climate. If the next fifty years are at all like the last fifty, Canada is going to get hotter. Canada's average temperature has already risen at roughly double the global average[13]—and it's expected to continue to rise throughout this century. That prospect, coupled with Canada's abundant fresh water supply, makes it an ideal candidate to become one of the world's future breadbaskets. In fact, Canada has been identified as one of only 5 out of 163 countries that have all the requisite characteristics to significantly boost agricultural production in the future.

While all regions of Canada have warmed, the greatest temperature increases have been seen in the higher-latitude regions of the Yukon and the Northwest Territories, and in the High Arctic. Seasonally, winter and spring have seen the greatest warming. In northwestern Canada, average winter temperatures have risen by more than 3 degrees Celsius.[14] Despite an increase in those scorchers that are so noticeable whenever they occur, summer temperatures have actually risen the least. However, a decided trend toward earlier springs and warming autumns has already had a significant lengthening impact on growing seasons across the country, particularly on the western Canadian prairies.

Temperatures have been recorded in measuring stations across the Prairies since 1895. Average temperatures have risen by 1.6 degrees

Celsius, with the warming trend accelerating since the 1970s. Compared with the thirty-year period ending in 1990, average temperatures are predicted to rise by 2 degrees Celsius by 2050 in southern Alberta, and by 3 degrees Celsius farther north, in Fort McMurray. Similar temperature increases are projected across the other Prairie provinces. Those temperature changes will have profound ecological impacts.[15]

It won't just be grassland coming north. Insects, birds and animals will also be heading in that direction—and not all will necessarily be welcome. Warming winters have already laid a path for the destructive mountain pine beetle to chew through a good chunk of Canada's western forests. And the ticks that carry Lyme disease are now more prevalent across the country. Generally speaking, most of the world's nasty critters can't handle bone-chilling Canadian winters. Climate change will give some a passport.

But for farmers and seed companies such as Monsanto and DuPont, the most important consequence of those temperature changes will be the critical impact on the number of frost-free days. In northern latitudes, crop-killing frost is much more of a constraint on food production than crop-killing heat waves. The growing season—defined by the number of frost-free days—can be half of what it is in more southern latitudes.

For most of Canada, then, the increase in the frost-free growing season promises to be significant. On what is currently the northern margin of agriculture, in places like the Peace River district in the Mackenzie basin in northern Alberta, the growing season could increase by as much as three to four weeks. It could be a week or two longer in the Prairies as well as in Ontario and Quebec. But the lengthened growing season will affect more than just crop yields. For western Canadian farmers, the traditional shortened growing season has been a barrier blocking access to the continent's most important and lucrative crop. That is about to change.

IS KING CORN MOVING NORTH?

The DuPont-sponsored talk in Morris, Manitoba, was only one of many taking place across the southern Canadian prairies these days. The federal government may not have figured it out yet, or even been inclined to think much about it, but some of the world's largest seed companies have already targeted the southern Prairies as a potential new hot spot for corn cultivation.

For companies that engineer new seed varieties ("genetically modified," in today's lexicon), understanding the implications of global climate change is vital for continued success. Finding new markets will become critically important when rising temperatures and water shortages start to take their toll on crop yields and production in the US Midwest.

There may still have been a few feet of snow outside the Morris auditorium in March, but the farmers weren't letting snowdrifts stand in the way of learning how a warming climate might provide opportunities for their businesses. Even those skeptical of the whole thesis of human-made climate change can see what's happening in their own backyards. When you work in the fields every day, it's hard not to notice what's going on with your weather.

Over time, it adds up. Historical records indicate that spring is already twenty-six days earlier in Alberta than it was half a century ago, and warmer autumns point to a growing season that will be anywhere from 25 to 40 percent longer than the average from 1961 to 1990. Numbers like that have the potential to turn a lot of golden fields of wheat into green fields of corn. And remember, average temperatures on the Prairies are expected to climb by as much as 3 degrees by 2050, with the growing season continuing to lengthen.

Already, corn acreage under cultivation is booming. In 2013, farmers in Manitoba, Saskatchewan and Alberta planted a record 405,000 acres of corn, double the amount planted only two years earlier.[16]

While that's still a pittance compared with the 95 million acres grown south of the border, production is clearly creeping north.

And seed companies like Monsanto are doing everything they can to facilitate that migration, by developing corn seeds that require shorter growing seasons, ideally suited for the crop's northern expansion. The company estimates that acreage devoted to corn cultivation on the Prairies could increase as much as twentyfold over the next decade. That scale of expansion could easily make Canada self-sufficient in the world's most important crop, if not an outright exporter. Corn imports from the United States have already fallen to about a quarter of their level only five years ago.[17]

The migration of the Corn Belt to the Canadian prairies could be a double win for Canadian farmers. By switching to corn (and other cash crops like soybeans), farmers would significantly increase the cash flow from their acreage, setting the stage for a marked appreciation in farmland values. Right now, land value is about the only comparative advantage western Canadian prairie farmers have in the US-dominated corn market. In Illinois, a corn farmer's cash rent per acre (the cost of leasing an acre of farmland) can be as high as $300; in southern Manitoba, it is as low as $25. Even compared with farmland prices in southwestern Ontario, where corn has always been grown, an acre of prairie wheat field can be purchased or leased at a fraction of the cost.[18]

But Canadian prairie corn farmers may garner an even more fundamental comparative advantage going forward. Rising temperatures and drought should reduce corn yields, and hence production, in the US Midwest, with some prime growing areas becoming unsuitable for corn cultivation. Given how important the USA is to world production, any reduction of US supply is almost certain to put upward pressure on world corn prices, making the crop all the more valuable for those who can grow it.

Those concerns regarding future US crop production were echoed in the National Climate Assessment—a collaborative effort by thirteen

US federal agencies drawing upon the work of six hundred climate change experts. Their findings warn that climate changes will have a growing influence on US crop yields over the next twenty-five years. By mid-century, the impact of temperature and precipitation changes will become significantly negative. The increased frequency of 35-degree-Celsius days, coupled with a sharp rise in the number of consecutive dry days (less than 0.25 millimetres of rainfall), is expected to adversely affect crop yields and agricultural production in the Great Plains, the Midwest and the Southwest. Not only will rising temperatures drop yields, they will cause increased evaporation of soil moisture, requiring more and more irrigation from already depleting sources of fossil water like the Ogallala Aquifer.[19] That sounds like bad news for Kansas corn farmers, but it's awfully good news for those new corn farmers 1,100 kilometres north, in Morris, Manitoba.

MARGINAL NO MORE

It's perhaps natural that so much climate change analysis focuses on the Prairies, which is, after all, the centre of Canada's grain industry. But the trend toward warmer average temperatures will also have an impact in other regions. Where soil conditions permit, once-marginal farmland elsewhere in the Canadian North will suddenly become productive in ways farmers have never seen before. Places like northeastern Ontario's long-forgotten Clay Belt—not to mention the other clay belts scattered like archipelagos across the Canadian Shield— could eventually fulfill the promise that once lured unsuspecting settlers north.

While nowhere near the size of the Prairies, the Clay Belt is nevertheless vast, covering over 180,000 square kilometres in northeastern Ontario and into Quebec's adjoining Abitibi county. The belt runs approximately 965 kilometres east-west and, at its widest point, over 400 kilometres north-south, encompassing an area from Kapuskasing in the north down to Lake Timiskaming at its southern extremity, and eastward to the town of Rouyn-Noranda in Quebec. Surrounded on all sides by rocky, muskeg-laced Canadian Shield, the Clay Belt is the bottom of preglacial Lake Ojibway, which drained away around ten thousand years ago, at the time of the last ice age. Similar clay formations are found in northern Quebec and Labrador.

Despite the outstanding fertility of the soil, short growing seasons have stunted agricultural development in the area. Of some 16 million acres, only a small fraction (a little under 190,000 acres) has been cultivated. It's not hard to understand why. As one discouraged settler put it decades ago, seven months of the year your field lies under a blanket of snow, two more months it's subjected to constant rain, and for the remaining three months it's covered by swarms of blackflies and mosquitoes.[20]

But crank the thermostat up 3 or 4 degrees Celsius and all of a sudden those growing seasons aren't so desperately short. In addition to growing oats and barley, farmers can start growing soybeans and corn. And when farmers start reaping the rewards that come from a cash crop, all of a sudden there are sufficient financial incentives to increase the acreage under cultivation. Instead of a backwoods resource region, dependent on highly cyclical industries such as forestry, pulp and paper, and mining, the Clay Belt could become prime agricultural land, just like southwestern Ontario.

CHÂTEAU MCMURRAY: GRAND CRU DE Y2Y

Discussions about global warming and the future of agriculture — like the one we've been having — can tend toward the serious. What happens when droughts and floods take their inevitable toll? Will there be enough food to feed our children and grandchildren? Keep at it long enough and you might find yourself reaching for a nice glass of wine to take the edge off. Sorry to disappoint, but the vineyard that supplied that lovely Brunello or Côtes du Rhône you just uncorked may be as endangered as the Kansas Corn Belt.

As any vintner knows, wine grapes are one of the most finicky crops you can grow, acutely sensitive to even the most minute changes in temperature, sunshine and moisture. The slightest year-to-year variation in any of these factors can mean the difference between an outstanding vintage and an indifferent one, which is why year-to-year changes in the weather are such a critical component of winemaking. But when you start talking about multiple-degree changes in average temperatures, the discussion is no longer about the difference between one vintage and another. Instead, you are talking about changes of a whole other magnitude.

Unfortunately for wine lovers such as myself, the climate in most of the world's primary wine-producing regions is going to become increasingly hostile to viniculture. The Mediterranean region, traditional home of the world's wine industry, is expected to be hit the hardest, losing as much as a third of its rainfall. Studies suggest that over the next century, Bordeaux, the Rhône and Tuscany, three of Europe's top wine-growing regions, could lose as much as 85 percent of their wine-growing acreage. The impact will be only marginally less severe in places such as Australia and California, which in recent decades have challenged the supremacy of European wines.[21] Each could lose as much as 70 percent of its land suited for vineyards. California's grape growers will need to hunker close to the coast or to the Oregon border to the north. Another study, this one by Stanford University, predicted that California's premium grape-growing territory could be cut in half within thirty years.[22] The cape area of South Africa is also expected to lose over half of its wine-grape acreage, while Chile will lose somewhere between 25 and 40 percent of its wine-growing terrain.

In most if not all cases, water will be more of an issue than temperature. Higher temperatures will increase evaporation of soil moisture, while simultaneously reducing precipitation. If California, for example, is to maintain its current area of cultivation, it will require massive amounts of imported water to douse its otherwise withering vineyards.

All other things being equal, these developments mean we'll be drinking a lot less wine in the future. But as we've already seen with the upward creep of North America's Corn Belt, all things will not remain equal. While changes in temperature and precipitation will render vast swaths of land through Bordeaux and Napa unsuitable for growing grapes, those same changes will simultaneously make other places more suitable. Much of the wine we'll be drinking in the decades to come will hail from strange new appellations.

Viniculture, like most agriculture, will generally shift from low-latitude regions to much higher-latitude areas. Move some 1,500 kilometres north of Napa's increasingly sun-baked and water-deprived vineyards and a changing climate is doing wonders for grape growers and winemakers in British Columbia's Okanagan Valley. The growing of wine varietals in the Okanagan is a relatively new development, with commercial activity not really taking hold until the 1960s. Since then, though, the region has seen explosive growth in its wine production—and a warming climate deserves most of the credit. The Okanagan region has seen above-average warming compared with the rest of the province, in terms of both maximum and minimum temperatures.

When it comes to growing most wine grapes, it's the bone-chilling winter lows that are most devastating to rootstocks. Rising winter temperatures, more than soaring summer highs, have made the greatest difference to viniculture in the Okanagan. In the past, the region's fledgling wine production was vulnerable to harsh winters, as evidenced in both 1968 and 1978, when severe freezes wiped out a significant portion of the vines. But since then, warming winters and a steadily extended growing season have allowed wine production to flourish—including varietals such as Merlot and Cabernet Sauvignon, both of which require a longer growing season.

And the region is expected to become even more suitable for wine cultivation in the future. Average temperatures in the Okanagan are expected to rise between 1.2 and 2.7 degrees Celsius by mid-century, which in turn would extend the frost-free growing season by anywhere from fourteen to thirty-seven days. The constraint, as we've seen elsewhere, will be water. Even in northern latitudes, warming temperatures are likely to lead to increasing soil moisture evaporation, resulting in a large increase in irrigation requirements. Within the next decade, the demand for crop water in the Okanagan could spike by as much as 20 percent; by 2050, it's expected to rise by almost 40 percent.

The Okanagan is not the only region in Canada where vintners have welcomed a changing climate. The wine industry has also flourished in southern Ontario, in regions such as the Niagara Peninsula and, more recently, Prince Edward County (along the northeastern shore of Lake Ontario). Like the Okanagan, the Niagara Peninsula was traditionally a fruit-growing area. Wine production has ramped up since the 1960s and 1970s, with the area originally producing what could only be described as "schlock wines"—the kind sold in cartons and consumed by college kids on camping trips.

But as in British Columbia, the southern Ontario industry matured and started producing more serious wines. Its signature product—ice wines made from the harvest of frozen Riesling or Vidal grapes—has become world renowned. While warming temperatures will improve the cultivation of red wine grapes here, there is a certain irony in the fact that the region's claim to fame may be forced to move north. Ice wine grapes need to be harvested at between minus-8 and minus-11 degrees Celsius for best results, and those kinds of January lows are predicted to become less common in Niagara in the future. Vintners are already considering shifting some of their ice wine production to more northern locations, such as Grey County on Georgian Bay.

The huge expansion of wine production from the Okanagan and Niagara regions in recent decades is only the beginning. According to a comprehensive US study, Canada could be one of the world's biggest beneficiaries when it comes to the geographical movement of viniculture.[23] The Okanagan and the Niagara Peninsula may represent only a fraction of the acreage that will be devoted to cultivating wine grapes in years to come. Already, vineyards are popping up in Nova Scotia's Annapolis Valley.

Wine lovers may be looking forward to tasting the unique nuances of new appellations from high-latitude vineyards where grapes have never been grown before, but environmentalists are considerably less thrilled. They're concerned about what the warming climate will do to wildlife. A joint American-Canadian grassroots environmental initiative, dubbed Y2Y, is trying to establish a wildlife corridor from Yellowstone National Park in Wyoming all the way up to the Yukon Territory to preserve habitat for animals that will likely be migrating in response to dramatic climate transformations. The potential northern expansion of agriculture could turn significant swaths of the boreal forest's wildlife habitat into wheat fields or even corn-growing areas. Some have even speculated that viniculture may eventually take root in the north.

If you take a look at the latitudes where wine grapes are likely to be grown in the future (for example, northern England), you might be surprised at what could be grown in sections of Canada's vast boreal forests, where soil conditions permit. Will Merlot soon be displacing moose as Château Rothschild gives way to Château McMurray?

It's intriguing to speculate about the future of Canadian agriculture, and the significant and varied opportunities that climate change will bring. Answering nature's call, however, is no slam dunk for Canadian farmers. Rising temperatures and lengthened growing seasons may indeed open up new vistas, but crop decisions—be they related to wheat, corn or grapes—will continue to depend critically on the availability of water.

CHAPTER 12

WATERWORKS

A THIN BLUE LINE separates abundance from desolation—on one side, a verdant mosaic of luscious crops; on the other, a barren, sun-baked wasteland of foreboding desert. The blue line that separates these two worlds is the All-American Canal—a 30-metre-wide marvel of engineering that is the longest irrigation canal on the planet. It snakes across the Sonoran Desert for 130 kilometres, bringing water to a region that nature has given none (the average annual rainfall here is just 7.6 centimetres).

Before the canal was built, this remote stretch of southwestern California was known as the Valley of Death, an apt-enough name for a place whose soaring temperatures and lack of water snuffed out many a desperate settler heading for the coast. But after the canal was completed in 1942, and began siphoning off millions of acre-feet of precious water every year from the Colorado River, that deadly desert was transformed into agricultural gold. The Imperial Valley, as it's now known, is one of America's great breadbaskets.

Today, the Imperial Valley is a half-million-acre oasis in the middle of the enormous desert that rises in Mexico and spills across the border into Arizona and California. If you're buying lettuce in a supermarket in Toronto or New York in the middle of January, chances are it was grown in this valley. The region supplies 80 percent of North America's fresh vegetables during the winter.

As for the canal itself, it has the dubious distinction of being America's most dangerous waterway. Through much of its course, the All-American Canal traces the US-Mexican border. The steep walls on either side of the channel, together with the cold and relatively swift current (the Colorado drops nearly 4,000 metres from the high Rockies), have proven to be a death trap for illegal migrants seeking entry to the United States. More than five hundred have died attempting to cross.[1]

But for farmers, the canal has been nothing short of a lifeline. Massive water diversion for irrigation — not only to the Imperial Valley but also to the Central Valley, its much bigger cousin — has enabled California to become the leading agricultural producer in a country that is itself the world's largest food supplier, producing nearly $330 billion worth of agricultural commodities each year.[2]

The miracle of irrigation is nothing new. Egyptian and Mesopotamian farmers were diverting water from the Nile as far back as 6000 BC, and the Hanging Gardens of Babylon — one of the Seven Wonders of the World — were watered by a complex irrigation system. Now, more than eight thousand years after those first canals were dug, our warming climate will make irrigation even more crucial. As we've seen, climate change will soon shift where food can be grown, and the new places that feature lengthened growing seasons and milder temperatures may not always be endowed with abundant supplies of water.

And as always, there will be competing uses for the water that is available. Ironically, one of the biggest competitors will be the very carbon industry whose emissions are driving climate change. The energy sector is very thirsty. It takes a lot of water to frack shale formations, and a lot more to grow biofuels like corn-based ethanol.

The FAO estimates that over 10 percent of cropland in developed countries has already been converted from producing food to producing biofuels.[3] According to the IEA, the energy sector already accounts for approximately 15 percent of the world's water use,[4] and the amount used in energy production will double from 66 billion cubic metres a year to 135 billion by 2035.[5] To put that number in perspective, it is equivalent to three years' worth of residential water consumption for every person in the United States. In a world with a skyrocketing population that will be in need of an ever-greater food supply, those statistics could be problematic indeed.

"GO ON, NOW. EAT YOUR WATER."

You might not recognize it when you're chomping on an ear of corn or tucking into a plate of pasta, but it takes an enormous amount of water to grow what is on your plate. When you're pondering the inputs that go into producing corn or wheat, it's likely that seeds, soil or even the land itself come quickly to mind; it's easy to forget the litres and litres of fresh water required. But we shouldn't forget, given that agriculture typically accounts for over 70 percent of water usage in most countries. This overwhelming dependence on the wet stuff means that a desert country like Saudi Arabia has to buy land in places like Ethiopia or Sudan in order to grow its food supply. Back in 1985, Saudi Arabia began an irrigation program with a view to becoming self-sufficient in wheat. Turns out that when you live in a desert and you try to grow your own food, you very quickly suck your aquifers dry of whatever fossil water nature has given you. In 2014, the Saudi government wisely announced that the kingdom was abandoning wheat cultivation.[6]

In distinct contrast to Saudi Arabia, Canada has more water than its agricultural sector can use; by some estimates, farming uses less than 10 percent of the country's total supply. Canadian food production, however, is limited by climate. If Canada had the growing season of Saudi Arabia, it wouldn't be the planet's eighth-largest exporter of food.[7] Instead, it would supplant America as the world's leading agricultural exporter. Alternatively, if Saudi Arabia had Canada's water, the desert kingdom could easily look like the Imperial Valley.

If one thinks about agricultural production in these terms, food is actually the embodiment of highly processed water. And if that's the case, then exporting food is really just a value-added way of exporting H_2O, in much the same way that exporting petrochemicals is a value-added way to export bitumen. Most of us don't think of food in those terms—at least not yet—but we will when we start making full use of Canada's greatest resource.

To get there, we'll have to overcome some pretty ingrained biases. For most Canadians, the notion of bulk water exports has traditionally been viewed as something akin to the rape of the country's most treasured resource. These same folk, however, have never been opposed to selling water in the form of wheat, lentils or canola. In fact, both federal and provincial governments have set up all kinds of programs to support farm exports, not the least of which was the creation of the Canadian Wheat Board.

Let's take a closer look at wheat. It takes a whopping 1,500 litres of water to grow a kilogram of wheat on the Canadian prairies. So when you are exporting wheat, what you're really doing is exporting processed water. In this sense, at least, the country is already a major water exporter—whether Canadians recognize it or not. In 2010, the country exported 78 billion cubic metres of water in the form of agricultural produce (the water needed to grow it). Based on that figure, Canada is already the third-largest water exporter in the world.[8]

ALL THE RIGHT STUFF IN ALL THE WRONG PLACES

It's really not at all surprising that Canada could benefit from exporting water—in either its straight-up or its value-added form. The country has a heck of a lot of the stuff. Depending on which definition you care to use, Canada has somewhere between 7 and 20 percent of the world's fresh water supply. The higher estimate refers to total fresh water resources, including the water frozen in glaciers and icefields as well as so-called fossil water in lakes and underground aquifers. The lower estimate refers to the country's far more accessible share of the world's renewable fresh water that is replenished through precipitation.

By either measure, it's a lot of water for a country of 35 million—a figure that represents only one half of 1 percent of the global population of 7 billion. In per capita terms, it makes Canada the Saudi Arabia of fresh water. And just as Saudi Arabia is a world leader in oil consumption per capita, Canada racks up an impressive ranking when it comes to how much water each of us sucks up.[9]

All of that water is a good thing, undoubtedly, and in a world where water can be turned into increasingly expensive food, we should be thanking our lucky stars that geography has endowed us with the natural resources we currently possess. But the story is not that simple. The trick with Canadian water (or any water, really) is that it doesn't always flow to where it is needed, or where it can best be put to use. Consider that more than half of Canada's water supply drains north, either directly into the Arctic Ocean or into Hudson Bay. The rivers of the Mackenzie basin, for example, dump over 7,000 cubic metres of fresh water into the Arctic Ocean every second—out of reach of more than 85 percent of the country's population.[10] A second but no less serious challenge is that Canada, with all of its water, just happens to be located on the other side of an invisible line, one that separates us from the much larger and thirstier American population to the south. Most agriculture in western Canada occurs within a 450-kilometre band north of the forty-ninth parallel.[11] That's a pretty thin strip of a country that stretches some 4,634 kilometres from north to south.[12] Furthermore, some of that prime agricultural land is water-stressed. Southern Alberta's South Saskatchewan River basin, for example, holds the province's most productive land and contains almost all of its 2 million acres under irrigation. While less than 4 percent of arable land in Alberta is irrigated, that 4 percent produces a fifth of the province's total agricultural output.[13]

Of all the rivers that drain eastward from the Continental Divide that runs along the spine of the Rockies, none is more important than the Saskatchewan. The Canadian province takes its name from the river that in Cree means "fast running water." It is as important to farmers in the Canadian prairies as the Colorado is to farmers in the US Southwest. And just like the Colorado, it runs through a number of different jurisdictions, with a drainage area that covers much of Alberta, Saskatchewan and southern Manitoba, and even extends into Montana.

The Saskatchewan is more a river system than a single river. Its two branches—the North and the South Saskatchewan—both rise from the glacial melt and run off from the icefields that straddle the Canadian Rockies. The fields are a remnant of past ice ages, but lately they have been shrinking to dimensions not seen in millennia. The Athabasca glacier—one of the Columbia icefield's most accessible, and the source of the water that the massive oil sands development depends on for its operations—has retreated one and a half kilometres since it was first measured in 1843, and has lost 60 percent of its volume. Meltwater from the icefields is declining at its fastest rate in the last hundred years, as are the icefields themselves. Ancient tree stumps, once entombed, are now visible for the first time since the last ice age. The culprit is warmer winters, which today produce far less snow than in the past; snow is the source for the field's ice.[14]

The North Saskatchewan flows from its glacial headwater in Alberta's Banff National Park. From the toe of the Saskatchewan glacier, it passes through the city of Edmonton then meanders across central Alberta and into Saskatchewan before joining with the South Saskatchewan about 30 kilometres east of Prince Albert, a journey of almost 1,300 kilometres.

The South Saskatchewan also has its headwaters in the eastern Rockies, starting with the glacial melt carried by its tributary the Bow River. After running through Calgary, the Bow heads south and meets the Oldman River near Grassy Lake, Alberta. The South Saskatchewan is born from the junction of those two rivers, flowing over 1,300 kilometres through southern Alberta and into Saskatchewan before meeting the northern branch at Saskatchewan Forks. After the two branches merge in central Saskatchewan, the river flows another 550 kilometres before draining into Lake Winnipeg. From there, the water travels via the lake's major outlet, the Nelson River, which discharges an average of 2,370 cubic metres of fresh water every second into Hudson Bay.

A little over a century ago, the Saskatchewan River supported huge herds of wild buffalo that roamed the grasslands. Today, those fertile grasslands have been tilled and converted into valuable farmland, and the river supports the breadbasket of an entire country. The Prairies hold 82 percent of the country's farmland;[15] at the same time, however, they are Canada's driest region. Without the Saskatchewan River's life-giving water, the Prairies wouldn't be producing a fraction of the food they now grow.

No province depends on the river more than Alberta. Alberta has more arable land than any other province aside from Saskatchewan. It also has 60 percent of all the irrigated farmland in the country (throw in the other two Prairie provinces and you're talking about three-quarters of all Canada's irrigated farmland).[16] As it turns out, Alberta needs irrigation ditches as badly as it needs pipelines.

But the meltwaters from the snowpack in the eastern Rockies—water that prairie agriculture is critically dependent on for irrigation—are already a casualty of a warming climate, and the situation will only get worse. There are water stresses in southern Alberta as reduced snowfall, and hence mountain runoff, has led to declining streams flowing from rivers such as the Bow, Milk and Oldman. At the same time, a warmer and drier climate has meant that evapotranspiration (water lost to the atmosphere as a result of evaporation and transpiration by plants) draws off 50 percent more water from southwestern Alberta farms than it did a century ago.[17]

Farmers already siphon off no less than 2.2 billion cubic metres every year from the South Saskatchewan River for irrigation, roughly 30 percent of the river's total flow.[18] As irrigation needs grow, perhaps exponentially, more and more attention is going to be focused on water diversion. Aside from a slice of southeastern Alberta and southwestern Saskatchewan that is part of the Missouri River basin, all the water flowing across the Prairies heads either to the Arctic or to Hudson Bay. It's not too hard to figure out where the water to meet tomorrow's irrigation needs is going to come from. Moving water to booming areas of agricultural production may become as important to tomorrow's Canadian economy as moving oil is to today's.

Just as the South and the North Saskatchewan Rivers drain the southern and middle runoff from the Rockies, the Athabasca and the Peace capture its more northern drainage. Both rise in the Rockies and flow into Lake Athabasca and then, ultimately, out the Mackenzie River to the Arctic Ocean. That water, however, may soon be coveted by farmers in the southern and much drier portions of the province.

The Peace River is certainly no stranger to waterworks. It's already home to two hydroelectric power stations and dams, and the provincial government in BC is currently mulling over a proposal for a third: the $7-billion-plus Site C dam and power station project that has already passed a provincial environmental assessment review.[19] In 1968, the province built what was eventually named the W.A.C.

Bennett Dam and the G.M. Shrum Generating Station, and in the process flooded some 1,700 square kilometres to create Lake Williston, a 250-kilometre-long lake that, at its widest point, stretches 155 kilometres. In 1980, it built the Peace Canyon Dam, creating a 21-kilometre-long reservoir, Dinosaur Lake.

The Athabasca, too, is Arctic-bound. It comes crashing out of the Rockies then plunges over the Athabasca Falls into the boreal forest. It starts off fresh and clean in Jasper National Park, but that's hardly how it ends. Its once-pristine flow of glacial meltwater is soon poisoned by the effluent from the oil sands. Deformed whitefish downstream in Lake Athabasca are testament to mercury levels up to thirty times greater than permitted by pollution guidelines.[20] In 2011, some 170 million cubic metres were sucked from the river for oil sands operations, an amount equivalent to the yearly domestic water usage of 1.7 million Canadians.[21] In a world of falling oil prices but rising food prices, farmers in the southern portion of the province may have more productive uses for that water.

With irrigation water becoming ever more scarce, it's only a matter of time before prairie farmers start looking at all the water flowing out to Hudson Bay and the Arctic and wishing it could be flowing their way instead.[22]

THIRSTY NEIGHBOURS

Chances are good that Canada's farmers won't be the only ones eyeing that water. Back in 2008, Peter Lougheed told the *Globe and Mail* that the United States would soon be coming after our water, and that we needed to prepare: "With climate change and growing needs, Canadians will need all the fresh water we can conserve, particularly in the western provinces . . . I hope that when the time comes, Canada will be ready. The reality is that fresh water is more valuable than crude oil."[23]

In early 2014, Lougheed's musings were echoed in surprisingly candid remarks from Gary Doer, Canada's ambassador to the United States and a former Manitoba premier. Doer predicted that current disputes between the two countries over pipelines and oil sands would soon pale in comparison with looming conflicts over water. Perhaps even more alarming was his prediction that those conflicts could be coming as soon as by the end of this decade.[24]

In fact, there have already been a number of minor skirmishes between the two countries over the shared resource. Doer's home province was involved in a tiff with neighbouring North Dakota about water diversions into the Red River. There have been a few scuffles over managed water levels in the shared Lake of the Woods and its drainage through the Winnipeg River system. There is the coming renegotiation of the Columbia River Treaty, which involves major-league water flows. And then there is the ever-present threat of water diversions from the jointly managed Great Lakes Basin. But as Doer warned, today's differences are likely to seem insignificant down the road, when demands for major inter-basin diversions— code words for redirecting water from its natural flow—could see massive amounts of Canadian water diverted to parched American landscapes.

Of course, the United States has its own considerable fresh water resources. By some estimates those resources are almost as large as Canada's. After all, over 50 percent of the Great Lakes are found in American territory. But the population of the USA is almost ten times that of Canada. Further exacerbating the issue is that the United States—the world's largest food producer, remember—has chosen to turn vast areas of desert scrub brush into prime agricultural land, a feat dependent upon massive water diversion and irrigation systems.

Water stresses have been building throughout the largely semi-arid region of the western United States for decades now. The massive Ogallala Aquifer, principal water source for no fewer than eight

western states and for much of the irrigation of the US wheat and
Corn Belt, is being drained at eight times the rate of replenishment.
Water tables in Texas, Oklahoma and Nebraska, three key grain-
growing states, have dropped by more than 30 metres.[25] Nearly one-
third of the Kansas portion of the Ogallala Aquifer has already been
pumped out. At current rates of water extraction, another 40 percent
will be gone by 2040, pointing to a peak in the state's agricultural production within the next two decades.

Other states are faring worse. Over the last three years, California
has experienced the worst drought in its modern history—a situation
that has left state reservoirs less than half full. Shasta Lake, the
state's largest reservoir, is down to 36 percent capacity, while the
second-largest reservoir, Lake Oroville, has dropped over 10 metres
and is down to a third of its capacity.[26]

Governor Jerry Brown has already declared a state of emergency,
calling for Californians to reduce their water use by 20 percent and
directing state officials to prepare for widespread water shortages.[27]
Some 70 percent of California's territory is experiencing either extreme
or exceptional drought—the two most severe classifications used by
the US Drought Monitor. In 2014, the California Farm Bureau predicted that as much as 500,000 acres of prime agricultural land would
go unplanted owing to a lack of water for irrigation. Thousands of
homeowners in California have torn out their lawns in an effort to
comply with increasingly stringent water rationing directives from
local authorities.[28]

And it's likely to get worse. Measurements by California's Department of Water Resources in January 2015 indicated that the water
trapped in mountain snowpacks is just a quarter of normal levels at
that time of year. Mountain snows account for a third of the state's
water supply, and January is typically the state's wettest month.[29]
Climate change models point to a warmer and even drier US Southwest in the future. It's worth noting that this area is home to some

91 million Americans.[30] As drought conditions threaten irrigation and food production all the way from the Midwest Corn Belt to California's breadbasket Central Valley, demands for inter-basin water transfers will rise. If you look at a water map of North America, it's not too hard to figure out where most of the water will be coming from. And it's sure not hard to imagine that the warnings from Lougheed and Doer were right.

SHARING THE WEALTH?

With a border that stretches 8,891 kilometres across the continent, it's no surprise that Canada and the USA share many watersheds. None, of course, is more important than the Great Lakes, home to the largest concentration of fresh water in the world. The joint management of this massive resource was set out more than a century ago in the historic International Boundary Waters Treaty Act of 1909. In 2001, Canada amended the act to explicitly prohibit bulk removal of water from the country in any of the watersheds shared with its neighbour to the south.

If Canadians seem a little paranoid about protecting our fresh water resources, we have good reason to be. Some of the schemes proposed over the years to divert water from Canada to the United States have been downright pharaonic.

NAWAPA (*North American Water and Power Alliance*)

It was hatched deep in the bowels of the Los Angeles Department of Water and Power in the early 1950s. The state was experiencing one of its recurrent droughts, forcing another round of water rationing that would pit the city's ever-growing water needs against those of surrounding farmers. Donald Baker, a planning engineer, had a vision so sweeping in scope that it would not only solve his city's chronic water problems but reshape the way water flowed across the entire continent.

For drought-stricken Californians, the snowmelt coming off the mountains that run along the western coastline of the continent was a precious resource going to waste, flowing, as it did, down watersheds that all drained into the Pacific Ocean. The Fraser River's outflow into the Pacific is greater than the entire runoff of California, while the Skeena's almost matches that of Texas.[31] The Pacific Ocean, Baker thought, had more than enough water. Farmers and communities in California and throughout the US Southwest, on the other hand, were battling each other over scarce water rights. Redirecting wasted water flows to more useful purposes would involve the greatest hydro engineering project the world had ever witnessed.

Salmon, steelhead and other spawning fish in these rivers might challenge Baker's definition of a "useful purpose" for water flow, but the needs of those species didn't register very highly on the LA water department's list of priorities at the time. They still don't. Water levels in California rivers such as the Sacramento are so low that not only are mature fish unable to swim upstream to spawn, but tiny fry can't swim downstream to get to the ocean. It's got so bad that the only native river water most salmon fry get to swim in is the stuff filling the barrels that wildlife officials use to transport them to the sea.

Baker's grand vision was grand indeed: it involved redirecting much of the water flow of Alaska, the Yukon and British Columbia. Such huge rivers as the Yukon, the Liard and the Peace would be diverted from their natural ocean-bound route through a series of huge reservoirs. Many would have exceeded the size of Lake Meade, America's largest impoundment, created by damming the Colorado River in the Grand Canyon. The biggest of NAWAPA's proposed reservoirs—a more than 800-kilometre-long behemoth created by flooding the Rocky Mountain Trench in central British Columbia—would have been *sixteen times* the size of Lake Meade.

It also would have flooded much of the province's interior, including the city of Prince George.

You can imagine the size of the dams needed to create those mega-reservoirs. NAWAPA featured 369 separate construction projects. Many of the proposed dams would have dwarfed anything the US Bureau of Reclamation had built up to that time, including the Grand Coulee Dam on the Columbia, or the Hoover or Glen Canyon Dams that had tamed the once-feral Colorado. Indeed, these colossi of American engineering would have measured as mid-sized dams compared with the monuments that NAWAPA had on the drawing board.

According to Baker's plot, some of the water would be diverted along the Peace River, which would connect to a 25-metre-wide and 10-metre-deep transcontinental canal cutting across the Canadian prairies and ultimately pouring into Lake Superior, connecting Alberta—and the meltwater coming off the Rockies—with the Great Lakes. Another branch would link up with the Mississippi. The diverted flow would have been sufficient to raise water levels in all of the Great Lakes (which even then was an issue of concern) and double the electric power output at Niagara Falls. Water diversion to the Mississippi basin would have raised the river's depth enough to allow ocean-bound freighters to travel as far upriver as St. Louis.

The rest of the water would be diverted to the Southwest, using tunnels through the Sawtooth mountain range in Idaho, and ultimately to California. No fewer than six nuclear stations would provide the power needed to drive the million-horsepower pumps that would push water over the St. Elias Mountains (Canada's highest range) and then later over the US Rockies so it could be diverted into the Colorado and the Rio Grande basins. Some of the water would travel from as far north as the Yukon River all the way to Mexico via the resulting enhanced water flow from rivers like the Colorado.

Baker took his bold plan to a Pasadena engineering firm, whose founder, Ralph Parsons, quickly became enthralled with the idea and made it a lifelong obsession. He created a foundation called the North American Water and Power Alliance — or NAWAPA, as it was known — to lobby for the grand scheme's implementation. Not surprisingly, the idea was popular among US politicians from the water-deprived Southwest. Secretary of State Dean Rusk was enamoured of the plan's sweeping ambition to divert otherwise "wasted" water to thirsty US farmers and households. At one point, even the Canadian prime minister, Lester Pearson, was quoted as saying that NAWAPA "can be one of the most important developments in our history."[32]

As it turned out, it wasn't.

Environmentalists on both sides of the border were horrified by what implementing the plan would do to the watersheds of the Pacific Northwest. Both the upper Fraser and the Columbia rivers would have disappeared within the newly formed contours of a mega-reservoir running hundreds of kilometres through flooded landscape. The plan would have wiped out the entire salmon fishery on the Pacific coast. Every major river from Alaska to Vancouver would have been dammed, including those with world-renowned salmon runs, such as the Fraser, Stikine, Dean, Skeena and Chilcotin. In the United States, a number of treasured scenic rivers — including the Salmon, Lochsa and Yellowstone — would also have disappeared within the contours of huge reservoirs.

Opposition was greatest in Canada, where, as we've seen, the notion of bulk water shipments to the States was and still is viewed with deep suspicion — even if such a move were to produce significant economic benefits. And to be sure, Canada *was* to receive significant economic benefits under the plan; in fact, by some measures, Canada would have received more benefits than the United States. The country would have gained 38 million kilowatts of additional electrical power from the new dams. Alberta and Saskatchewan would have received 19 million acre-feet of new irrigation water. And through a maze of interlocking canals, the resource-rich northern Canadian hinterlands, like Ontario's Ring of Fire, would have gained shipping access to the Mississippi and, ultimately, the Gulf of Mexico.

In the end, however, NAWAPA was simply too expensive. Even back in the 1970s, the cost of the project was pegged at $100 billion — over $400 billion in today's dollars, and roughly the same amount that was spent on building the Interstate Highway System. For all of its sweeping vision and supporters in the US Southwest, the scheme never got off the ground.

WATER WARS

Will a warming planet revive plans like NAWAPA? Or will new, hitherto unimaginable schemes find their way onto the table? When we take into account the growing population and the havoc climate change is going to wreak on the world's breadbaskets, it's not too hard to imagine that water diversion—with its inevitable ecological and social fallout—will replace pipelines as the environmental movement's key battlefront.

It's also not hard to imagine that environmentalists will have some company on the front lines. The minute you start talking about inter-basin water transfers, you are talking about conflict. And that conflict isn't necessarily the Canada–USA showdown that Gary Doer warned about. With the exception of the Milk River, which drains south into the Missouri, all watersheds in the region are wholly in Canadian territory.

But that fluke of geography means nothing when it comes to disputes. When you divert water upstream, the action has consequences downstream, even if downstream is in the same community. And when upstream and downstream communities happen to lie in different provinces? Well, then you have the makings of an inter-provincial conflict.

The United States provides some textbook examples of what the coming water wars might look like. Even a cursory examination at the long history of water diversion from the Colorado River underscores the tensions that can arise. In California—which was literally populated and built thanks to massive water diversion to the southern regions of the state—there has always been bad blood between the farmers and the city-dwellers competing for the state's scarce water supplies. That conflict was dramatized in the 1974 film classic *Chinatown*, in which Hollis Mulwray, chief engineer of the Los Angeles Department of Water and Power (the birthplace of NAWAPA), is murdered in a sinister plot to divert the city's water to thirsty orange groves in the surrounding countryside.

Like the waterways themselves, the fight for fresh water often crosses state lines. In the case of the Colorado, no fewer than seven states have laid claim to the water flowing through the river's watersheds: Colorado, Utah, Wyoming, New Mexico, Nevada, Arizona and, of course, California, which has siphoned off the lion's share of the river's once-mighty flow. By the time the Colorado empties into Mexico's Sea of Cortez, it's been reduced to a small stream; in some years, it's virtually dry. Disputes over water usage by the states in the Colorado basin have frequently landed in federal court.

Canada's Prairie provinces should take note. As irrigation claims on the Saskatchewan and other prairie rivers mushroom in the face of a warming climate, those types of conflicts may soon be heading north. The more water Alberta takes upstream, the less will be available to divert to farmers downstream in Saskatchewan and Manitoba.

It's possible that things won't get quite as dicey in Canada as they are in the USA. Alberta's take from the all-important Saskatchewan River is limited by an arrangement with neighbouring Saskatchewan that guarantees the latter no less than 50 percent of the river's flow. The apportioning ratios stem from a 1948 agreement between the federal government and the provincial governments of Alberta, Saskatchewan and Manitoba that established the Prairie Provinces Water Board (PPWB)—a body that jointly administers the management of watersheds across the region. But will that agreement stand in the face of the mounting need for irrigation that climate change will bring?

Only time will tell. Canada, as we've seen, is well positioned to take advantage of the sea change that a warming climate is about to unleash on agricultural production. Blessed with both an abundant supply of fresh water and vast amounts of land that may soon be better suited to grow much-needed and increasingly lucrative crops like corn, this country could find that there is a lot more economic value added—and a lot more jobs created—by exporting highly processed water in the form of food than through bulk water exports, all the more so in a world of rising food prices. However it shakes out, one thing is clear: water is the key. And if that's the case, it's entirely possible that the PPWB—now an obscure regulatory body that most Canadians have never heard of—may soon have the same prominence as today's National Energy Board.

CHAPTER 13

POWER PLAYS

VALUE-ADDED WATER EXPORTS in the form of food may be an opportunity-in-waiting for Canada's economy, but it's not the only prospect on the table. Water, after all, is a multi-tasking element, and irrigation is just one of its many uses. Donald Baker undoubtedly had parched acres of farmland uppermost in his mind when he hatched his grandiose water diversion scheme, but the implementation of that scheme would have both depended on and unleashed a massive amount of hydro power. Some sixty years later, that same power source is being considered with increasing favour by a world looking to drastically cut carbon emissions.

As we saw in chapter 2, however, not every country has the ability to take advantage of the relatively clean energy that hydro provides. Canada does. In fact, Canada has been harnessing the power of its rivers for almost as long as it's been a country. In 1881, the Ottawa Electric Light Company installed a water wheel at Chaudière Falls on the Ottawa River; the resulting power was used for street lights and local mills. Today, with the exception of Prince Edward Island, every province in Canada produces hydro power. In fact, when it comes to global ranking, Canada turns out to be a much greater hydro power than it is a petro power. Some 475 hydroelectric power

stations scattered across the country produce more than 370 terawatts
of power every year. It's an amount that puts Canada second only to
China. Hydroelectric power currently accounts for over 60 percent of
Canada's electricity generation, and that percentage is almost certain
to grow in the future.[1]

It's one thing to be blessed—as Canada clearly is—with an
abundance of the very resource one needs in order to become a
hydro power; it's another thing altogether actually to turn that
blessing into a long-standing and effective source of power. The
fact that Canada has managed to do so stems in part from the same
type of pie-in-the-sky dreaming that inspired Donald Baker and his
NAWAPA plans.

GRAND-IOSE PLANS

About five years after the LA Department of Water and Power brain-
stormed the broad outlines of NAWAPA, a Canadian mining engineer on the other side of the continent was thinking similar grand
thoughts. Thomas Kierans had grown up in the dust bowls of the
1930s and saw first-hand the growing need for fresh water supplies
for farmers across North America. In 1959, he proposed a water
diversion scheme for James Bay that rivalled in scale NAWAPA's
ideas for rechannelling water on the western side of the continent.

The Great Recycling and Northern Development Canal, or
GRAND as it became known, would have converted James Bay into
an enormous fresh water lake by sealing off its entrance to Hudson
Bay through a network of sea-level dikes. In effect, the scheme
meant recycling the entire James Bay watershed by capturing the out-
flows of a massive drainage area of the La Grande, Eastmain, Rupert,
Broadback, Nottaway and Harricana Rivers in Quebec, and the
Moose, Albany, Kapiskau, Attawapiskat and Ekwan Rivers in Ontario.
In total, the project would have captured and redirected almost

20 percent of the entire fresh water supply of the provinces of Ontario and Quebec.

Once collected in James Lake—the new fresh water body created out of the diked James Bay—the water would have been pumped south into the Harricana River and ultimately to Lake Timiskaming and the connecting Ottawa River, where it would then cross over to Lake Nipissing and through the French River into Georgian Bay and Lake Huron.

Like NAWAPA's master plan, GRAND would have significantly raised water levels throughout the Great Lakes by pouring in the equivalent of two and a half times the flow of Niagara Falls. Once levels there had been raised sufficiently, subsequent flow would have been redirected to western farmers in both Canada and the United States through an interlocking network of canals.

All of that pumping and redirecting—back over the James Bay watershed and into the Great Lakes basin—would have been powered by multiple nuclear power plants, ensuring that GRAND, like NAWAPA before it, wouldn't come cheap: in the early 1990s, it would have cost some $100 billion to build.

Kierans's Great Recycling and Northern Development project never got off the drawing board. It did, however, attract the attention of then Quebec premier Robert Bourassa, who commissioned some feasibility studies on the project. What Bourassa really had in mind, though, was an entirely different plan for the James Bay watershed. With the help of one of the world's largest hydroelectric sites—built and run, naturally, by Hydro-Québec—Bourassa dreamed of harnessing the energy created by all that water. Instead of exporting *water* south, Quebec would export *power*.

During the 1970s and 1980s, no fewer than eight power stations were built along the La Grande system, with a combined power capacity of over 16,000 megawatts. In order to increase water flow through the stations, the neighbouring Eastmain and Caniapiscau Rivers were diverted into the La Grande. The biggest of the projects was the massive Robert-Bourassa Dam, which still ranks among the world's ten largest. It's an engineering marvel. Carved into the side of a mountain, the dam reaches 140 metres below the surface, giving it bragging rights as the world's largest underground plant. From a height equivalent to Niagara Falls, the water tumbles down a "giant's staircase" (each "step" is the size of two football fields) at a discharge rate of 16,280 cubic metres of water per second—about twice the flow of the St. Lawrence at Montreal.[2]

In addition to generating a steady stream of much-needed export revenues, Bourassa's plan also gave the province a supply of relatively cheap power for its own domestic needs. Hydroelectric stations in the James Bay watershed now provide almost half of the power produced in the province. Quebec has one of the lowest domestic power rates on the continent. And no doubt thanks to that cheap hydro, Quebecers consume more power than anybody else in the world. Per capita electricity consumption in the province is double that of Ontario and three times that of New York, neither of which are shining examples of energy conservation.[3]

TWO SOLITUDES

While hydro power seems an obvious replacement for either coal- or gas-fired power in an emissions-constrained world, further growth in hydro power in Canada is more likely to come at the expense of nuclear. In part, that is because coal and gas play a much smaller role in power generation in Canada than they do in the United States, so there is much less to replace. Moreover, spare hydro capacity isn't always located near where hydrocarbons are being burnt to generate power.

But nuclear is a whole other story. Ontario, home to all but one of the country's aging nuclear power plants, has wisely put plans to refurbish them on hold. Over the next fifteen years, though, the province will have to overhaul some 8,500 megawatts (roughly one-third of its peak power demand) of nuclear capacity at a staggering cost. The Darlington nuclear power plant just outside Toronto will require a minimum of $13 billion in capital spending if it's going to continue to operate past 2020.[4] And costs of past nuclear projects in Ontario have come in, on average, at two and a half times their original estimate, leaving ratepayers on the hook for stranded debt charges tacked on to their hydro bills.[5]

Instead of committing billions of dollars to refurbishing reactors that no other country in the world has bought in two decades, Ontario premier Kathleen Wynne has wisely chosen to contemplate what no previous Ontario premier has ever been willing to consider: importing surplus hydro power from Quebec.

You might think that option would be a natural one for neighbouring provinces, but Quebec and Ontario have long operated as two solitudes when it comes to coordinating power generation. Quebec, given its natural water resources and topography, has championed hydro while Ontario, home to the CANDU reactor, went nuclear.[6] Cheap and reliable power was considered key to the broader industrial strategies of both provinces. Quebec used its comparative advantage in generating hydro power to attract power-intensive industries like aluminum to its economy. Ontario used the power supplied by Niagara Falls, and later the power from a massive expansion of nuclear energy, to attract industries like auto assembly.

If there was one common denominator between the provinces' power utilities, it was that both Hydro-Québec and Ontario Hydro were permeated with an engineering culture that had only one imperative: build—and do it with little regard for economics. In Ontario, that resulted in too many costly nuclear power plants, based on forecasted power demand growth that never materialized. In Quebec, that same engineering culture resulted in an overbuild of hydro capacity. But economics always finds a way of reasserting itself over time, and at least in Ontario, power costs have risen hand in hand with Ontario's aging nuclear-powered grid.

Instead of producing the "too cheap to meter" power once promised, Ontario's nuclear plants have left Ontario residents paying some of the highest power costs in the country.[7] Premier Wynne's recent overtures to Quebec signal a long-overdue realization that Ontario's traditional pursuit of energy self-sufficiency is a mug's game, at best. What matters today to Ontario households and businesses is the cost of power, not its province of origin. Ontario has already squandered billions of taxpayers' dollars on natural gas–fired power plants that were never built, and the province could potentially squander many more billions on refurbishing aging nuclear stations in a futile bid to preserve what is left of the province's shrinking nuclear industry.

Premier Wynne would be wise to follow Ottawa's lead on the CANDU reactor. The federal government severed its life-support line to the industry back in 2011 when the Atomic Energy Corporation of Canada (a Crown company) sold its CANDU reactor business to SNC-Lavalin for the princely sum of $15 million. Of course, the real motivation for the sale was to get the taxpayer off the hook for subsidizing an ailing nuclear division that had racked up over a billion dollars in losses over the previous five years.

Quebec has sufficient surplus capacity to provide Ontario with almost the entire power output of the Darlington nuclear plant.[8] And it can supply that power for about a third less than the best-cost estimate from a refurbished Darlington.

A deficit-strapped Ontario shouldn't be handing out any more blank cheques to its homegrown nuclear industry. Even the industry's low-ball estimate of $13 billion for the refurbishment of Darlington is more than the province can afford, never mind the inevitable cost overruns. That money would be better earmarked for Premier Wynne's stated priority of funding desperately needed new public transit to redress the now-permanent state of gridlock on roads around the Greater Toronto Area—home to roughly 5 million people. Fortunately, she doesn't have to pour billions more of taxpayers' dollars into the province's nuclear sinkhole. Some estimate a cost as low as $500 million to put in place the transmission system upgrades needed for the province to take full advantage of Quebec's power. That's less than 4 percent of the cost of rebuilding Darlington (again, based on optimistic estimates of the rebuild cost). The investment would pay for itself in less than one year.[9] The Ontario government is not expected to make a final decision on refurbishing the reactors until the first quarter of 2016, following the tabling of final cost estimates for the project.

A WIN-WIN PROPOSITION

Ontario wouldn't be the only winner from an interprovincial deal. Quebec has an abundance of surplus hydro power and urgently needs to find new markets. Its traditional export markets in the northeastern USA are becoming more reliant on the cheap power provided by burning shale gas, available from the Marcellus Formation in nearby states such as Pennsylvania and Ohio. Even states that don't allow fracking of their own shale deposits, like New York, are all too happy to import cheap power from neighbouring states that do.

To stay competitive with cheap gas-fired power, Quebec has had to slash its export prices to the States in half in the last few years. A recent contract signed with Vermont set prices as low as 5.7 cents a kilowatt, some 30 percent lower than the best-case cost estimate from a refurbished Darlington, and likely much lower than the true cost of that nuclear power once the inevitable cost overruns are factored in.[10] But here's something to keep in mind: while cheap electricity from burning shale gas may be the commercial benchmark in today's North American power markets, the goalposts in energy markets, as we have seen before, can shift in a hurry. It wasn't

222 THE CARBON BUBBLE

so long ago, after all, that coal held the same position. Then the regulatory goalposts moved—and quite dramatically. Is it really so far-fetched to imagine that tomorrow's goalposts could move just as much against shale gas and, in the process, open up new export markets for Canadian hydro power?

As we noted earlier, shale's claim of a lighter carbon footprint isn't as straightforward as some might have us believe. One side effect of the far from perfect fracking process is the release into the atmosphere of "fugitive methane"—gas that either isn't captured at the fracking site or leaks away later, during refining or transport. And methane, like most GHGs, is nasty stuff. Although it's got a much shorter shelf life than CO_2, it's also twenty times as damaging to the climate over a period of one hundred years.[11] Add to that the risk of local groundwater contamination as well as fracking-induced seismic activity and it's not too hard to imagine a future EPA cracking down on shale gas the same way the agency is cracking down on coal today. In fact, we may already be seeing the first signs. In the United States, fifteen senators have submitted a letter to the White House urging President Obama to regulate methane emissions in the oil and gas industry. The letter, signed by Senator Sheldon Whitehouse and members of the Climate Action Task Force, asks the president to direct the Bureau of Land Management and the EPA to establish mandatory steps to curb leakage.[12]

If such action is taken, there may yet be a greater market for Canadian hydro power in the USA in the future. In any event, there is already a market for Quebec hydro power in Ontario. Instead of the Energy East pipeline sending over a million barrels a day of unrefined bitumen from Alberta through Ontario to Quebec, we are more likely to see a steady current of electrons travelling the other way. Not only would an Ontario–Quebec power accord not require the construction of any new pipelines, but the production and use of that energy wouldn't leave a huge carbon trail in the sky.

BUMPS IN THE ROAD

Whether we're talking about interprovincial or international deals, hydro power appears destined to play a bigger role in Canada's economic development in the coming decades. On the surface, at least, it would seem that our resources are up to the task: according to the Canadian Electricity Association, the country houses twice as much untapped hydro potential as what has already been developed.[13] That's quite a circuit load, considering Canada is already the second-largest hydro producer in the world. But to what extent can all that hydro be developed?

Hydro power has always come with challenges. Consider Bourassa and his James Bay scheme. In many respects, that project was the defining economic policy of his government; he saw it as the principal engine of economic growth for the province, much in the same way that Prime Minister Harper currently views the development of Alberta's oil sands. But just as in the case of today's oil sands projects, the environmental impact of Quebec's massive hydro development in the James Bay watershed was far from benign.

While the project didn't go so far as to reverse the natural flow of water over the James Bay watershed, it nevertheless dramatically altered seasonal flows over the contours of a reconfigured wilderness area the size of New York State. The hydro project flooded thousands of square kilometres of the boreal forest, the traditional hunting grounds of some five thousand native Cree and Inuit who still lived primarily off hunting and fishing. The thousands of decaying trees submerged in the huge reservoirs created by the project released so much mercury into the water that levels of the element in native whitefish and northern pike were six to seven times higher than before the project started. Eventually, the Cree and neighbouring Inuit were awarded $150 million in compensation for the permanent loss of their ancestral hunting and fishing grounds.[14]

Unlike in the early 1970s, when most James Bay power stations were built, today's power projects require extensive environmental assessments. And as we have already seen where pipelines are concerned, Native communities are not passive about protecting the environment of their traditional homelands, be they near Newfoundland's proposed Muskrat Falls generating facility or British Columbia's controversial Site C.

And then there's the problem of transmission lines. Transmission lines are to hydro what pipelines are to oil and gas. Without them, electrons don't move from the power plant to your light switch. Much of the country's hydro potential is in places like the James Bay watershed or the Romaine river basin in the remote north shore of the St. Lawrence River in Quebec. Building new transmission lines to distant markets materially changes the economics of hydro power and its competitiveness against other sources of power. Lines can easily cost over $2 million a kilometre to build. For example, BC Hydro's recently completed 344-kilometre Northwest Transmission Line that runs north of Terrace cost $736 million.[15]

HYDRO POWER'S SECOND WIND?

Challenges aside, hydro's potential is too huge to ignore, and there is hope on the horizon for less problematic ways to tap into all that power. We could see the development of more modest-sized "run-of-the-river" hydro sites—projects that create power using the natural water flow of rivers without distorting it through massive dams that leave behind huge reservoirs of flooded forest. British Columbia, which currently has thirty-five run-of-the-river power installations, is a world leader in this field.[16] With its mountainous terrain that is inundated with more rain than in any other province in the country, BC's topography and climate are ideally suited for these installations. The demand for power from such sources can only grow as more provinces and states in North America move their grids toward renewable energy sources.

Harnessing the incredible kinetic power generated by the movement of the country's running fresh water is yet another way in which Canada can capitalize on its most important resource. But in a world of global climate change, it's not just the country's fresh water resources that may provide new economic opportunities. A melting Arctic looks set to unlock long-sought sea routes and their commercial promise.

CHAPTER 14

FRANKLIN'S DREAM

BY ALL ACCOUNTS IT WAS A GRISLY END, and certainly not what Sir John Franklin expected when he set sail from England in 1845 on an expedition to find the elusive Northwest Passage. With him aboard the HMS *Erebus* and HMS *Terror* were 128 officers and men, a good deal of research equipment, and provisions expected to last for three years. But the mood upon sailing was optimistic, and many believed it would take only a year to make it through. It wasn't to be. On July 26, whalers in Baffin Bay spotted the expedition. After that, Franklin and his ships were never seen again.

Nearly 170 years later, we know a great deal about the fate of Franklin and his men. We know that the ships entered Lancaster Sound and spent their first winter at Beechey Island. We know that during the summer of 1846 they ventured south, through Peel Sound and into Victoria Strait. And we know that they then became trapped in the ice off King William Island—ice that even in the summer months refused to melt and release the ships from its death grip. Franklin is reported to have died on June 11, 1847, which spared him the horrors that would follow. His men, who abandoned their ships the following April, may have gone mad (perhaps as the result of lead poisoning), and almost certainly resorted to cannibalism in a desperate attempt to survive.

Franklin's lost expedition has fascinated archaeologists and historians for more than a century. It's also fascinated Canadians, including Stephen Harper. In 2008—just two years after he took office—Parks Canada announced a well-publicized search for the remains of the expedition, and in 2012, on one of his annual visits to Nunavut, Harper himself announced stepped-up efforts to find the lost ships.

Little surprise, then, that the announcement on September 9, 2014, that the *Erebus* had been found was greeted with much excitement. The Canadian media tripped over themselves in proclaiming the discovery the culmination of Harper's long-standing commitment to and interest in the Canadian North. The prime minister used the event as an opportunity to talk about history, mysteries and, most important, Canadian sovereignty over Franklin's route. Calling the lost ships a "truly important part of Canadian history," Harper went on to say that the expedition "laid the foundations of Canada's Arctic sovereignty."[1]

Leaving aside the dubious historical logic of the claim (Franklin was working for the British Crown at the time, and Canada was not yet a country) and focusing instead on the message, we can see the driving force behind the government's interest in the North. It's not about Franklin—not really. It's about the need to establish sovereignty over this vast, largely uninhabitable territory. And when Prime Minister Harper is talking sovereignty, you know oil isn't too far from his mind. The International Energy Agency estimates that the Arctic contains roughly 13 percent of the world's oil reserves (not to mention 30 percent of the world's undiscovered natural gas volumes).[2] Is it any wonder that Canada's energy-obsessed PM is chomping at the bit to establish a claim?

THE BIG MELT

There are certainly oil and natural gas deposits in the Beaufort Sea, and in other regions of the Canadian Arctic as well; thanks to the warmer temperatures and melting ice packs brought on by global warming, those reserves are easier to access than ever before. Even so, the question of whether those Arctic reserves will ever be developed is open to debate. Both the logistics and the costs of drilling in the Arctic are challenging, to say the least. Shell's decision to abandon its development plans in the Chukchi Sea is a case in point. The company's supposedly state-of-the-art *Kulluk* drilling platform was crippled by brutal seas before it got anywhere close to the planned drilling site.

Undaunted, Russia has announced ambitious plans to develop its arctic oil, but the latest round of economic sanctions in the intensifying cold war between NATO and Russia has at least temporarily put on hold Exxon's joint venture with Rosneft (Russia's state-owned oil company) to develop the underwater oil fields in the Arctic's Kara Sea. And then there's the question of whether, in a world of carbon constraints, we'll be able to burn anything we do manage to haul up from the depths.

Will Arctic oil exploration lead to lucrative new finds of commercially extractable oil, or are the billions slated for the region destined to be written off as wasteful cap ex spending? Not only is arctic oil very costly to extract, and hence dependent on sky-high oil prices, it is also a problem from an environmental perspective. A well blowout of the kind experienced at the *Deepwater Horizon* drilling platform in the Gulf of Mexico back in 2010 would have catastrophic consequences in this remote and environmentally fragile region of the world.

However, a world of melting polar ice caps exposes more than just previously inaccessible hydrocarbon reserves. Other economic opportunities lurk beneath that once-frozen landscape. All kinds of resources have suddenly become accessible—from iron deposits on the Mary River in Baffin Island to uranium, nickel, rare earth[3] and even emerald deposits beneath the rapidly retreating glaciers in Greenland. Global mining giants have taken notice, and are now on the hunt for Arctic treasure. And as more Arctic resources are developed, there will be an increasing need to transport them to southern markets.

It's not a stretch to imagine that the frigid waters of the Arctic may soon be dotted with freighters hauling not only local resources but also cargo from all around the world. In the same way that international airlines fly over the Arctic to shave off costly miles on long-haul flights, shipping companies may soon find that climate change will allow them to do the same. Travelling through an ice-free Arctic passage would cut 7,000 kilometres from the 23,000-kilometre journey a ship travelling from Tokyo to London would make via the Panama Canal.[4] That's two weeks in travel time, and huge dollar savings in fuel and other shipping costs. Those kinds of savings have the potential to reroute much of today's global shipping.

If you're thinking this is a vision of the distant future, think again. Circumnavigating the Arctic Ocean is no longer the dream of intrepid explorers like John Franklin. China's *Yong Sheng*, a 19,000-ton cargo ship, made history in 2013 when it sailed from the Chinese port of Dalian to the European port of Rotterdam. Normally, the journey would have taken the Chinese freighter down the South China Sea and through the Strait of Malacca to the Indian Ocean. After crossing the latter, the ship would have moved up the Red Sea to the Suez Canal, which would connect it with the Mediterranean, and through the Straits of Gibraltar to the North Atlantic seacoast and Rotterdam. The 10,500-nautical-mile route would have taken forty-eight days to complete. But unlike the seventeen thousand other ships that move through the Suez Canal in any given year, the *Yong Sheng* instead chose a route that no cargo ship had ever taken before.

Instead of going south from Dalian, the *Yong Sheng* headed north, past the volcano-laden coast on the Kamchatka Peninsula, and up across the top of the world through the once-frozen Arctic Ocean. The ship traversed the entire length of Russia's Arctic coastline, rounded the northern tip of Norway, and made a beeline to the port city of Rotterdam. The Northern Sea Route, as it is called in Russia, shaved 2,400 nautical miles from the route through the Suez, whittling travel time from forty-eight days to thirty-five.[5]

Today, the route taken by the Chinese freighter is only seasonal (July to November), but it may not stay that way for long. For shipping companies, global warming is a good news story. As recently as 1979, Arctic sea ice covered 4.5 million square kilometres. By 2012, that coverage had shrunk by slightly more than 50 percent, to 2.15 million square kilometres. There's no great mystery as to why. At the rate the Arctic ice cover is melting, the Northern Sea Route may soon be open year-round, and the *Yong Sheng* may find itself with lots of company.

Russia's Northern Sea Route isn't the only one that climate change will open up in the High Arctic. Average summer temperatures in the eastern Canadian Arctic are already the highest they have been in more than 40,000 years, and possibly in as many as 120,000 years.[6] In just the last fifty years, temperatures in the Canadian Arctic have risen by almost 4 degrees Celsius.[7] Ships may soon be navigating through waters that Franklin explored—waters over which Canada now claims sovereignty.[8] Like its Russian counterpart, the Canadian Arctic is becoming much more user-friendly than it was in the days when it locked Franklin's *Erebus* and *Terror* in a frozen grave. A month after the *Yong Sheng* completed its historic journey, the *Nordic Orion*, a 225-metre ice-strengthened carrier loaded with BC coal, sailed to Finland through the Northwest Passage.[9] This time, it wasn't the Suez Canal that was being bypassed, but the Panama Canal. Instead of travelling more than 8,000 kilometres—south down the

Pacific coast from Vancouver to Panama before coming out in the tropical Gulf of Mexico and then sailing across the Atlantic Ocean to the northern Baltic Sea—the *Orion* tracked a much shorter route. It sailed north up the Pacific coast, around Alaska and across the Beaufort Sea before needling its way through a now-open Northwest Passage. The Arctic journey shaved four days off the travel time, and around a thousand kilometres. Moreover, no longer bound by the weight restrictions required to pass through the Panama Canal's many locks, the freighter was able to carry 25 percent more coal than it would normally hold.

The *Yong Sheng* and *Nordic Orion* are both signs of things to come. Some climate change models are forecasting that significant sections of the Arctic will be ice-free within decades. In that scenario, today's seasonal routes through Arctic waters could become year-round shipping lanes. Millions of tons of cargo could be diverted from the Panama and Suez Canals—just how much is anyone's guess—and equally unimaginable savings could accrue as a result of the shorter routes and lower transport costs. Not surprisingly, a world in which Franklin's dream is a bright new reality is a world in which Arctic shipping could soon be growing at an exponential rate. If so, there will be an urgent need for shipping infrastructure—such as deepwater Arctic ports and search and rescue stations—as the commercial stakes in the Arctic get that much higher.

RUSSIA BULKS UP WHILE CANADA DITHERS

Russia is certainly recognizing and responding to those infrastructure needs. President Vladimir Putin has made the development of Arctic shipping infrastructure a national priority. The country's current fleet of nuclear-powered submarines and icebreakers is operating continuously in the region, and in 2017 Russia will welcome the world's largest nuclear-powered icebreakers, able to navigate

Arctic waters year-round.[10] Putin is also re-establishing northern military bases that were abandoned after the collapse of the Soviet Union, with the aim of providing a formidable search and rescue capacity. And perhaps most important, Russia is poised to become a major shipping hub.[11] The Russian port of Murmansk is the largest seaport north of the Arctic Circle now open to year-long ice-free shipping. Since 2004, Russia has invested over 4 billion euros (roughly $5.5 billion Canadian) in expanding and upgrading the port's facilities, as shipping tonnage is expected to double over the decade.[12] In addition to Murmansk, Russia has fifteen other Arctic seaports currently in operation.[13]

Russia's Arctic strategy is already paying off. Arctic shipping in the country has seen a tenfold increase over the last four years.[14] While Arctic shipping may never be the cash cow that the canal locks are to Panama, it can nevertheless become an increasing source of revenue[15]—and strategic clout—for Arctic nations.

And what of Canada? Canada has the largest Arctic coastline in the world.[16] Unlike Russia, however, it has done little to develop any infrastructure in the region. While Harper certainly knows how to talk up the Arctic on his annual sojourns, many of his ideas for enforcing Canadian sovereignty in the region have failed to get off the ground. Once-grandiose plans for three nuclear icebreakers were quickly downsized to one—and even that won't be delivered for at least another half decade. There is no search and rescue capacity in the area (aside from thirty civilian spotters in Arctic Bay and Pond Inlet, Nunavut[17]), and the country has no deepwater seaports on the Arctic Ocean proper. The Port of Churchill, in the southern section of Hudson Bay, is the country's only northern seaport capable of handling the Panama Canal–sized vessels that today are standard for international shipping—and it's located 2,000 kilometres south of the Northwest Passage. The port is linked by rail to the Prairies, providing an outlet for western grain shipments that otherwise would have to be sent along the more lengthy Great Lakes–St. Lawrence Seaway route. Of course, in keeping with Canada's national priorities, Churchill and its rail connection has recently been discussed as a possible route to move bitumen to markets in the Atlantic basin. The current shipping season runs from July to November, but that is almost certain to be extended in the future with a further warming of Hudson Bay waters. The Harper government has promised to build a new Arctic port around the old mining town of Nanisivik on Baffin Island, to be used for both military and commercial purposes, but so far, at least, the project remains on the shelf.

At first glance, Harper's neglect of this country's Arctic priorities is hard to reconcile with his seemingly passionate commitment to the region, especially when you compare it with the path Putin has chosen to follow. But stop and think for a moment and perhaps the apparent disconnect isn't really that puzzling. After years of denying the very existence of climate change, is it so surprising that Harper would be ill equipped to take advantage of the opportunities those changes present? After all, why prepare for an eventuality you refuse to recognize? In the end, however, Harper's lip-service-only approach to the North may prove costly to the Canadian economy. As Wayne Gretzky once said, "You miss one hundred percent of the shots you don't take."

EMBRACING CHANGE

IN THE SPACE OF THE YEAR it has taken to write this book, the goal-posts have moved as decisively on Canada's bitumen-fuelled carbon dreams as they had already moved on the dreams of coal producers around the world. (I've spent the better part of the editing process changing verb tenses from future to present.) Oil prices have already tanked, falling by over 50 percent during the latter half of 2014 as slug-gish growth in the global economy together with a flood of high-cost North American supply took a heavy toll on oil markets. While the short-term outlook for oil prices remains uncertain, the longer-term outlook is crystal clear. The inevitable adoption of measures to cap oil-fired emissions must mean lower global demand, lower global pro-duction and, most of all, lower oil prices in the future.

We may not yet have a green world economy, but it's certainly a slow-growing one. Insofar as oil prices are concerned, that's just as bad—if not worse. All the more so when the world is simultaneously being flooded with a torrent of new high-cost oil supply, which, as oil sands producers can surely appreciate, is not easy to turn off.

As you read these pages, the carbon bubble that has pretty much encapsulated the Canadian economy for the better part of the last decade has burst. The price of oil has plummeted, and it's taken the value of the Canadian dollar right along with it. Combined, these two events have unleashed a great deal of uncertainty into this country's economic picture. Alberta's premier, Jim Prentice, has acknowledged that his province's budget surplus is now a sizeable deficit—one that will only grow over time without decisive fiscal action. He has also intimated that the province will have to slash program spending by billions of dollars to help make up for the loss of expected bitumen royalties. Even the federal government, whose revenues are not nearly as exposed to oil as Alberta's, has been quick to use collapsing oil prices as a reason to delay the federal budget—in an election year, no less—also warning that the drop has resulted in the loss of billions of dollars of revenue. And over at the Bank of Canada, Governor Stephen Poloz has used the plunge in oil prices as an excuse for a surprise interest rate cut.

Clearly, Canada is no longer poised to become an energy super-power. As we've seen, the rapid expansion of the country's high-cost oil sands is simply unsustainable in today's marketplace. And still ahead (in the not too distant future) are the environmental challenges that oil sands companies will face when the world finally moves to limit carbon emissions. Survival, not growth, is the oil sands industry's new economic imperative.

But all is not lost. As devastating as a deflated carbon bubble has been to Alberta, it and the other Prairie provinces may yet get another turn at the helm of the Canadian economy. Although the dictates of climate change will devalue the oil sands, they will at the same time boost the value of much of Canada's arable land and its water resources. And therein lies enormous economic opportunity in a changing world. As we saw in part 4, Prime Minister Harper's folly isn't just about betting the house on a losing sector; it's just as much about not seeing the opportunities that climate change can bring. Having spent so much political capital—not to mention so many tax-payer dollars—on coddling the oil sands and denying climate change, it's probably too late for this prime minister to change course now. But it's certainly not too late for the Canadian economy, or for your investment portfolio.

SEIZING A GREEN FUTURE

As investors these days are painfully aware, virtually every commodity market has fallen in value in recent years. Since 2011, metallurgical prices are down over 60 percent, iron prices over 50 percent, and even copper, widely seen as a barometer of economic growth, is down by over a third. Those declines have pretty well put to rest the notion that the world is in some kind of "super cycle" for resource demand, as renowned investment bank Goldman Sachs once dubbed it.

That so-called super cycle was driven by exceptionally and ultimately unsustainably strong economic growth during the last decade, particularly in resource-hungry economies like China. For coal and oil markets, that oversized reliance on Chinese demand has proven to be a double-edged sword. Now that growth in the Chinese economy, as well as in the rest of the BRIC economies, is slowing, that sword is cutting the other way—into oil and coal prices, as well as into a raft of other resource markets. Investors who clung to the super-cycle notion and stayed long in those markets have been severely punished, none more so than those owning oil and coal (giving the lie to the long-held belief that "going green" means risking your portfolio; these days, as we've seen, going green is more of a passport to avoiding the worst-performing segments of the stock market).

But amidst this mad sell-off in commodity markets is one group that has more or less kept its pricing power: food. Not that there haven't been some wild swings in prices from year to year based on weather-related changes in annual harvests. Comparing the American 2012 and 2014 corn and wheat harvests, for example, is a night-and-day contrast: crop prices dropped by a good 30 percent after initially rising by as much as 50 percent on the heels of the 2012 drought in the US Midwest. But as a whole, agricultural prices have proven to be far more resilient than those of other resources, be they hydrocarbons, base metals or even gold.

If you want to invest in a sector with pricing power, food should be high on your shopping list. And climate change is likely to push it even higher. The United Nations FAO Food Price Index, which tracks monthly price changes for a broad basket of international food commodities, has more than doubled over the last decade. While the same could have been said for many other commodities, most have since given back a good portion of their gains. Not food. Even today, the index is not far from its 2011 high. By comparison, and as measured by the same index, world food prices were roughly flat over the preceding two decades (1980–2000).

There are, of course, many ways to invest in agriculture. You could start with Monsanto or DuPont or any of the other seed companies that will try to re-engineer the genetic characteristics of crops so that they are better suited to the requirements of a changing climate. Or you could explore the fertilizer companies, like potash producers, that will provide those seeds with nourishment. And then there are farm equipment companies such as John Deere and Brandt, makers of the tractors and harvesters and other machines that will plant those seeds and reap those crops. In short, you can invest in all of agriculture's technical inputs. The problem, of course, is that farming technology is constantly changing the need for those technical inputs. Farmers today invest in everything from satellite imagery to soil chemistry to try to coax the most value out of their land. Modern farming is as much about technology as it is about sweat equity. And with the challenges brought about by a shifting climate, tomorrow's farmer will need to be even more technologically sophisticated to adapt to changes in temperature and soil moisture. Undoubtedly, farming technology will continue to change, and with it the technical inputs for growing and harvesting crops. That said, there are two inputs that will remain absolutely, unequivocally critical to farming: water and land. Without them, all the technology embodied in today's hybrid seeds, potent fertilizers and powerful tractors won't grow a thing.

WHERE LAND AND WATER MEET

Canada is, by any measure, blessed with an abundance of fresh water; it could also soon be blessed with strategic control over potentially year-round Arctic shipping routes. The Canadian economy could clearly benefit from seizing opportunities on these fronts. Can investors do the same? The answer is yes—and no.

It will be hard, for example, to invest in Franklin's dream of shipping through the Northwest Passage until the federal government provides some bare-bones infrastructure in the region. At a minimum, Ottawa needs to build a deepwater port that can become a commercial nucleus on which private investment can build.

And while investing in hydro power seems attractive in an emissions-constrained world, investment opportunities are limited to small, independent generator companies that sell their power to provincial government–regulated grids. There could be more of these independents in the future—especially with the growth of smaller-scaled "run of the river" hydro projects—but the big players such as Hydro-Québec, Manitoba Hydro and BC Hydro are all Crown corporations. And even if you could invest in them, you might think twice about doing so. Carbon-neutral power generation sounds awfully appealing, but what happens on the power transmission side of the business when more and more households start to install solar and disconnect from the grid?

Of course, there are many other ways to invest in water these days. In fact, the promoters of these opportunities often proclaim water to be "the new oil." You can invest in municipal water infrastructure (or those who will build it), in desalination plants and in the ever-burgeoning bottled-water business. And these opportunities can be played through individual stock selections, mutual funds or even exchange-traded funds. But the greatest economic opportunity that climate change will bring when it comes to the value of water is in the need for irrigation, particularly in potentially expanding and increasingly productive breadbaskets like western Canada.

Since water is a public good in Canada, there is no way to own it directly. The closest you can get to investing in irrigation is investing in the land that will be irrigated. If what has happened in water-stressed California is any guide, irrigation is about to become an even bigger part of how prairie land values are determined. If you had bought worthless desert in the Imperial Valley just before the government decided to build the All-American Canal, you would have made a fortune. Some did.

And land? Well, that you *can* own. Just ask the growing number of investors who are already buying Canadian farmland—and with good reason. Even aside from the recent upturn in interest connected to climate change, Canadian farmland as an asset class has not disappointed investors. Between 1951 and 2010, the value of Canadian farmland rose at an average annual rate of over 7 percent. If you bought land and leased it to a farmer at a 3 percent annual rate, you are looking at a total return of 10 percent a year, as good as or better than the return you would have got from the TSX Composite over the same period—and with a lot less volatility. Aside from five years associated with the bursting of the farm bubble in the mid-1980s, an investment in farmland would have yielded a stream of steady returns. By comparison, over the last six decades the TSX provided negative annual returns in fifteen separate years—three times as many as in the farm sector.

As good as the long-term results have been, Canadian farmland prices have recently gone into overdrive. Farmland has been far and away the hottest segment of the Canadian real estate market; farm prices have averaged a 12 percent annual increase since the Great Recession, outpacing gains in both commercial and residential real estate. During the same period, oil sands stocks have lost roughly half of their value.

According to Farm Credit Canada, the federal agency that provides financial services to the agricultural community, farmland prices shot up over 20 percent across the country in 2013, and by almost 30 percent in Saskatchewan. The agency noted these were the largest increases in the value of farm property that it had seen in its last two decades of monitoring prices.[1]

Not surprisingly, those numbers led some commentators to speculate that the recent runaway increases had set the stage for the bursting of a farmland bubble, much like what was witnessed in North America during the early 1980s.[2]

The fallout back in the farm bust of the early 1980s was the worst for farmers since the dust bowl and the Great Depression of the 1930s. The media was full of stories about desperate farmers like the one facing bankruptcy in Hills, Iowa, who shot his wife, his neighbour, his banker and then himself.[3] Or the one in Ruthton, Minnesota, who walked into his local lending institution with his son and shot two bank officials.[4] Between 1981 and 1985, farmland prices in the Midwest had dropped by as much as 60 percent, with bank foreclosures rippling across America's breadbasket.[5] In Iowa, the heartland of American corn production, farmland values fell within the space of five years from $2,147 an acre to as low as $787 an acre, while a third of the state's farms went out of business.[6]

While it may be tempting to speculate about the similarities between then and now, there are some fundamental differences between the two periods. The rise in food prices leading up to that bubble was more a product of spiralling oil-led rates of inflation than of any specific move in food prices per se. Food prices were simply following the trend triggered by the Middle East oil shocks. The recent rise in food prices, in contrast, is taking place in decidedly disinflationary times.

Hence, instead of the Federal Reserve Board cranking up lending rates to as high as 20 percent to rein in galloping inflation, it and other central banks around the world, including the Bank of Canada, have been keeping rates at record lows to support stumbling economic growth. Moreover, unlike today's farm sector, the one in the 1980s was highly leveraged, and hence very vulnerable to soaring financing rates. Today's farm sector is largely financed by equity, not debt. If it's not institutional funds like large pensions buying land, it's farmers themselves plowing their record-high incomes from soaring crop prices back into expanding their farmland.

BUYING THE FARM

That, of course, doesn't mean that farmland prices won't hit some bumps along the way—or that crop prices won't continue to fluctuate. Bumper crops in the United States in 2014 following the 2012 drought have led to substantial declines in both corn and wheat prices in North America. While those declines have taken some of the sizzle out of North American farmland, Canadian farmland prices have remained remarkably resilient.

How much of that resilience reflects an investment in the positive spinoffs of climate change is, at this point, impossible to say. But for investors, the situation is well worth pondering. The expected improvement in crop yields that will come with longer growing seasons, combined with the potential shift to higher-value-added grains like corn and soybeans, will undoubtedly make the economics of owning Canadian farmland even more attractive in the future. And the recent example of the havoc that drought conditions in the US Midwest can wreak on crop prices and production has given investors a good glimpse of how Canadian farmland can be an effective hedge against the impact of climate change elsewhere on the continent.

There's only one catch: for individuals, investing in farmland isn't quite as simple as investing in the stock market. Few of us are in a position to buy a commercial farm. Even fewer would be able to provide their own sweat equity and operate one. There are no liquid exchange-traded funds that can readily deliver the returns from farmland as there are for the TSX Composite (or any other of the world's bourses). But that doesn't mean you can't invest in it. Pension plans are sure doing it.

The Canada Pension Plan Investment Board (CPPIB) acquired the $128-million Assiniboia Farmland Limited Partnership. Toronto-based Bonnefield Financial has launched three different closed-end Canadian farmland funds totalling over $325 million. Bonnefield's funding comes mainly from pension plans, and the firm's farmland funds hold some fifty thousand acres of leased farmland in Alberta, Saskatchewan, Manitoba, New Brunswick and Nova Scotia. These funds typically acquire farmland and then lease the land back to the farmer, who continues to operate the farm.

To be sure, the sector is not without its growing pains. Saskatchewan has threatened to prohibit the sale of additional farmland to pension plans following the CPPIB purchase. While farmers wanting to cash out of their rapidly appreciating land are all in favour of big institutional money chasing their assets, those wanting to expand their acreage aren't crazy about competing with the likes of $234-billion pension plans such as the CPPIB. Who will prevail in this tug-of-war is far from clear, but if climate change keeps pushing up the value of Canadian farmland, there may soon be more sellers than buyers in the farm community, tipping the scales in favour of institutional investment.

Investment restrictions aside, closed-end funds aren't for everybody. As a general rule, they are not as liquid or transparent as exchange-traded funds. Often, they trade on the market at a value less than that of their underlying assets. And valuation can be problematic since there is no transparent benchmark—like the daily level of the TSX Composite, for example—that can be referenced every trading day to let you know how your index fund is performing. That said, farmland as a financial asset class is still in an embryonic stage. As it becomes increasingly apparent that climate change is adding more and more value to Canadian farmland, and as farmers themselves become ever more eager to capitalize on those gains, you can bet that always-opportunistic financial markets will find new ways of allowing them to do so, and, in the process, make this asset far more accessible to the investing public.

LOOKING BACK TO MOVE FORWARD

Stephen Harper may ultimately be right on the money in his belief that the centre of the country's economy lies to the west. But it won't be Alberta's bitumen fuelling growth, either in the economy or in your investment portfolio. There's no longer any doubt that the world will need to cut back its combustion of oil, particularly high-cost, emissions-intensive bitumen. There's also no doubt that this very same world, one that features a rapidly growing global population that is moving toward a more protein-rich diet, will want—and, more important, pay a high price for—all the grain that expanded crop production on a warming and potentially expanding Canadian prairies can produce. The dictates of the global market will once again dramatically change the makeup of the Canadian economy. Only this time, the global marketplace will incent Canada to produce more food instead of more oil. And in the process, those price signals will start making the economy much greener.

Today, the oil and gas sector may have three times the weighting of agriculture in this country's GDP. That won't be the case tomorrow. Instead of supertankers plowing up and down our Atlantic and Pacific coasts to pick up boatloads of bitumen from pipelines or rail terminals, we're likely to see more freighters—perhaps even some following the *Nordic Orion*'s route—carrying western grain to hungry overseas markets.

It's an image that blends well with the country's past. Farming is as much a part of this country's history as the east coast fisheries, the fur trade or the timber industry. In the very early 20th century, the Canadian Northern Railway Company advertised the untapped farming potential of the Prairies as the "key to prosperity in the bread basket of the world."[7] Acres upon acres of free or cheap farmland drew legions of settlers to the vast Canadian prairies, and once there, those settlers flourished. The wheat grown on that land— King Wheat, as it soon became known—became an engine of economic growth.

Little wonder, then, that when Alberta and Saskatchewan joined Confederation in 1905, the crests designed for the new provinces paid homage to their biggest provider. Today, those crests can still be seen on the provincial flags. On Saskatchewan's, three wheat sheaves are prominent. In Alberta's crest, a golden field of wheat sits beneath prairie, foothills and the majestic Rocky Mountains.

If you look closely at these flags, you'll notice something else: there are no symbols representing pipelines or bitumen mines. Not even a single oil pump. It is a stark and effective reminder of a simple fact: long before these provinces became major producers of oil, they were major producers of agriculture. As it turns out, they will be even bigger agricultural producers in the future.

In tomorrow's world—a time of climate change and ever-tightening restrictions on carbon emissions—Canada stands a much better chance of becoming an agricultural superpower than it ever had of becoming an energy superpower. Growing food for a burgeoning global population instead of extracting bitumen for a shrinking oil market isn't just an urgently needed change for our carbon-choked atmosphere. In a world of plunging oil prices and soaring food prices, that transition will be just as vital to our economic future.

[SOURCE NOTES]

CHAPTER ONE: **RUNNING OUT OF TIME**

1   Statistics Canada, *National Household Survey: Education and Labour*, Statistics
    Canada Catalogue no. 99-012-X, available online.

2   US Energy Information Administration, "International Energy Outlook, 2014,"
    September 9, 2014.

3   NASA, "Climate Change: How Do We Know? Global Climate Change:
    Vital Signs of the Planet," accessed November 14, 2014.

4   Intergovernmental Panel on Climate Change, "IPCC Fourth Assessment
    Report: Climate Change 2007," http://www.ipcc.ch/publications_and_data
    /ar4/wg1/en/tssts-2-1-1.html.

5   Melanie Fitzpatrick, "The New 400ppm World: CO_2 Measurements
    at Mauna Loa Continue to Climb," Union of Concerned Scientists,
    The Equation (blog), March 20, 2014, http://blog.ucsusa.org/400ppm
    -co2-mauna-loa-455.

6   Qiancheng Ma, "Greenhouse Gases: Refining the Role of Carbon Dioxide,"
    Goddard Institute for Space Studies, March 1998, http://www.giss.nasa.gov
    /research/briefs/ma_01/.

7   Michael Carlowicz, "Global Temperatures: 1880–1889," NASA Earth
    Observatory, http://earthobservatory.nasa.gov/Features/WorldOfChange
    /decadaltemp.php.

8   Caitlin E. Werrell, Francesco Femia and Anne-Marie Slaughter, "The Arab
    Spring and Climate Change," Center for American Progress, February 28,
    2013. https://www.americanprogress.org/issues/security/report/2013/02/28
    /54579/the-arab-spring-and-climate-change/.

9   Jae Hur and Rudy Ruitenberg, "Wheat Jumps to Highest since 2008 as
    Chinese Crop Faces Drought," Bloomberg.com, February 9, 2011, http://
    www.bloomberg.com/apps/news?pid=newsarchive&sid=aauQfPyYKiD8.

10 Brian Clark Howard, "West Antarctica Glaciers Collapsing, Adding to Sea-Level Rise," *National Geographic*, May 12, 2014.

11 Global Green USA, "Sea Level Rise: The Risk, the Facts," http://www.globalgreen.org/articles/global/95.

12 Andrea Thompson, "As Hurricane Season Begins, New Storm Surge Maps Emphasize Importance of Preparedness," *Huffington Post*, June 2, 2014.

13 You may occasionally see this figure expressed as 10 billion metric tons of carbon. Carbon emissions, and hence carbon budgets, can be expressed in two ways. For the IPCC and others, emissions are measured in metric tons of carbon. But emissions can also be measured in metric tons of CO_2, the actual gas that is released through the combustion of carbon fuels such as coal and oil. When you add the mass of both carbon and oxygen in carbon dioxide, the result is about 3.7 times the mass of the carbon alone. So a carbon budget based on the mass of CO_2 will be about 3.7 times bigger than one that uses the mass of carbon.

14 Jeff Rubin, *The End of Growth* (Toronto: Vintage Canada, 2013).

15 Michelle Nijhuis, "Can Coal Ever Be Clean," *National Geographic*, April 2014, 40.

16 Shawn McCarthy, "SaskPower Unveils World's First Carbon Capture Coal Plant," *Globe and Mail*, October 3, 2014.

17 Ibid.

18 MIT Energy Initiative: Carbon Capture and Sequestration Technologies, "Kemper County IGCC Fact Sheet: Carbon Dioxide Capture and Storage Project," last modified September 15, 2014, https://sequestration.mit.edu/tools/projects/kemper.html.

19 *World Energy Outlook 2012*, IEA, 58.

20 World Nuclear Association, "Fukushima Accident," November 2014; Danielle Demetriou, "Japan Earthquake, Tsunami and Fukushima Nuclear Disaster: 2011 Review," *Daily Telegraph* (London), December 19, 2011.

21 Chris Dalby, "Au Revoir, Nuclear Power? France Eyes an Energy Shift of Its Own," *Christian Science Monitor*, October 20, 2014.

22 Canadian Hydropower Association, "Hydro Facts," 2014, https://canadahydro.ca/hydro-facts/hydro-in-5-points.

23 European Wind Energy Association, "Wind Energy Basics," http://www.ewea.org.

24   James Hawkins, "The State of Solar Power in Europe," *Clean Technica*, February 16, 2012.

25   European Commission, "Renewable Energy," http://ec.europa.eu/energy /renewables/index_en.htm.

26   Barbara Lewis, "'Tar Sands,' but Not Tarred," *Globe and Mail Report on Business*, special edition, *Oil Sands: The Biggest Business Story of the Decade*, November 2014, 45–46.

27   Reuters, "Solar Market to Nearly Triple by 2018 as Asia Leads Europe," *Star* online, June 2, 2014.

28   Worldwatch Institute, "Solar Power Installations Jump to a New Annual Record," press release, July 29, 2014.

CHAPTER TWO: **GROW GREEN OR DON'T GROW**

1   As of November 24, 2014. Tesla's stock price is $247.03. The IPO price was set at $17. At one point, the stock traded as high as $291.42.

2   Hannah Elliott, "The Tesla Model S Is the Most-Loved Car in America," *Forbes*, February 26, 2014, http://www.forbes.com/sites/hannahelliott/2014 /02/26/the-tesla-model-s-is-the-most-loved-car-in-america/.

3   Usage data taken from the US Energy Information Administration (www.eia.gov, accessed June 12, 2014).

4   According to the US Energy Information Administration, for example, China's energy mix for 2011 was 69% coal, 18% oil, 6% hydroelectric, 4% natural gas, <1% nuclear and 1% other renewables; Brazil's was 47% oil, 35% hydroelectric, 8% natural gas, 5% coal and 1% nuclear; and Canada's was 32% petroleum, 26% hydro, 22% natural gas, 8% coal, 7% nuclear and 5% non-hydro renewables. All figures taken from the US Energy Information Association website (www.eia.gov/countries, accessed June 12, 2014).

5   For a detailed discussion of what a limited-growth scenario might entail, see *The End of Growth* (Toronto: Random House, 2012).

6   There's no question that climate change is taking a toll on economic growth. Back in 2006, in a landmark report to the British Parliament, Lord Nicholas Stern argued that climate change could reduce the global economy by as much as 20 percent. In more recent estimates coming from the London School of Economics' Grantham Research Institute on Climate Change, Stern and his co-author, Simon Dietz, suggest that even larger economic impacts may be on the horizon as climate change forces an increasing share

of investment dollars to be diverted to repairing damaged infrastructure, and as entire industries have to relocate to avoid low-lying areas at risk from rising sea levels. And the bad news just keeps on coming. *Risky Business*, an in-depth assessment of the vulnerability of the US economy to climate change, sponsored by ex–New York major Michael Bloomberg and former Treasury secretary and Goldman Sachs executive Henry Paulson, estimates that the damage from events like Superstorm Sandy will run between $2 and $3.5 billion a year. The report also projects that by 2050, between $66 and $106 billion of existing coastal property, much of it high-priced, will be below sea level. (Simon Dietz and Nicholas Stern, "Endogenous Growth, Convexity of Damages and Climate Risk," Centre for Climate Change Economics and Policy Working Paper No. 180, Grantham Research Institute on Climate Change and the Environment Working Paper No. 159, June 2014. http://www.lse.ac.uk/GranthamInstitute/wp-content/uploads/2014/06 /Working-Paper-180-Dietz-and-Stern-2014.pdf; *Risky Business Project, Risky Business: A Climate Risk Assessment for the United States* (June 2014).

7   The Paris-based International Energy Agency was set up in the 1970s by major oil-consuming nations to keep tabs on world energy markets, with an eye toward safeguarding its members' energy security. Its *World Energy Outlook* has become the reference for global energy statistics and forecasts.

8   Carbon Tracker, "Unburnable Carbon 2013: Wasted Capital and Stranded Assets," 2013, http://www.carbontracker.org/wp-content/uploads/2014/09 /Unburnable-Carbon-2-Web-Version.pdf.

9   Dina O'Meara, "Companies Respond to Shareholder Activism on Carbon Risks," *Financial Post*, April 10, 2014, http://business.financialpost. com/2014/04/10/companies-respond-to-shareholder-activism-on-carbon -risks/?__lsa=fa4a-caa5.

10 Ian W.H. Parry, Dirk Heine and Eliza Lis, *Getting Energy Prices Right: From Principle to Practice* (Washington, DC: International Monetary Fund, 2014).

11 Damian Carrington, "Carbon Bubble Will Plunge the World into Another Financial Crisis—Report," *Guardian* (Manchester), April 19, 2013, http://www.theguardian.com/environment/2013/apr/19/carbon-bubble -financial-crash-crisis.

CHAPTER THREE: **PARIAH**

1   Oxfam, for one, has argued that while every country needs to be part of the effort to keep climate change in check, "rich countries must make the deepest cuts and support poor countries so they can switch to low carbon development

and adapt to worsening impacts" (http://oneworld.org/2014/04/06/rich-must
-lead-in-cutting-climate-emissions-to-avoid-hunger/, accessed June 23, 2014).
And in the wake of the IPCC's 2014 report on climate change, Britain's
climate change secretary, Ed Davey, urged the European Union to lead
the fight to reduce carbon emissions (http://www.bbc.com/news/uk
-politics-27008750, accessed June 23, 2014). The World Bank, the *Financial
Times* and the Global Policy Forum have also supported this approach.

2   Coral Davenport, "In Climate Deal with China, Obama May Set 2016
Theme," *New York Times*, November 12, 2014, http://www.cbc.ca/news/world
/barack-obama-sets-2030-emissions-target-for-u-s-power-plants-1.2661384.

3   George Monblot, "Canada's Image Lies in Tatters. It Is Now to Climate
What Japan Is to Whaling," *Guardian* (Manchester), November 30, 2009,
http://www.theguardian.com/commentisfree/cif-green/2009/nov/30/canada
-tar-sands-copenhagen-climate-deal.

4   Climate Action Network, "Canada Wins 'Lifetime Unachievement'
Fossil Award at Warsaw Climate Talks," press release, November 22, 2013,
http://climateactionnetwork.ca/2013/11/22/canada-wins-lifetime
-unachievement-fossil-award-at-warsaw-climate-talks/.

5   Address by the prime minister at the Canada–UK Chamber of Commerce,
July 14, 2006, http://pm.gc.ca/eng/news/2006/07/14/address-prime-minister
-canada-uk-chamber-commerce.

6   The jerker-line system improved on the steam-engine system (in which
individual wells were powered by one steam engine). Power from a single
engine is transmitted to wooden rods through belts, pulleys, gears, cranks
and horizontal wheels. The rods connect to a beam that moves the pump
rods in each well. (Description taken from "Technology at Fairbank Oil,"
www.fairbankoil.com/section5.swf.)

7   Earle Gray, *Ontario's Petroleum Legacy: The Birth, Evolution and Challenges
of a Global Industry* (Calgary: Heritage Community Foundation, 2008).

8   Ironically, the company faced widespread criticism for choosing a shorter and
therefore less costly route, to Superior, Wisconsin, instead of going through to
Thunder Bay. These days, with American opposition to transborder pipelines,
distance is the least of the pipeline companies' concerns (see chapter 5).

9   According to the Pembina Institute, GHG emissions for oil sands extraction
and upgrading are between 3 and 4.5 times more intensive per barrel than for
conventional oil produced in North America. However, since the majority of
emissions are created upon combustion, on a well-to-wheels basis, the GHG

emissions intensity is only 8 to 37 percent higher than for conventional crude. (Pembina Institute, "Oil Sands 101: Climate Impacts," http://www.pembina.org /oil-sands/os101/climate, accessed November 24, 2014.)

10 http://www.oilsandstoday.ca/whatareoilsands/Pages/WhatareOilSands.aspx, accessed June 25, 2014.

11 Citi Research, *Global Oil Vision*, September 12, 2012, https://drive .google.com/viewerng/viewer?a=v&pid=forums&srcid=MTYwMTE1NjEw NDIzMzc2MzgyOTkkBMDU3MjgwMjkxOTg4MTQ2MjMzMDABdnhpd G5Ib3Q0bHNKATAuMQEBdjI.

12 *Globe and Mail Report on Business*, special edition, *Oil Sands: The Biggest Business Story of the Decade*, November 2014, 54.

13 Tom Parry, "High-Five on Repealed Carbon Tax Draws Criticism for Canada," CBCNews.ca, November 15, 2013, http://www.cbc.ca/news/politics/high -five-on-repealed-carbon-tax-draws-criticism-for-canada-1.2427706.

14 David McLaughlin, "How Harper Should Speak About Climate Change," *Huffington Post*, June 16, 2014, http://www.huffingtonpost.ca/david -mclaughlin/climate-change-harper_b_5497297.html?utm_hp_ref=tw.

15 Shawn McCarthy, "Ottawa's New Anti-terrorism Strategy Lists Eco-Extremists as Threats," *Globe and Mail*, February 10, 2012.

16 Speech to the Economic Club of New York, September 20, 2006, www.pm.gc .ca/eng/news/2006/09/20/speech-economic-club-new-york.

17 Emily Atkin, "'A Government of Thugs': How Canada Treats Environmental Journalists," *Climate Progress*, May 20, 2013, http://thinkprogress.org /climate/2014/05/23/3428984/canada-war-on-environmentalists/.

18 Raveena Aulakh, "Audits of Environmental Charities Linked to Position on Oilsands," *Toronto Star*, February 7, 2014, http://www.thestar.com/news /world/2014/02/07/audits_of_environmental_charities_linked_to_position _on_oilsands.html.

19 Stephen Luntz, "Canadian Weather Forecasters Forbidden from Discussing Climate Change," *Reader Supported News*, http://readersupportednews.org /news-section2/312-16/23954-canadian-weather-forecasters-forbidden-from -discussing-climate-change, accessed June 4, 2014.

20 QMI Agency, "Most Canadians Support Oilsands Development: Poll," *Toronto Sun*, October 15, 2012, http://www.torontosun.com/2012/10/15/ most-canadians-support-oilsands-development-poll.

21   World Bank, GDP growth (annual %) data table, http://data.worldbank.org
/indicator/NY.GDP.MKTP.KD.ZG.

CHAPTER FOUR: **THE FRACKERS**

1   Fiona Harvey, "George Mitchell" (obituary), *Guardian* (Manchester),
August 4, 2013, http://www.theguardian.com/environment/2013/aug/04
/george-mitchell.

2   John Richardson, "The History of Fracking (A Timeline)," *Quora*, February 23,
2013, http://energywithjr.quora.com/The-History-of-Fracking-A-Timeline.

3   Harvey, "George Mitchell."

4   When US secretary of state John Kerry travelled to Geneva in November 2013
to begin talks with Iran over its nuclear weapons program, several news
outlets theorized that the meeting would not have been possible without the
American oil boom. "Over the last two years, the U.S. has increased its crude
production by about 2 million barrels a day," wrote Matthew Phillips in
Businessweek. "That's like swallowing Norway, the fourteenth largest oil
producer in the world. This new U.S. crude supply has allowed the West
to put the squeeze on Iran without disrupting the global market or jacking
up the price." (Matthew Phillips, "There Would Be No Iranian Nuclear
Talks If Not for Fracking," *BloombergBusinessweek*, November 9, 2013,
http://www.businessweek.com/articles/2013-11-08/there-would-be-no
-iranian-nuclear-talks-if-not-for-fracking.)

5   "What Goes In and Out of Hydraulic Fracturing," website,
http://www.dangersoffracking.com; Nick Logan, "N.B. Election:
Did Shale Gas and Fracking Sway the Vote?" GlobalNews.ca,
September 23, 2014, http://globalnews.ca/news/1577434/n-b-election-did-shale
-gas-and-fracking-sway-the-vote/.

6   "The Father of Fracking," *Schumpeter* (blog), *Economist*, August 3, 2013,
http://www.economist.com/news/business/21582482-few-businesspeople-have
-done-much-change-world-george-mitchell-father.

7   "Fracking: Frequently Asked Questions," *Bigger Pie Forum*, http://www
.biggerpieforum.org/How-does-fracking-work#Q7, accessed July 15, 2014.

8   Credit Suisse Securities, Research and Analytics, "The Shale Revolution,"
Connections Series (December 2012), https://doc.research-and-analytics.csfb.
com/docView?language=ENG&format=PDF&document_id=1005321471
&source_id=em&extdocid=1005321471_1_ENG_pdf&serialid=0sD72
ky5PVE69YdSxRIsei9L5gnDVssxzgAuLedlEiQ%3d.

9   Phil Milford, Sonja Elmquist and Dawn McCarty, "Coal Company Pain
     Accelerates as Bankruptcy Cases Rise," Bloomberg.com, July 25, 2014,
     http://www.bloomberg.com/news/articles/2014-07-24/coal-bankruptcies
     -loom-on-pain-from-cheap-gas-new-rules.

10   Ben Lefebvre, "US Refineries Export More Fuel Than Ever," *Wall Street
     Journal*, October 8, 2013, http://www.wsj.com/articles/SB10001424052702304
     44140457912360428785486 2.

11   Mark Trumbull, "Oil Export Ban 101: Why Does US Have It? Why Is It Now
     Easing?" *Christian Science Monitor*, June 25, 2014, http://www.csmonitor
     .com/USA/DC-Decoder/2014/0625/Oil-export-ban-101-Why-does-US-have
     -it-Why-is-it-now-easing.

12   In October 2012, the *Wall Street Journal* detailed the decline in US oil
     imports: "Five years ago, the U.S. was importing 60% of its oil, a figure that
     had been rising since the early 1980s. Today, the U.S. imports just over 40% of
     its oil, the smallest share in 20 years." ("Renaissance in U.S. Oil Production,"
     Real Time Economics (blog), *Wall Street Journal*, October 23, 2012, http://
     blogs.wsj.com/economics/2012/10/23/renaissance-in-u-s-oil-production/.)

13   Melanie Cruthirds, "U.S. Crude Oil Imports Dependency to Decline 32%
     by 2020," *World Oil Online*, August 20, 2013, http://www.worldoil.com
     /US-crude-oil-imports-dependency-to-decline-32percent-by-2020.html.

14   Figures taken from the US Energy Information Administration.

15   *Merriam-Webster's Collegiate Dictionary*, 11th ed. (online),
     http://www.merriam-webster.com/info/newwords09.htm.

16   Angie Schmitt, "For Eighth Year in a Row, the Average American Drove
     Fewer Miles in 2012," Streetblog USA, February 7, 2013, http://usa.streetsblog
     .org/2013/02/27/for-eighth-year-in-a-row-the-average-american-drove-fewer
     -miles-in-2012/.

17   Daily Mail Reporter, "American Suburbs Turning into Ghost Towns,"
     Daily Mail (London), April 5, 2012, http://www.dailymail.co.uk/news
     /article-2125507/American-suburbs-turning-ghost-towns-How-homeowners
     -ditching-town-areas-live-big-cities.html.

18   Kate Lunau, "For Today's Youth, Cars No Longer Represent Freedom,"
     Maclean's, June 5, 2012.

19   Bill Vlasic, "U.S. Sets Higher Fuel Efficiency Standards," *New York Times*,
     August 28, 2012, http://www.nytimes.com/2012/08/29/business/energy
     -environment/obama-unveils-tighter-fuel-efficiency-standards.html?_r=0.

20 Brad Pulmer, "Cars in the U.S. Are More Fuel-Efficient Than Ever. Here's How It Happened," *Wonkblog* (blog), *Washington Post*, December 13, 2013, http://www.washingtonpost.com/blogs/wonkblog/wp/2013/12/13 /cars-in-the-u-s-are-more-fuel-efficient-than-ever-heres-how-it-happened/.

21 Reuters, "Europe Oil Demand: 20-Year Low and to Slide Further," cnbc.com, January 11, 2013, http://www.cnbc.com/id/100372251; United States Energy Information Administration, http://www.indexmundi.com/energy.aspx/? region=eu&product=oil&graph=consumption, accessed February 17, 2015.

22 The EIA is the statistical and analytical arm of the US Department of Energy—not to be confused with the IEA (International Energy Agency).

23 Daniel Tencer, "Canadian Imports of U.S. Oil Double in a Year, Posing New Challenge to Oilsands," *Huffington Post*, July 15, 2014, http://www.huffington post.ca/2014/07/15/us-oil-exports-canada_n_5587730.html?utm_hp_ref=canada.

24 Jeff Lewis, "Even in Canada, Booming U.S. Petroleum Elbowing Out Alberta Producers," *Financial Post*, July 14, 2014, http://business.financialpost. com/2014/07/14/even-in-canada-booming-u-s-oil-exports-are-elbowing -out-albertas-crude/?__lsa=1986-70d8.

25 Gordon Isfeld, "'We Have to Find New Customers,' Says Joe Oliver as Canada's Landlocked Energy Sector Adapts to Self-Reliant U.S.," *Financial Post*, June 10, 2014, http://business.financialpost.com/2014/06/10/canada -energy-joe-oliver/?__lsa=101f-51d4.

CHAPTER FIVE: **PIPE DREAMS**

1 Rachel Mendleson, "Why Aren't We Building Refineries in Canada? Because It's Too Late, Experts Say," *Huffington Post*, May 24, 2012, http:// www.huffingtonpost.ca/2012/05/23/canada-oil-refineries_n_1539701.html.

2 The Sturgeon County refinery, just north of Edmonton, is scheduled to be open for business in 2017. (Brent Jang, "Not So Refined," *Globe and Mail Report on Business*, special edition, *Oil Sands: The Biggest Business Story of the Decade*, November 2014, 56.)

3 "The Bitumen Bubble: What Does That Mean?" *Edmonton Journal*, January 7, 2014, http://www.edmontonjournal.com/business/Bitumen+ Bubble+What+does+that+mean/9306461/story.html?__federated=1.

4 The situation for Alberta producers has improved recently, thanks to the southern leg of Keystone (which didn't require presidential approval, since it doesn't cross a border) and the reversal of the existing Seaway pipeline

that runs from Cushing, Oklahoma, to the Gulf Coast. With these two developments, Alberta bitumen is now able to get to coastal refineries along the US Gulf Coast. But without approval of the Keystone XL pipeline, there won't be pipeline capacity to move the planned increase in production, likely resulting in future transit bottlenecks and the return of those crippling price discounts.

5   TransCanada, "TransCanada Received NEB Approval to Construct and Operate the Keystone Oil Pipeline," news release, September 21, 2007, http://www.transcanada.com/3115.html.

6   National Energy Board, "National Energy Board Approves Keystone XM Pipeline Project," press release, March 11, 2010, https://www.neb-one.gc.ca /bts/nws/nr/archive/2010/nr06-eng.html.

7   James Hansen, "Game Over for the Climate," *New York Times*, May 9, 2012, http:// www.nytimes.com/2012/05/10/opinion/game-over-for-the-climate.html?_r=0.

8   Steven Mufson, "Keystone XL Pipeline May Threaten Aquifer That Irrigates Much of the Central U.S.," *Washington Post*, August 6, 2012, http://www .washingtonpost.com/national/health-science/keystone-xl-pipeline-may -threaten-aquifer-that-irrigates-much-of-the-central-us/2012/08/06/7bf0215 c-d4db-11e1-a9e3-c5249ea531ca_story.html; Jim Meyer and Nikki Burch, "Keystone Komics: The Incredible Illustrated History of the Keystone XL Oil Pipeline," *Grist*, March 28, 2013, http://grist.org/slideshow/keystone -komics-the-incredible-illustrated-history-of-the-keystone-xl-oil-pipeline/.

9   Stream Team, "A History of Keystone (Timeline)," Aljazeera America, December 11, 2013, http://america.aljazeera.com/watch/shows/the-stream /multimedia/2013/multimedia/2013/12/a-history-of-keystonetimeline.html.

10   Even if the vote had passed, it was widely assumed that Obama would veto the bill, which was specifically designed to bypass the White House's environ- mental review process. Still, it's likely that the "no" vote did little more than buy some time for those opposed to Keystone. As a result of the 2014 midterm elections, the political makeup of the Senate is set to change in 2015, with pro-Keystone Republicans taking control. Once that happens, the bill will likely be put forward again. (Canadian Press, "Keystone Vote: U.S. Senate Rejects Pipeline Bill," *Huffington Post*, November 18, 2014, http://www .huffingtonpost.ca/2014/11/18/keystone-vote-us-senate_n_6176320.html.)

11   Bloomberg News, "Keystone XL Cost May Surge to $10-Billion, TransCanada Says," *Globe and Mail*, September 19, 2014.

12   Susana Mas, "Harper Won't Take No for an Answer on Keystone XL," CBCNews.ca, September 26, 2013, http://www.cbc.ca/news/politics /harper-won-t-take-no-for-an-answer-on-keystone-xl-1.1869439.

13 "Peter Mansbridge Talks with Stephen Harper," transcript, CBCNews.ca, January 18, 2012, http://www.cbc.ca/news/politics/transcript-peter -mansbridge-talks-with-stephen-harper-1.1192774.

14 "West-East Pipeline Key to Open New Markets for Canadian Oil: Oliver," CTVNews.ca, April 2, 2013, http://www.ctvnews.ca/business/west-east -pipeline-key-to-open-new-markets-for-canadian-oil-oliver-1.1220400.

15 Ibid.

16 According to the NEB website, the factors considered during an environ- mental assessment include: physical and meteorological environment; soil, soil productivity and vegetation; wetlands, water quality and quantity; fish, wildlife and their habitats, species at risk; heritage resources; traditional land and resource use; and human health (www.neb-one.gc.ca).

17 In 2002, before he was prime minister, Stephen Harper sent a letter to supporters of the Canadian Alliance (eventually reborn as the Conservative Party of Canada). In it, he urged the faithful to gear up for the "biggest struggle" the party had faced since it had entrusted him with its leadership: "the battle of Kyoto." The letter makes for interesting reading. It clearly establishes Harper's deep distrust of the environmental movement. Kyoto, he claims, is "based on tentative and contradictory evidence about climate trends" that focus on "carbon dioxide, which is essential to life, rather than upon pollutants." Implementing Kyoto, he writes, "would cripple the oil and gas industry, which is essential to the economies of Newfoundland, Nova Scotia, Saskatchewan, Alberta, and British Columbia." The accord, he continues, "is essentially a socialist scheme to suck money out of wealth- producing nations." Clearly, Obama and Harper have different agendas when it comes to climate change and the efforts needed to combat it. (Climate Action Network Canada, "Stephen Harper Talks Kyoto Accord," http://climateaction network.ca/archive/e/issues/harper-talks-kyoto.html, accessed July 23, 2014.)

18 Ngalo Hotte and Ussif Rashid Sumaila, "Potential Economic Impact of a Tanker Spill on Ocean-Based Industries in British Columbia," Fisheries Centre research report, University of British Columbia, April 9, 2013, http://www.fisheries.ubc.ca/node/3679.

19 Ken Coates and Dwight Newman, "Tsilhqot'in Ruling Brings Canada to the Table," *Globe and Mail*, September 11, 2014.

20 Still to come is the development of China's own shale gas reserves, estimated to be among the largest in the world. In July 2014, the Chinese government confirmed shale gas reserves in Sinopec's Fuling field. Located in the Chongqing, in southwest China, the Fuling field has verified proven reserves

of nearly 350 billion cubic feet. The announcement by the government is believed to confirm the official launch of the commercial development of the country's first large shale gas field. ("Sinopec's Fuling Verified as China's First Large Shale Gas Play," Reuters.com, July 17, 2014, http://af.reuters.com /article/commoditiesNews/idAFL4N0PS2BX20140717.)

21   Wood Mackenzie, "Energy East Pipeline Project: Impacts to Ontario's Natural Gas Market," Presentation to the Ontario Energy Board, January 29, 2015, http://www.ontarioenergyboard.ca/html/oebenergyeast/documents /PartTwo/StakeholderForum/Panel%203/3.2B%20Wood%20Mackenzie%20 (on%20behalf%20of%20Union%20Gas).pdf.

CHAPTER SIX: **TICK, TICK, TICK**

1   Mr. Buffett has since changed his tune. In June 2013, it was revealed that Berkshire Hathaway held nearly 18 million shares of Suncor—the largest of Canada's oil sands producers. And with BNSF already well entrenched in the oil business, it's not surprising that Buffett has recently suggested that he supports the building of Keystone XL. (Matthew J. Belvedere, "I'd Vote 'Yes' on Keystone Pipeline: Warren Buffett," CNBC.com, March 3, 2014, http://www.cnbc.com/id/101460011.)

2   Steve Horn, "Warren Buffett Invests Big Time in Tar Sands," *Alternet*, August 19, 2013, http://www.alternet.org/environment/warren-buffett-buys-over-500 -million-suncor-tar-sands-stock.

3   Andy Kroll, "How Obama Banks on Warren Buffett—for Campaign Cash," *Mother Jones*, April 24, 2012, http://www.motherjones.com/politics/2012/04 /barack-obama-warren-buffett-campaign-cash.

4   BNSF Railway, http://www.bnsf.com, accessed July 25, 2014.

5   Ross Marowits, "CN Taps into Growing Shale Demand with New Alberta Frack Sand Terminal," *Globe and Mail*, July 3, 2013, http://www.theglobe andmail.com/report-on-business/industry-news/energy-and-resources /cn-taps-into-growing-shale-demand-with-new-alberta-frack-sand-terminal /article12959153/.

6   Leslie Young, "Crude Oil Spills Are Bigger From Trains than Pipelines," GlobalNews.ca, January 8, 2014, http://globalnews.ca/news/1069624 /how-do-crude-spills-compare-by-rail-truck-pipeline-you-may-be-surprised/.

7   Guy Dixon, "First Six Months on Job Prove Lucrative for CP Chief Harrison," *Globe and Mail*, March 22, 2013, http://www.theglobeandmail.com/report

-on-business/first-six-months-on-job-prove-lucrative-for-cp-chief-harrison
/article10202261/.

8   Thomas Black, "Fracking Sand Spurs Grain-Like Silos for Rail Transport,"
Bloomberg.com, April 17, 2014, http://www.bloomberg.com/news/2014-04-17
/fracking-sand-spurs-grain-like-silos-for-rail-transport.html.

9   Barrie McKenna and Colin Freeze, "Amid Lac-Mégantic fallout, Irving
Oil pledges rail-safety upgrade," *Globe and Mail*, February 17, 2014.
http://www.theglobeandmail.com/report-on-business/industry-news
/energy-and-resources/irving-scuttles-rail-car-model-at-centre-of-lac
-megantic-derailment/article16922759/

10   Yadullah Hussain, "Demand for Tank Cars to Ship Crude Oil by Rail Rises
at Breakneck Speed," *Financial Post*, February 22, 2013.

11   In July 2014, the Norfolk Southern Corp.—an eastern rail company—actually
sued the state of Maryland in an effort to block the media from learning about
crude shipments through the state through Public Information Act requests.
(Maria Gallucci, "US Oil Trains' Routes Should Remain Secret, Railroad
Company Argues in Lawsuit," *International Business Times*, July 25, 2014,
http://www.ibtimes.com/us-oil-trains-routes-should-remain-secret-
railroad-company-argues-lawsuit-1639118.)

12   Jeffrey Jones, "The oil trains are here to stay—pipelines or not," GlobeAdvisor.
com, January 2, 2014. https://secure.globeadvisor.com/servlet/ArticleNews
/story/gam/20140102/RBJONESCOLUMN0101ATL.

13   United States Department of Transportation, "U.S. DOT Announces
Comprehensive Proposed Rulemaking for the Safe Transportation of
Crude Oil, Flammable Materials," press briefing, July 23, 2014,
http://www.dot.gov/briefing-room/us-dot-announces-comprehensive
-proposed-rulemaking-safe-transportation-crude-oil.

14   Murray Brewster and Benjamin Shingler, "Lac Megantic: Oil shipments by
rail have increased 28,000 per cent since 2009," *Toronto Star*, July 8, 2013.
http://www.thestar.com/news/canada/2013/07/08/lac_megantic_oil
_shipments_by_rail_have_increased_28000_per_cent_since_2009.html.

15   Edmonton's Alberta Crude Terminal (a joint venture of Kinder Morgan and
Keyera) has a planned capacity of 40,000 barrels a day; TORQ's Kerrobert Rail
Terminal in Saskatchewan has a planned capacity of 68,000 barrels a day;
Gibson Energy's Hardisty, Alberta, terminal is expected to handle 120,000;
the Canexus Bruderheim terminal is planning for 50,000 a day. More recently,
Exxon announced plans for a rail terminal in Edmonton to move its Kearl

oil sands product to the United States, while Imperial Oil and Kinder Morgan have announced plans for a terminal in Strathcona. (Nia Williams, "For Canada's Oil-Rail Terminal Firms, Muted Glee over Keystone," Reuters.com, April23,2014,http://www.reuters.com/article/2014/04/23/canada-keystone-railway-idUSL2N0NE20J20140423; Keyera Corp., Kinder Morgan Energy Partners LP, "Keyera and Kinder Morgan to Construct Alberta Crude Terminal, *Oil & Gas Financial Journal*, July 30, 2013, http://www.ogfj.com/articles/2013/07 /keyera-and-kinder-morgan-to-construct-alberta-crude-terminal.html; "TORQ to Build 168,000 bpd Western Canada Crude-by-Rail Terminal," Reuters.com, August 14, 2013, http://www.reuters.com/article/2013/08/14/canada-crude -rail-idUSL2N0GF0Z520130814; "Canada's First Oil-Sands Unit Train to Run in November," Reuters.com, October 3, 2103, http://www.reuters.com /article/2013/10/03/canada-rail-canexus-idUSL1N0HR2A120131003; "Exxon Says Considering Edmonton Rail Terminal to Move Kearl Crude," Reuters. com, October 31, 2013, http://www.reuters.com/article/2013/10/31/us-exxon -kearl-idUSBRE99U10120131031.)

16 The Council of Canadians recently published a "disaster spotter's" guide to DOT-111s; the website MoveOn.org features a petition asking the United States House of Representatives, the Senate and President Barack Obama to "stop transporting explosive & hazardous crude oil via rail using unsafe and outdated DOT-111 tanker cars"; and the Riverkeeper watchdog group, whose mandate is to protect the Hudson River and its tributaries, has called on the Department of Transportation to "stop the bomb trains" that currently transport more than 7 billion gallons of crude oil through New York each year. And in July 2014, the "Oil by Rail Week of Action" was organized by a coalition of environmentalists, and saw protests in Chicago, Detroit and Washington, among other cities. (Michael Butler, "DOT-111 Detecting Disasters Spotters Guide," Council of Canadians, April 21, 2014, http://www.canadians.org/blog/dot-111-detecting-disaster-spotters-guide; MoveOn.org, "Stop Transporting Explosive & Hazardous Crude Oil via Rail Using Unsafe and Outdated DOT-111 Tanker Cars," petition by Alan Stankevitz, http://petitions.moveon.org/sign/stop-transporting -explosive, accessed July 30, 2014; "Stop the Bomb Trains," Riverkeeper.com, https://secure3.convio.net/river/site/Advocacy?cmd=display&page= UserAction&id=449, accessed July 20, 2014; Meagan Clark, "Oil by Rail Protests Are Rippling Nationwide This Weekend," *International Business Times*, July 10, 2014, http://www.ibtimes.com/oil-rail-protests-are-rippling -nationwide-weekend-1624546.)

17 Joel Connelly, "The Fine Print: U.S. Government Fudges Phase-Out of Old Oil Tank Cars," Seattlepi.com, July 23, 2014, http://blog.seattlepi.com /seattlepolitics/2014/07/23/the-fine-print-u-s-government-fudges-on-phaseout -of-old-oil-tank-cars/.

18   Meagan Clark, "Oil by Rail Protests Are Rippling Nationwide This Weekend," *International Business Times*, July 10, 2014, http://www.ibtimes.com/oil -rail-protests-are-rippling-nationwide-weekend-1624546.

19   Dave Battagello, "Windsor Stands Firm on Confidentiality Fight with Railways," *Windsor Star*, July 14, 2014, http://blogs.windsorstar.com/news /windsor-stands-firm-on-confidentiality-fight-with-railways.

20   Jim Snyder and Thomas Black, "Puncture-Prone Rail Cars May Be Phased Out in Two Years," Bloomberg.com, July 23, 2014, http://www.bloomberg .com/news/print/2014-07-23/obama-administration-said-to-plan-oil-by -rail-rules.html.

21   Connelly, "The Fine Print."

22   Ibid.

23   Kim Mackrael, "Railways Face Higher Insurance Costs in Review of Lac-Mégantic Crash," *Globe and Mail*, September 16, 2013, http://www.the globeandmail.com/news/national/lac-megantic-crash-prompts-review-of -railway-insurance-rules/article14331237/.

24   Betsy Morris, "Fiery Oil-Train Accidents Raise Railroad Insurance Worries," *Wall Street Journal*, January 8, 2014, http://online.wsj.com/news/articles /SB10001424052702304773104579268871635384130.

25   Transportation Safety Board of Canada, "Lac-Mégantic Runaway Train and Derailment Investigation Summary," last modified October 28, 2014, http://www.tsb.gc.ca/eng/rapports-reports/rail/2013/r13d0054/r13d0054 -r-es.asp.

26   "Prairie Pile-Up," *Economist*, March 5, 2014, http://www. economist.com/blogs/americasview/2014/03/canadas-grain-crisis.

27   Ibid.

28   Ibid.

29   Ibid.

30   Farmers were forced to use rail providers and tracks within thirty kilometres of their farms—a regulation that made it difficult to "shop" for better prices.

31   In September 2014, CN faced the first fine under the Fair Rail Act, for failing to move enough grain. (Eric Atkins, "CN Faces First Fine under Fair Rail Act for Failing to Move Enough Grain," *Globe and Mail*, September 17, 2014.)

CHAPTER SEVEN: **HOLLOWED OUT**

1 Fabrice Taylor, "No Better Place To Be Than Fort McMurray," *Winnipeg Free Press*, April 21, 2012, http://www.winnipegfreepress.com/business/finance /no-better-place-to-be-than-fort-mcmurray-148365415.html.

2 Sarah Dobson, Nathan Lemphers and Steven Guilbeault, *Booms, Busts and Bitumen* (Calgary: Pembina Institute, November 2013), http://www.pembina .org/reports/booms-busts-bitumen-en.pdf. The Calgary and Edmonton averages were $527,429 and $417,836 respectively.

3 Toronto Real Estate Board, "GTA Realtors Release Mid-Month Resale Housing Figures," press release, June 18, 2013, http://www.torontorealestate board.com/market_news/release_market_updates/news2013/nr_mid _month_0613.htm. According to the Toronto Real Estate Board, the average Toronto house price in June 2013 was just over $500,000.

4 *Globe and Mail Report on Business*, special edition, *The Oil Sands: The Biggest Business Story of the Decade*, November 2014, 74.

5 Statistics Canada, *Canada Year Book*, Table 9.1 "Gross domestic product, expenditure-based, by province and territory, 1996 to 2010," Statistics Canada Catalogue no. 11-402-X, http://www.statcan.gc.ca/pub/11-402-x/2012000/chap/ econo/tbl/tbl01-eng.htm.

6 Statistics Canada, "Canada's total population estimates, 2013," *The Daily*, September 26, 2013, http://www.statcan.gc.ca/tables-tableaux/sum-som/l01/ cst01/econ15-eng.htm.

7 Ibid.

8 Statistics Canada, *Canada Year Book*, Table 9.1.

9 Labour was also brought in from other countries. The Alberta Federation of Labour (AFL) estimates that there were 57,843 temporary foreign workers in Alberta in December 2008, an increase of 55 percent in one year, and a fourfold increase over five years—and that number is growing. In 2010 alone, the ALF reported that Alberta brought in 22,992 temporary foreign workers (while the province itself "lost" 8,600 jobs). ("Exploitation of Foreign Workers Continues Unabated," Alberta Federation of Labour, www.afl.org/index.php /Temporary-Foreign-Workers/overview.html; and "TFW: From Last Resort to First Choice," Alberta Federation of Labour, May 1, 2013, http://www.afl.org /index.php/View-document-details/848-2013-TFW_From-Last-Resort-to-First -Choice.html.

10 *Globe and Mail Report on Business, Oil Sands*, 41.

11   Ibid.

12   Ibid.

13   Adam Radwanksi, "After the Gold Rush: The Long, Slow Decline of the Nation's Industrial Heartland," *Globe and Mail*, May 30, 2014, http://www .theglobeandmail.com/news/politics/after-the-gold-rush/article18923563/.

14   Rob Ferguson, "New 'Fiscal Gap' Study Finds Ottawa Milking Ontario of $11 Billion a Year," *Toronto Star*, April 1, 2013, http://www.thestar.com/news /canada/2013/04/01/star_exclusive_new_fiscal_gap_study_finds_ottawa _milking_ontario_of_11_billion_a_year.html.

15   In 2012, Ontario's share of the country's GDP dropped to 37.1 percent from a peak of 42.2 percent in 1989. (Livio Di Matteo, Jason Clemens, and Milagros Palacios, *Can Canada Prosper without a Prosperous Ontario?* (Vancouver: Fraser Institute, April 2014), http://www.fraserinstitute.org/uploadedFiles /fraser-ca/Content/research-news/research/publications/can-canada-prosper -without-a-prosperous-ontario-rev.pdf.)

16   Shawn McCarthy, "Environmental Group Uses Poll to Battle Oil Sands PR," *Globe and Mail*, July 4, 2014, http://www.theglobeandmail.com/report -on-business/industry-news/energy-and-resources/environmental-group-uses -poll-to-battle-oil-sands-pr/article19475437/.

17   Dobson, Lemphers and Guilbeault, *Booms, Busts and Bitumen.*

18   In 2001, Sherry Cooper of BMO Nesbitt Burns called for Canada to abandon the loonie and embrace a common currency with the USA. (Gordon Pitts, "Time to Scrap the Loonie, Nesbitt Economist Says," GlobeAdvisor.com, November 9, 2001, https://secure.globeadvisor.com/servlet/WireFeed Redirect?cf=sglobeadvisor/config&date=20011109&slug=RDOLL&archive= gam.) Six years later, she was at it again, claiming that the idea made even more sense in 2007 than it had in 2001. (Canwest News Service, "Merge the Canadian, U.S. Dollars, Says Economist," Canada.com, September 20, 2007, http://www.canada.com/montrealgazette/story.html?id=968f9da1-65d7-43d8 -b31a-3a4ada80ba68.)

19   David Gewirtz, "The Dot-Com Bubble: How to Lose $5 Trillion," *AndersonCooper360* (blog), November 24, 2009, http://ac360.blogs.cnn.com /2009/11/24/the-dot-com-bubble-how-to-lose-5-trillion/.

20   Chris Alden, "Looking Back on the Crash," *Guardian* (Manchester), March 10, 2005, http://www.theguardian.com/technology/2005/mar/10/newmedia.media.

21 OECD, "Prices and Purchasing Power Parities, 2008 PPP Benchmark Results" (Table 1.1), last updated December 2010, http://stats.oecd.org/Index. aspx?DataSetCode=PPP2008#.

22 To satisfy your curiosity: In 2014, the average price of a Big Mac in the USA was $4.80. The same sandwich cost $2.73 in China (suggesting that the Chinese yuan was undervalued by 43 percent). In Canada, the Big Mac cost $5.75, suggesting a 9.5 percent overvaluation. (D.H. and R.L.W., "The Big Mac Index," *Economist*, July 24, 2014, http://www.economist.com/content /big-mac-index.)

23 Statistics Canada, Real Gross Domestic Product By Expenditure Account CANSIM Table 380-0064; Bureau of Economic Analysis, US Department of Commerce.

24 "Exports of Goods and Services (% of GDP) in Canada," *Trading Economics*, http://www.tradingeconomics.com/canada/exports-of-goods-and-services -percent-of-gdp-wb-data.html.

25 Statistics Canada, Canada's International Merchandise Trade, CANSIM Table 228-006.

26 Ibid.

27 "Maritime Bus Alberta Offers Luxury Ride to Oilsands," *Huffington Post*, June 5, 2014, http://www.huffingtonpost.ca/2014/06/05/maritime-bus -alberta_n_5454616.html.

28 Eric Atkin and Tavia Grant, "Kellogg's Ontario Plant Closing a Casualty of Changing Tastes," *Globe and Mail*, December 10, 2013, http://www.theglobe andmail.com/report-on-business/kellogg-to-close-london-ont-plant-next-year /article15840106/.

29 Tristin Hopper, "Brine Drain: Pickle Maker Moves South," *National Post*, January 26, 2012, http://news.nationalpost.com/2012/01/26/brine-drain-pickle -maker-moves-south/.

30 Rachel Mendleson, "Canada Manufacturing Job Losses: Study Finds Laid-Off Auto Workers Still Struggling Years Later," *Huffington Post*, July 12, 2012, http://www.huffingtonpost.ca/2012/07/12/manufacturing-layoffs-study-caw _n_1667869.html.

31 Dobson, Lemphers and Guilbeault, *Booms, Busts and Bitumen*.

32 Ibid.

33   Deloitte Canada, "Declining Productivity Most Significant Threat to Canada's Standard of Living," *Financial Post*, October 9, 2012, http://business.financial post.com/2012/10/09/marketing-feature-declining-productivity-most-significant -threat-to-canadas-standard-of-living/. Some indicators are now pointing to modest improvements based on a stronger US economy and—not surprisingly— a weaker Canadian dollar. (Julian Beltrame, "Canadian Manufacturing Shows Signs of Growth After Long Decline," CTVNews.ca, April 1, 2014, http://www.ctvnews.ca/business/canadian-manufacturing-shows-signs -of-growth-after-long-decline-1.1755409.)

34   Bank of Canada, annual report, 2012, www.bankofcanada.ca/wp-content /uploads/2013/04/annualreport2012.pdf.

35   Bank of Canada, Mark Carney, Remarks, Spruce Meadow Round Table, Calgary, Alberta, September 7, 2012, http://www.bankofcanada.ca/2012/09 /dutch-disease/.

36   Daniel Wyatt, "Regina—The Motor City," *High on History* (blog), June 18, 2013, http://danielwyatt.blogspot.ca/2013/06/regina-motor-city.html.

37   Canadian Energy Research Institute, "Canadian Economic Impacts of New and Existing Oil Sands Development in Alberta" (Calgary: CERI, November 2014).

38   Dobson, Lemphers and Guilbeault, *Booms, Busts and Bitumen*.

39   Ibid.

40   Greg Keenan, "Canada Left Behind in Auto Race as U.S., Mexico Make Gains," *Globe and Mail*, February 5, 2014, http://www.theglobeandmail.com /report-on-business/canada-left-behind-in-auto-race-as-us-mexico-make-gains /article16722514/.

41   Greg Keenan, "Mexico Races Ahead in Auto Industry as Canada Stalls," *Globe and Mail*, February 9, 2015, http://www.theglobeandmail.com /report-on-business/international-business/latin-american-business /mexico-races-ahead-in-auto-industry-as-canada-stalls/article22885336/.

42   Paul Stenquist, "Camara Production Returning to the United States," *Wheels* (blog), *New York Times*, December 19, 2012, http://wheels.blogs.nytimes. com/2012/12/19/camaro-production-returning-to-the-united-states/? _php=true&_type=blogs&_r=0.

43   Rick Westhead, "PC's Elliott Holds Whitby-Oshawa but NDP's French Surprising in Oshawa in Ontario Election," *Toronto Star*, June 12, 2014.

44   Curtis Rush, "Canada Simply Gives Up Competing for the American Tourist," *Toronto Star*, May 11, 2013, http://www.thestar.com/business/2013/05/11 /canada_simply_gives_up_competing_for_the_american_tourist.html.

CHAPTER EIGHT: **SHIFTING GOALPOSTS**

1   Thermal coal (also known as steam coal) is primarily used for energy production. Metallurgical coal (also known as coking coal) is primarily used in the production of steel.

2   Gaelle Gourmelon, "Greenhouse Gas Increases Are Leading to a Faster Rate of Global Warming," Worldwatch Institute, December 17, 2014, http://blogs .worldwatch.org.

3   Energy Information Administration, Quarterly Coal Report, Table 32; Rebecca Smith, "Rush to Natural Gas Has Coal-Fired Utilities Seeing Red," *Wall Street Journal*, January 24, 2013, http://www.wsj.com/articles/SB1000142 4127887324296604578179471763404196.

4   Under the executive authority granted to him by the Clean Air Act, Obama instructed the EPA to impose a requirement that new power plants built in America emit no more than 1,000 pounds of carbon per megawatt hour of power generated. That standard is benchmarked to the emissions per kilowatt-hour from an average gas-powered utility. But emissions from your average coal-fired utility in the USA are around 1,900 pounds per kilowatt-hour, meaning that without carbon capture and sequestration, no new coal plants can possibly meet the new federal standard.

5   US Energy Information Administration, International Energy Statistics, "China Consumes Nearly as Much Coal as the Rest of the World Combined," January 29, 2013, http://www.eia.gov/todayinenergy/detail.cfm?id=9751.

6   In 2006, China overtook the USA as the world's leading producer of greenhouse gas emissions ("China Overtakes U.S. in Greenhouse Gas Emissions," *New York Times*, June 20, 2007). As of 2010, China's 26.43 percent of the world total is a good deal higher than the USA's share, which comes in second at 17.33 percent. The European Union sits third, with 13.33 percent (figures taken from US Department of Energy's Carbon Dioxide Information Analysis Center, for the United Nations).

7   "Airpocolypse in China Kills 1.2 Million: Record Air Pollution Causes Beijing State of Emergency," *International Science Times*, April 2, 2013, http://www.isciencetimes.com/articles/4830/20130402/airpocolypse-china -kills-1-2-million-record.htm.

8   Josh Chin and Brian Spegele, "China Details Vast Extent of Soil Pollution," *Wall Street Journal*, April 17, 2014, http://online.wsj.com/news/articles/SB100 01424052702304626304579507040557046288.

9   "New Premier Li Keqiang Pledges to Use 'Iron Fist' on China's Pollution," Climate Group, March 18, 2013, http://www.theclimategroup.org/what -we-do/news-and-blogs/china-announces-ten-tough-measures-to-combat -atmospheric-pollution/.

10   "China Announces Ten 'Tough Measures' to Combat Atmospheric Pollution," Climate Group, June 25, 2013, http://www.theclimategroup.org/what-we -do/news-and-blogs/china-announces-ten-tough-measures-to-combat -atmospheric-pollution/.

11   Jonathan Kaiman, "China Strengthens Environmental Laws," *Guardian* (Manchester), April 25, 2014, http://www.theguardian.com/environment/2014 /apr/25/china-strengthens-environmental-laws-polluting-factories.

12   Associated Press, "China to Ban All Coal Use in Beijing by 2020," August 5, 2014.

13   Timothy Gardner, "U.S., China Agree to Cut Emissions from Vehicle, Coal," Reuters.com, July 10, 2013, http://www.reuters.com/article/2013/07/10/us -climate-usa-china-idUSBRE9690VM20130710.

14   Julie Makinen and Neela Banerjee, "China, U.S. Sign Groundbreaking Deal to Curb Emissions," *Toronto Star*, November 17, 2014.

15   Greenpeace, "Keeping an Eye on China," Ban Ki-moon UN Climate Summit, September 2014, http://www.greenpeace.org/international/Global /international/briefings/climate/2014/Ban-Ki-moon-UN-Climate-summit.pdf.

16   Energy Information Administration.

17   Bob Davis, "China Growth Seen Slowing Sharply over Decade," *Wall Street Journal*, October 20, 2014, http://www.wsj.com/articles/china-growth -seen-slowing-sharply-over-decade-1413778141.

18   Damian Carrington, "China's Coal Use Falls for First Time This Century, Analysis Suggests," *Guardian* (Manchester), October 22, 2014, http://www .theguardian.com/environment/2014/oct/22/chinas-coal-use-falls-for-first-time -this-century-analysis-suggests.

19   In early 2014, Goldman Sachs estimated that marginal production costs (the cost of producing one additional unit) for thermal coal were 15 percent higher than plunging thermal coal prices. Since that analysis, coal prices have dropped by almost another $20 a ton.

20 Daniel Gilbert and Justin Scheck, "Big Oil Companies Struggle to Justify Soaring Project Costs," *Wall Street Journal*, January 28, 2014, http://online .wsj.com/news/articles/SB10001424052702303277704579348332283819314.

21 Between 2009 and 2013, the figures are as follows: ExxonMobil—cap ex rose 51%, production rose 6%; Royal Dutch Shell—cap ex rose 39%, production rose 1%; Chevron—cap ex rose 89%, production fell 3%. Figures taken from Econbrowser, "Big Oil Companies Spending More and Producing Less," *Wall Street Journal*, January 31, 2014, http://econbrowser.com/archives /2014/01/big-oil-companies-spending-more-and-producing-less.

22 Geraldine Amiel and Selina Williams, "Production at Kazakhstan's Kashagan Oil Field Halted Until 2016," *Wall Street Journal*, June 10, 2014. http://www.wsj.com/articles/production-at-kazakhstans-kashagan-oil-field -halted-until-2016-1402400700.

23 EIA.

24 For more on the subprime mortgage bubble, see chapter 7, "Just How Big Is Cleveland," in Rubin, *Why Your World is About to Get a Whole Lot Smaller* (Toronto: Random House, 2009).

25 The group comprised seventy global investors managing more than $3 trillion in assets. They launched a coordinated effort to make forty-five of the world's top oil and gas, coal and electric power companies assess the financial risks that changes in demand and price pose to their business plans. (Janet McFarland, "Global Investment Funds Pledge 'Carbon Footprint' Disclosure," *Globe and Mail*, September 25, 2014; "Investors Challenge Fossil Fuel Companies," Carbon Tracker Initiative, http://www.carbontracker.org/site /investors-challenge-fossil-fuel-companies#/.)

CHAPTER NINE: **MEAN REVERSION**

1 Government of Alberta, "Alberta Overview: Economic Results," http://albertacanada.com/business/overview/economic-results.aspx, accessed August 18, 2014.

2 A. Stephenson, "Redford Budget Bets on Continued Oilsands-Driven Economic Growth," *Calgary Herald*, March 6, 2014, http://www2.canada .com/calgaryherald/iphone/news/latest/story.html?id=9588296.

3 Government of Alberta, Treasury Board and Finance, "2014–15 Second Quarter Fiscal Update and Economic Statement," November 26, 2014, http://finance.alberta.ca/publications/budget/quarterly/2014/2014-15-2nd -Quarter-Fiscal-Update.html.

4   Jeremy van Loon and Rebecca Penty, "Oil Rout to Weigh on Alberta's Carbon Emissions Policy," Bloomberg.com, November 3, 2014, http://www.bloomberg .com/news/2014-11-03/oil-rout-to-weigh-on-alberta-s-carbon-emissions-policy.html.

5   Dean Bennett, "Tumbling Oil Prices Mean Alberta Surplus This Year Now $500M deficit," *Globe and Mail*, January 8, 2015, http://www.theglobe andmail.com/news/alberta/tumbling-oil-prices-mean-alberta-surplus-this -year-now-500m-deficit-premier/article22372108/.

6   *Globe and Mail Report on Business*, special edition, *Oil Sands: The Biggest Business Story of the Decade*, November 2014, 67.

7   Ibid.

8   Ibid.

9   According to a Fraser Institute paper, if Alberta had consistently put away 25 percent of its non-renewable resource revenue between 1982 and 2011, as Alaska is constitutionally bound to do, total contributions would have been $42.2 billion, not the $9 billion the province actually managed to save during this period. If Alberta had followed in Norway's somewhat radical footsteps, and set aside *all* revenues during that same period, the total contribution would have been $169.5 billion. ("How Much Would Alberta's Heritage Fund Be Had It Followed Alaska's or Norway's rules," Fraser Forum, May/June 2013, http://www.fraserinstitute.org/uploadedFiles/fraser-ca/Content/research-news/ research/articles/how-much-would-albertas-heritage-fund-be-had-it-followed.pdf.)

10 Dan Woynillowicz, "Shine a Light on the Oil Sands Boom," *Globe and Mail*, June 1, 2012, http://www.theglobeandmail.com/globe-debate/shine-a-light-on -the-oil-sands-boom/article4223728/.

11 "The Bitumen Bubble: What Does That Mean," *Edmonton Journal*, January 7, 2014, http://www.edmontonjournal.com/business/Bitumen+Bubble+ What+does+that+mean/9306461/story.html.

12 John Gray, "The Second Coming of Peter Lougheed," *Globe and Mail*, August 29, 2008, http://www.theglobeandmail.com/report-on-business/rob -magazine/the-second-coming-of-peter-lougheed/article659021/?page=all.

13 In 2007, Premier Ed Stelmach tried to raise the province's royalty rates. Although the move failed, it nevertheless pitted him against the oil and gas industry for the rest of his tenure. (*Globe and Mail Report on Business, Oil Sands*, 51.)

14 Carbon Tracker Initiative, "Carbon Supply Cost Curves: Evaluating Financial Risk to Oil Capital Expenditures," May 2014.

15   Carrie Tait, "Total Shelves $11-Billion Alberta Oil Sands Mine," *Globe and Mail*, May 29, 2014, http://www.theglobeandmail.com/report-on-business /joslyn/article18914681/.

16   Jeff Lewis, "Shell Halts Work on Pierre River Oil Sands Mine in Northern Alberta," *Financial Post*, February 12, 2014, http://business.financialpost. com/2014/02/12/shell-halts-work-on-pierre-river-oil-sands-mine-in-northern -alberta/?__lsa=52ba-43a8.

17   Jeffrey Jones, "Statoil Retreats from Oil Sands as Industry Costs Rise," *Globe and Mail*, September 26, 2014.

18   Jeffrey Jones, "Cenovus Energy Slashes Spending by 15 Per Cent, Warns of Deeper Cuts," *Globe and Mail*, December 11, 2014, http://www.theglobeand mail.com/report-on-business/industry-news/energy-and-resources/cenovus-to -slash-capital-spending-amid-oil-plunge/article22037485/.

19   Dan Healing, "Suncor cuts $1B in capital spending, plans to chop 1,000 positions," *Calgary Herald*, January 14, 2015, http://calgaryherald.com /business/energy/suncor-cuts-1b-in-capital-plans-to-chop-1000-positions.

20   Yadullah Hussain, "Almost $60-Billion in Canadian Projects in Peril as 'Collapse' in Oil Investment Echoes the Dark Days of 1999," *Financial Post*, January 2, 2015, http://business.financialpost.com/2015/01/02/almost -60-billion-in-canadian-projects-in-peril-as-collapse-in-oil-investment -echoes-the-dark-days-of-1999/?__lsa=9516-aa8a.

21   Tasmin McMahon, "Calgary's Housing Market Slumps as Oil's Fall Takes a Toll," *Globe and Mail*, February 2, 2015, http://www.theglobeandmail.com /report-on-business/economy/housing/the-real-estate-beat/calgary-housing -market-hits-seven-year-low/article22749863/.

22   Canadian Press, "Honda to Invest $857M in Ontario Plant to Build Next Generation of Civic Car," *Financial Post*, November 6, 2014.

23   Steven Chase and Greg Keenan, "General Motors to invest $560-million in Ontario's Ingersoll plant," *Globe and Mail*, February 12, 2015, http://www .theglobeandmail.com/report-on-business/gm-to-invest-450-million-in-ontarios -ingersoll-plant/article22933182/.

CHAPTER TEN: **SAVE YOUR PORTFOLIO BEFORE YOU SAVE THE WORLD**

1   Marc Lee and Brock Ellis, *Canada's Carbon Liabilities: The Implications of Stranded Fossil Fuel Assets for Financial Markets and Pension Funds* (Ottawa: Canadian Centre for Policy Alternatives, March 2013), https://www.policyal ternatives.ca/publications/reports/canadas-carbon-liabilities.

2   As of September 2014, the TSX energy sector weighting was 26.23 percent; the S&P 500 energy sector accounted for 10.3 percent.

3   "Quakers (Society of Friends)," http://abolition.e2bn.org/people_21.html, accessed September 3, 2014. Also: John Wesley, "The Use of Money," Global Ministries, http://www.umcmission.org/Find-Resources/John-Wesley-Sermons /Sermon-50-The-Use-of-Money.

4   Michael Wines, "Stanford to Purge $18 Billion Endowment of Coal Stock," *New York Times*, May 7, 2014, http://www.nytimes.com/2014/05/07/education /stanford-to-purge-18-billion-endowment-of-coal-stock.html?_r=0.

5   Sean McElwee, "The Oil Industry Is Not Only Hurting the Environment—It's a Bad Investment, Too," *Week*, April 9, 2014, http://theweek.com/article/index /259571/the-oil-industry-is-not-only-hurting-the-environment-mdash-its-a-bad-investment-too.

6   Charlotte Bancillhon, "Is Divestment from Fossil Fuels Going Mainstream?," Business for Social Responsibility, October 28, 2014, http://www.bsr.org/en /our-insights/blog-view/is-divestment-from-fossil-fuels-going-mainstream? utm_source=feedburner&utm_medium=email&utm_campaign=Feed% 3A+bsrblog+%28BSR+Blog%3A+The+Business+of+a+Better+World%29.

7   Divestment Commitments, Fossil Free, http://gofossilfree.org/commitments/, accessed September 4, 2014.

8   John Schwartz, "Rockefellers, Heirs to an Oil Fortune, Will Divest Charity of Fossil Fuels," *New York Times*, September 21, 2014, http://www.nytimes.com /2014/09/22/us/heirs-to-an-oil-fortune-join-the-divestment-drive.html?_r=0.

9   McElwee, "Oil Industry."

10   Benjamin Storrow, "Peabody Energy Reports $787M Loss in 2014; Powder River Coal Remains Strong," *Casper Star-Tribune*, January 27, 2015, http://trib.com/business/energy/peabody-energy-reports-m-loss-in-powder -river-coal-remains/article_4c23332a-c28c-5050-9e50-855399c4105c.html.

11   On September 19, 2014, Peabody Energy was removed from the S&P 500 index. When Peabody joined the S&P 500 in November 2006, its market capitalization was about $10 billion. In September 2014, it was down to $3.9 billion. The size of a company's market cap is a key factor when it comes to inclusion in the index. ("Peabody Energy to Be Removed from S&P 500 Index," *St. Louis Post-Dispatch*, September 12, 2014, http://www.stltoday. com/business/local/peabody-energy-to-be-removed-from-s-p-index/article _601ff555-f353-5df4-8f02-6ecae78e79d4.html.)

12   Shawn McCarthy, "Oil-Reliant Firms at Risk as World Moves Toward
     Low-Carbon Future: Report," *Globe and Mail*, September 16, 2014,
     http://www.theglobeandmail.com/report-on-business/industry-news
     /energy-and-resources/oil-reliant-firms-at-risk-report/article20607843/.

13   *Globe and Mail Report on Business*, special edition, *Oil Sands: The Biggest
     Business Story of the Decade*, November 2014, 61.

14   Jeff Lewis, "CNOOC's Operating Costs Jump 7 Per Cent since Nexen
     Takeover," *Globe and Mail*, August 28, 2014, http://www.theglobeandmail.com
     /report-on-business/industry-news/energy-and-resources/cnoocs-operating
     -costs-jump-7-per-cent-since-nexen-takeover/article20259197/.

15   CTI, *Carbon Supply Cost Curves: Evaluating Financial Risk to Oil Capital
     Expenditures* (London: Carbon Tracker Initiative, May 2014), http://www
     .carbontracker.org/wp-content/uploads/2014/05/CTI_Oil_Report_Oil_May
     _2014_13-05.pdf.

16   "Oil Price Decline Threatens One-Quarter of New Canadian Projects: IEA,"
     Huffington Post, October 14, 2014, http://www.huffingtonpost.ca/2014/10/14
     /oil-prices-oilsands-canada_n_5983614.html?utm_hp_ref=mostpopular&ir=
     Canada+Business.

CHAPTER 11: **BREADBASKET**

1   Alan Bjerga, "Canada's Corn Belt Attracts the Hot Money,"
     BloombergBusinessweek, November 8, 2012, www.businessweek.com/articles
     /2012-11-08/canadas-corn-belt-attracts-the-hotmoney#r=read.

2   Hanspeter Schreier and Chris Wood, "Better by the Drop," Blue Economy
     Initiative (June 2013), 20.

3   Ibid.

4   Ibid.

5   IPCC, *Climate Change 2014* (Geneva: IPCC, 2014).

6   Megan Willett, "How People Consume Meat Around the World," *Business
     Insider*, January 13, 2014, http://www.businessinsider.com/
     how-we-eat-meat-around-the-world-2014-1.

7   Colleen Scherer, "Observations on the Protein Gap in India and China,"
     AG Professional, May 12, 2011, http://www.agprofessional.com/news
     /Observations-on-the-protein-gap-in-India-and-China-121725224.html.

8   FOA, "World Agriculture: Towards 2015/2030 Summary Report," FOA
     Corporate Document Repository, http://www.fao.org/docrep/004/y3557e
     /y3557e09.htm.

9   Combined, Monsanto (USA), DuPont (USA) and Syngenta (Switzerland)
     account for $10,282 million—or 47 percent of the global proprietary seed
     market. ("The World's Top 10 Seed Companies: Who Owns Nature?,"
     GMWatch 2014, http://www.gmwatch.org/component/content/article
     /10558-the-worlds-top-ten-seed-companies-who-owns-nature.)

10   If you doubt the degree to which engineering has already transformed corn,
     compare today's grocery-store peaches-and-cream variety with the crop's
     original form, teosinte, or even with early varieties of maize grown by Native
     Americans. Tweaking corn's genetic composition for growth in more northern
     latitudes is a minor adjustment compared with the crop's previous evolutions.

11   Mychaylo Prystupa, "NASA Says Canada in 'Hot Spot' of Ecological Change,"
     CBCNews.ca, January 12, 2012, http://www.cbc.ca/news/canada/manitoba
     /nasa-says-canada-in-hot-spot-of-ecological-change-1.1158179.

12   Ibid.

13   Canada's rate of warming since 1947 is 1.3 degrees Celsius. (Raveena Aulakh,
     "IPCC Report: Canada at Greater Risk from Climate Change," *Toronto Star*,
     September 30, 2013, http://www.thestar.com/news/world/2013/09/30/great
     _lakes_climate_expected_to_warm_more_than_global_rise_says_un_report.html.)

14   "Overview of Climate Change in Canada: Figure 8," Statistics Canada,
     http://www.nrcan.gc.ca/environment/resources/publications/impacts
     -adaptation/reports/assessments/2008/ch2/10321.

15   There is already evidence that climate change is affecting plant behaviour in
     Canada. A recent study by the University of Toronto noted that the date of
     the first flower bloom in nineteen different Canadian plant species advanced
     on average by about nine days during the 2001–12 period, with the greatest
     change being recorded in the boreal forest region. Early blooming also implies
     a number of other physiological processes in plant life, including leaf
     expansion, root growth and nutrient uptake, which are all of critical impor-
     tance to agricultural yields. The study attributed almost three-quarters of this
     phenomenon of early flowering to the change in Canadian temperatures,
     which warmed by about 0.6 degrees Celsius during the 1961–1990 period.
     The warming temperatures associated with climate change imply not only
     earlier blooming but a longer growing season, potentially changing the type
     of plants that can be grown for agricultural purposes and opening the door for
     rotation into higher-value-added crops. (Alemu Gonsamu, Jing M. Chen and

Chaoyang Wu, "Citizen Science: Linking the Recent Rapid Advances of Plant Flowering in Canada with Climate Variability," *Scientific Reports*, July 2013, no. 3: 2239, doi:10.1038/srep02239.)

16 Alan Bjerga, "Canada's Corn Belt Attracts the Hot Money," *BloombergBusinessweek*, November 8, 2012, www.businessweek.com /articles/2012-11-08/canadas-corn-belt-attracts-the-hotmoney#r=read.

17 Ibid.

18 Alan Bjera, "Canada's Climate Warms to Corn as Grain Belt Shifts North," Bloomberg.com, April 15, 2014, http://www.bloomberg.com/news/2014-04 -15/canada-s-climate-warms-to-corn-as-grain-belt-shifts-north.html.

19 2014 National Climate Assessment, US Global Change Research Program (Washington, DC), http://nca2014.globalchange.gov/highlights/report-findings /agriculture.

20 "Kapuskasing," Reference.com, last modified October 7, 2008, http://www .reference.com/browse/kapuskasing.

21 Lee Hannah et al., "Climate Change, Wine, and Conservation," *Proceedings of the National Academy of Sciences of the United States of America* 110 (17), April 23, 2013, 6907–12, doi:10.1073/pnas.1308923110.

22 Sascha Zubryd, "Global Warming Could Significantly Alter the U.S. Premium Wine Industry within 30 Years, Say Stanford Scientists," *Stanford Report*, June 20, 2011, http://news.stanford.edu/news/2011/june/wines-global -warming-063011.html.

23 Hannah et al., "Climate Change."

CHAPTER 12: **WATERWORKS**

1   "The Deadly Passage of the All-American Canal," CBSNews.com, April 30, 2010, http://www.cbsnews.com/news/the-deadly-passage-of -the-all-american-canal/.

2   2014 National Climate Assessment, US Global Change Research Program (Washington, DC), http://nca2014.globalchange.gov/highlights/report-findings /agriculture.

3   "Biofuels: Prospects, Risks and Opportunities," in *The State of Food and Agriculture 2008*. Food and Agriculture Organization of the United Nations (Rome, 2008), http://www.fao.org/publications/sofa/2008/en/.

4   International Energy Agency, "For World Water Day, IEA Shares In-Depth
Analysis of Energy Sector's Use," press release, March 17, 2014, http://www
.iea.org/newsroomandevents/pressreleases/2014/march/for-world-water-day
-iea-shares-in-depth-analysis-of-energy-sectors-use.html.

5   Marianne Lavelle and Thomas K. Grose, "Water Demand for Energy to
Double by 2035," *National Geographic*, January 30, 2013, http://news
.nationalgeographic.com/news/energy/2013/01/130130-water-demand-for
-energy-to-double-by-2035/.

6   The trend of buying arable land in other countries is on the rise, so much so
that some economists are calling it "outsourcing's third great wave" (following
manufacturing in the 1980s and information technology in the 1990s). The
International Food Policy Research Institute, a think tank in Washington, DC,
reports that 15 to 20 million hectares of farmland in poor countries has been
acquired or is under discussion for acquisition. The United Arab Emirates,
South Korea and Qatar have all completed deals, and in 2010, China
announced a whopper of a transaction—the lease of 30,000 square kilometres
in Ukraine, which amounts to one-twentieth of the entire country. In 2013,
Spiegel Online reported that this "land grabbing," which it calls a "new form
of colonialism," has led to some alarming statistics, particularly in Africa:
Liberia has outsourced 100 percent of its arable land, while Gabon is not
far behind at 86 percent. (Dan Stone, "Why China Wants (and Needs)
Foreign Farm Land," *National Geographic*, September 25, 2013, http://voices
.nationalgeographic.com/search/foreign+farm+land; "Land Grabbing: Foreign
Investors Buy Up Third World Farmland," *Der Spiegel* (international edition),
February 19, 2013, http://www.spiegel.de/international/world/foreign-investors
-are-buying-up-farmland-in-third-world-a-884306.html.)

7   "Top Ten Countries by Agricultural Exports," Maps of World, http://www.maps
ofworld.com/world-top-ten/world-top-ten-agricultural-exporters-map.html.

8   Hanspeter Schreier and Chris Wood, "Better by the Drop," Blue Economy
Initiative (June 2013), 35.

9   According to a 2009 study, the average Canadian uses 329 litres of water per
day—second only to the USA in the developed world, and more than twice as
much as Europeans. (Thomas Jolicouer, "New Study Calls Average Water
Use by Canadians 'Alarming,'" *National Post*, March 18, 2009, http://www
.nationalpost.com/Life/pets/study+calls+average+water+Canadians+alarming
/1402591/story.html.)

10   F. Ghassemi and I. White, *Inter-Basin Water Transfer* (Cambridge: Cambridge
University Press, 2007), 264–68.

11 Schreier and Wood, "Better by the Drop," 30.

12 Canada's northernmost point is Ellesmere Island; its southernmost is Middle Island, in Lake Erie.

13 Schreier and Wood, "Better by the Drop," 45.

14 Cameron Stranberg, "Columbia Icefield Shrinking Fast," University of Saskatchewan, February 4, 2010, http://www.usask.ca/ip3/download/Rocky%20Mountain%20Outlook%204%20Feb%202010%20-%20Columbia%20Icefield%20shrinking%20fast.pdf.

15 Government of Canada, Environment Canada, "Threats to Water Availability in Canada," NWRI scientific assessment report series, ISSN 1499-5905; no. 3 (2004), http://www.ec.gc.ca/inre-nwri/default.asp?lang=En&n=0CD66675-1&offset=12&toc=show.

16 Ibid.

17 Schreier and Wood, "Better by the Drop," 30.

18 Government of Canada, "Threats to Water Availability."

19 Not surprisingly, the plans for Site C are controversial. The province's First Nations communities, among others, are stressing that BC Hydro must address decades of lingering resentment over the W.A.C. Bennett Dam—specifically concerning resource rights and interests—before considering another project in the area. ("A Dam Never Forgotten," Canada.com, October 28, 2005, http://www.canada.com/vancouversun/specials/websterawards/story.html?id=20cd8141-bc0c-4c8a-86d4-ef6867f056fb.)

20 Andrew Nikiforuk, "A Smoking Gun on Athabasca River: Deformed Fish," *Tyee*, September 17, 2010, http://thetyee.ca/News/2010/09/17/AthabascaDeformedFish/. In addition, a study of lakes near the oil sands found that levels of polycyclic aromatic hydrocarbons—pollutants that are linked to fish deformities—were twenty-three times pre-development levels. (*Globe and Mail Report on Business*, special edition, *Oil Sands: The Biggest Business Story of the Decade*, November 2014, 52.)

21 "Oil Sands: Water Impacts," Pembina Institute, http://www.pembina.org/oil-sands/os101/water.

22 In fact, water diversion from both the Peace and the Athabasca Rivers was considered in the late 1960s. The Central North America Water Project (CeNAWAP) would have redirected the natural flow of both rivers. Another variation on this theme, the Kuiper Diversion Scheme, would also have tapped the Athabasca and the Peace, along with the Nelson and Churchill

river systems in northern Manitoba, and diverted their flows southward. While all of these schemes were proposed for the purpose of bulk water exports to the USA, a much more likely imperative for future water diversion from these rivers will be meeting the irrigation needs of western Canadian farmers.

23 John Gray, "The Second Coming of Peter Lougheed," *Globe and Mail*, August 29, 2008, http://www.theglobeandmail.com/report-on-business/rob -magazine/the-second-coming-of-peter-lougheed/article659021/?page=all.

24 Gary Mason, "In a Water War, Canada Could Get Hosed," *Globe and Mail*, February 28, 2014, http://www.theglobeandmail.com/globe-debate/in-a-water -war-canada-could-get-hosed/article17139638/.

25 Rick Mills, "Water, An Endangered Global Resource," AheadoftheHerd.com, http://aheadoftheherd.com/Newsletter/2012/Water-An-Endangered-Global -Resource.htm.

26 Andrea Thompson, "What Will Winter Hold for Drought-Plagued California?," *Climate Central*, October 23, 2014, http://www.climatecentral .org/news/weak-el-nino-calif-drought-winter-18222.

27 Anthony York, "Gov. Jerry Brown Declares Drought Emergency in California," *Los Angeles Times*, January 17, 2014, http://articles.latimes.com /2014/jan/17/local/la-me-pc-jerry-brown-declares-drought-emergency-in -california-20140117.

28 Omar el Akaad, "In California, Not a Drop to Drink," *Globe and Mail*, February 10, 2014, http://www.theglobeandmail.com/news/world/in-california -not-a-drop-to-drink/article16794043/.

29 Warren Cornwall, "California's 'Dismally Meager' Snowpack Signals More Drought," *National Geographic*, January 30, 2015, http://news.national geographic.com/news/2015/01/150130-snowpack-snow-drought-california -environment-united-states/.

30 States included in population figure are California, Arizona, New Mexico, Texas, Nevada, Utah, Colorado, Kansas and Oklahoma. Figures taken from United States Census Bureau, "Population Estimates," http://www.census.gov /popest/data/state/totals/2013/index.html.

31 Information on NAWAPA taken from Marc Reisner, *Cadillac Desert: The American West and Its Disappearing Water* (New York: Penguin Books, 1993).

32 Michael Kirsch, "The History of NAWAPA: Reviving the Spirit of John F. Kennedy," *Canadian Patriot*, February 12, 2013, http://canadianpatriot.org /archives/484.

CHAPTER 13: **POWER PLAYS**

1   "Hydropower in Canada: Past, Present and Future," Canadian Hydropower
    Association (2008), https://canadahydro.ca/system/resources/BAhbBls
    HOgZmSSJHMjAxMy8wNS8wOS8xOC8xNC81Ny81OTAvMjAwOF9ooe
    WRyb3Bvd2VyX3Bhc3RfcHJlc2VudF9mdXR1cmVfZW4ucGRmBjoGRVQ
    /2008%20hydropower_past_present_future_en.pdf

2   Hydro-Québec, "Spillways," http://www.hydroquebec.com/learning
    /hydroelectricite/evacuateurs-crue.html; Michael Seo, "The World's 18
    Strangest Dams," *Popular Mechanics*, http://www.popularmechanics.com
    /technology/engineering/architecture/the-worlds-18-strangest-dams-robert
    -bourassa-dam#slide-7.

3   Jean-Thomas Bernard and Jean-Yves Duclos, "Quebec's Green Future:
    The Lowest-Cost Route to Greenhouse Gas Reductions," C.D. Howe
    backgrounder no. 118 (October 2009).

4   John Barber, "Ontarians Have No Excuse for Being Naïve about Nuclear,"
    Toronto Star, July 9, 2014, http://www.thestar.com/opinion/commentary
    /2014/07/09/ontarians_have_no_excuse_for_being_naive_about
    _nuclear.html.

5   The original phase of Darlington Nuclear Generating Station came in over
    four times the budget.

6   The CANDU (Canada Deuterium Uranium) reactor is Canadian invented,
    the result of a partnership in the late 1950s and early 1960s between Atomic
    Energy of Canada Limited, the Hydro-Electric Power Commission of Ontario
    (now Ontario Power Generation) and Canadian General Electric (now
    GE Canada). The partnership actively marketed the CANDU reactor
    overseas, and as a result, units are operating in India, Pakistan, Argentina,
    South Korea, Romania and China. ("CANDU History," Candu website,
    http://www.candu.com/en/home/candureactors/canduhistory.aspx.)

7   Generous feed-in tariffs for wind and solar power have also contributed to
    those costs.

8   The electricity transfer capacity between Quebec and Ontario is 2,788,000
    kilowatts per hour. There are 8,760 hours in a year; hence, the annual transfer
    capacity is 24.4 billion kilowatts. By comparison, Darlington's annual power
    output in 2013 was 25.1 billion kilowatts ("Maximizing the Value of OPG,"
    Ontario Clean Air Alliance and Environmental Defence (August 2014).

9   Ibid.

10 Jeffrey Simpson, "Hydro Imports: When Will the Bulb Go On for Ontario and Quebec?," *Globe and Mail*, June 6, 2014, http://www.theglobeandmail.com /globe-debate/when-will-the-hydro-bulb-go-on-for-ontario-quebec/article 19011993/.

11 "Overview of Greenhouse Gases," United States Environmental Protection Agency, last modified July 2, 2014, http://epa.gov/climatechange/ghgemissions /gases/ch4.html.

12 "Senators Urge Administration to Address Methane Pollution," press release, Sheldon Whitehouse website, September 26, 2014, http://www.whitehouse .senate.gov/news/release/senators-urge-administration-to-address -methane-pollution.

13 "Study of Hydropower Potential in Canada: Final Report," Canadian Hydropower Association, 2006.

14 "James Bay Project," Historica Canada, http://www.thecanadianencyclopedia .ca/en/article/james-bay-project/.

15 "BC Hydro Power Line Cost Soars," *Terrace Standard*, June 26, 2013, http://www.terracestandard.com/news/212632771.html.

16 Independent Power Producers BC, "Fact Sheet: Run of the River Hydro Power," http://www.bcenergyblog.com/uploads/file/IPPBC_Fact_Sheet _runofriver.pdf.

CHAPTER 14: **FRANKLIN'S DREAM**

1 Government of Canada, "Statement by the Prime Minister of Canada Announcing the Discovery of One of the Ill-Fated Franklin Expedition Ships Lost in 1846," September 9, 2014, Ottawa, http://pm.gc.ca/eng /news/2014/09/09/statement-prime-minister-canada-announcing -discovery-one-ill-fated-franklin.

2 International Energy Agency, "Resources to Reserves 2013," https://www.iea .org/media/presentations/Resourcestoreserves2013web.pdf.

3 Rare earth refers to a set of seventeen chemical elements in the periodic table, specifically the fifteen lanthanides plus scandium and yttrium. They are not often found in concentrated deposits, hence the designation "rare."

4 "Northwest Passage: The Arctic Grail," CBCNews.ca, August 8, 2006, http://www.cbc.ca/news2/background/northwest-passage/.

5   Leo Lewis, "China in Numbers: Yong Sheng Breaks Ice for New Golden Waterway," *Times* (London), September 10, 2013, http://www.thetimes.co.uk/tto/business/economics/article3864666.ece.

6   Emily Chung, "Eastern Arctic Temperatures Likely at 120,000-Year High," CBCNews.ca, October 25, 2013, http://www.cbc.ca/news/technology/eastern-arctic-temperatures-likely-at-120-000-year-high-1.2251709.

7   "Arctic Climate Impact Assessment (2004)," Arctic Council and the International Arctic Science Committee, Climate Impact Assessment (2004), http://www.acia.uaf.edu.

8   The entire Arctic region, it seems, is subject to debates over sovereignty. In late 2014, Denmark submitted a claim on the North Pole to the United Nations. "The North Pole: Does Denmark Have a Legitimate Claim," CBCNews.ca, December 15, 2014, http://www.cbc.ca/news/technology/the-north-pole-does-denmark-have-a-legitimate-claim-1.2873953.

9   John McGarrity and Henning Gloystein, "Northwest Passage Crossed by First Cargo Ship, the Nordic Orion, Heralding New Era of Arctic Commercial Activity," *National Post*, September 27, 2013, http://news.nationalpost.com/2013/09/27/northwest-passage-crossed-by-first-cargo-ship-the-nordic-orion-heralding-new-era-of-arctic-commercial-activity/.

10   Hege Eilersten, "New Russian Icebreakers Ready to Operate from 2017," *High North News*, August 12, 2014, http://www.highnorthnews.com/new-russian-icebreakers-ready-to-operate-in-2017/.

11   Michael Byers, "The (Russian) Arctic Is Open for Business," *Globe and Mail*, August 12, 2013, http://www.theglobeandmail.com/globe-debate/the-russian-arctic-is-open-for-business/article13696054/.

12   "Arctic Ports," Arctic Knowledge Hub, 2009, http://www.arctis-search.com/Arctic+Ports.

13   Kandalaksha, Vitino, Onega, Arkhangelsk, Mezen, Naryan-Mar, Varandey, Amderma, Dikson, Dudinka, Igarka, Khatanga, Tiksi, Pevek and Provideniya. ("Russian Arctic Ports," Arctic Knowledge Hub, 2009, http://www.arctis-search.com/Russian+Arctic+Ports&structure=Marine+Transport+and+Logistics.)

14   Byers, "The (Russian) Arctic."

15   Russia currently charges $100,000 for providing icebreakers and search and rescue pilots for tankers travelling along its Northern Sea Route.

16   Ivan Semeniuk, "Heading into Uncharted Waters," *Globe and Mail*, October 6, 2014.

17   Government of Canada, Royal Canadian Air Force, "CASARA Establishes New Search and Rescue Units in the Arctic," January 23, 2014, http://www .rcaf-arc.forces.gc.ca/en/article-template-standard.page?doc=casara-establishes -new-search-and-rescue-units-in-the-arctic/hqrtfljo.

CONCLUSION: **EMBRACING CHANGE**

1   Farm Credit Canada, "Farmland Values Report, 2013."

2   Don Pittis, "Soaring Farmland Prices a Crisis in the Making: Don Pittis," CBCNews.ca, November 11, 2013, http://www.cbc.ca/news/canada /soaring-farmland-prices-a-crisis-in-the-making-don-pittis-1.2420223.

3   AP, "Four Dead in Rampage in Iowa Town," *New York Times*, December 10, 1985, http://www.nytimes.com/1985/12/10/us/4-dead-in-rampage-in-an-iowa -town.html.

4   AP, "Suspect in Bankers' Killings Found Dead on Texas Farm," *New York Times*, October 3, 1983, http://www.nytimes.com/1983/10/03/us/suspect-in -bankers-killings-found-dead-on-texas-farm.html.

5   Department of Agriculture, Economic Research Service, "The U.S. Farm Sector: How Is It Weathering the 1980's?" AIB-506 (April 1987, iv, 12).

6   Christopher Doering, "Farmland Prices: Is the Bubble About to Burst?" USAToday.com, March 24, 2013, http://www.usatoday.com/story/money /business/2013/03/24/farm-land-prices-bubble/2013451/.

7   Caroline Leiffers, "Food for Thought," ActiveHistory.ca, http://active history.ca/2013/11/food-for-thought/.

[ACKNOWLEDGMENTS]

WRITING A BOOK is a bit like completing a jigsaw puzzle. Even
when you have assembled all the required pieces, knowing where
they go is critical. To that end, Linda Pruessen, my editor, has
been the best yet—and I have been blessed to work with great edi-
tors before.

Once again I must thank Anne Collins, my publisher at Random
House Canada, for her support and encouragement, both for this
project and for my previous two books. Similarly, I am indebted to
publicist Sharon Klein, who has again organized a whirlwind cross-
country promotional tour. Nick Garrison of Penguin Random House
Canada was instrumental in furnishing me with an original idea for
this book, as has been his custom in the past.

There are many people whom I have called upon for advice or
research in the course of writing this book, none more important than
Keith Brooks, director of clean energy at Environmental Defence.
Aside from graciously allowing me to use their diagram for Trans-
Canada's Energy East pipeline, Keith has been an invaluable source
of information on a variety of topics, particularly regarding proposed
pipeline projects in Canada.

I would also like to thank Mark Rudolph, CEO at Just Environment,
an environmental public policy consulting firm serving a number of
key oil sands producers, for his generous assistance. Mark might not
have known all the answers to my questions, but he invariably referred
me to someone who did.

Many thanks to Robert Fernandez of the Alberta Economic
Development Authority for calculating the conversion of China's
annual coal consumption into an energy equivalent in natural gas.

Dr. John Stone, research professor at Carleton University and board
member of the Pembina Institute, was kind enough to furnish me
with information regarding global emission growth. He initially presented this information during a conference on stranded carbon assets
at which he and I both spoke, sponsored by RBC and Suncor on

November 4, 2014, in Toronto.

I would like to thank Charlie Fairbank for his tour of Fairbank Oil, one of the first oil-producing properties in North America.

David Crane, former economics writer at the *Toronto Star*, was helpful in furnishing me with a number of examples of manufacturing plant closures in southern Ontario.

Thanks, also, to Erich Hartmann of the Ontario Ministry of Finance for his discussion of provincial-federal transfer payments and tax remittances.

Tom Eisenhauer, president of Bonnefield Financial Inc., provided a number of useful insights into the opportunities and challenges of investing in Canadian farmland, as did Jack Gibbons of the Ontario Clean Air Alliance regarding Ontario's power dilemma.

A number of former colleagues at CIBC World Markets also deserve mention.

Maurice Smith, my fishing buddy of many years, was kind enough to supply a good example of the principle of mean reversion. Larry Berman, another former colleague and now partner at ETF Capital Management, directed me to the KOL index and to sources for the individual weightings of stocks within the TSX Composite. Harvey Bradley, ex-colleague, fishing buddy and fellow biker, was kind enough to provide me with historical GDP and trade data. The venerable Karl Kainz, still going strong as a broker at CIBC Wood Gundy, was kind enough to send me a *National Geographic* article on coal use that provided a number of useful insights into the challenges facing carbon sequestration. I would also like to thank my old boss and mentor, former chief economist at Wood Gundy, Dr. John Grant, for alerting me to the agricultural potential of his birthplace, the Northern Ontario clay belt, in the warming world that lies ahead.

Last but not least, I would like to thank Aaron Milrad once again for his skill and guidance in negotiating my book contracts.

JEFF RUBIN is the author of *Why Your World Is About to Get a Whole Lot Smaller*, a #1 national bestseller and the winner of the National Business Book Award. His second book, *The End of Growth*, was also a #1 bestseller and made multiple best-book-of-the-year lists in 2012. Rubin was the Chief Economist at CIBC World Markets, where he worked for over twenty years. He lives in Toronto.

www.jeffrubinssmallerworld.com